Sexual, Marital and Familial Relations

THERAPEUTIC INTERVENTIONS FOR PROFESSIONAL HELPING

By

ROBERT HENLEY WOODY, PH.D.
The Ohio University

and

JANE DIVITA WOODY, PH.D., M.S.W.
The Ohio University

With an Original Chapter by

LUCIANO L'ABATE, PH.D.
The Georgia State University

and by

PAUL G. SCHAUBLE, PH.D.
The University of Florida

CHARLES C THOMAS · PUBLISHER
Springfield · Illinois · U.S.A.

Published and Distributed Throughout the World by

CHARLES C THOMAS • PUBLISHER
Bannerstone House
301-327 East Lawrence Avenue, Springfield, Illinois, U.S.A.

© *1973, by* CHARLES C THOMAS • PUBLISHER

ISBN 0-398-02803-6

Library of Congress Catalog Card Number: 73-231

With THOMAS BOOKS careful attention is given to all details of manufacturing and design. It is the Publisher's desire to present books that are satisfactory as to their physical qualities and artistic possibilities and appropriate for their particular use. THOMAS BOOKS will be true to those laws of quality that assure a good name and good will.

Printed in the United States of America
C-1

Dedicated To

Our Parents

PREFACE

SEXUALITY, MARRIAGE, AND FAMILY: it is doubtful that any other words hold the potential for so much personal importance as these three words. The universal relevance is, probably, a major explanation for the myriad of available treatises–books, scholarly research, articles in popular magazines, and seemingly endless discussions in private, at social gatherings, and on the mass communication media. Indeed, so great is the flood of material on the subject that, as we contemplated the development and writing of this book, we found that even our strong professional commitment seemed undermined by the feeling: "Oh no, not another marriage book."

After becoming more immersed in the project, however, and even with the risk of contributing to "publication pollution," we began to believe that there was a real need for the chapters herein. It seems that most treatises are directed at either a professional or a lay audience. Many are highly opinionated and, if scientific at all, often become esoteric and abstract, pursuing a maze of theoretical constructs at the expense of practicality; or the reverse may be true, i.e. simplistic notions about techniques are presented in absentia from the requisite theoretical foundations. Also, there are the numerous writings on sex, marriage, and the family that end up proselytizing for a given approach to the subject. The format presented in this text was developed to overcome these kinds of shortcomings.

It should be noted that throughout this book, the term *professional helping* has been used instead of more conventional terms, such as marriage counseling and psychotherapy. To be sure, the traditional therapeutic role definitions are useful, but *professional helping* is intended to go beyond the restricted perimeters imposed by any one professional discipline and to recognize that the contemporary state of affairs is such that helping for sexual, marital, and familial relations comes and should come from a variety of sources. Some of these disciplines–such as medicine (particularly psychiatry), psychology, and social work–have in the past and will in the future hold a critical responsibility for serving public needs in these areas. There are, however, many new identities developing in other disciplines that must not be by-passed as part of the human service system; most notably perhaps are professionals functioning in education, religion, law, and a host of other areas. Similarly, there are many professionals who tend to see their roles as practitioners exempt from involvement with direct professional helping for sexual, marital, and familial issues, even if they are in such disciplines as medicine, psychology, social work, and the other social-behavioral sciences. It would definitely lead to improved service if all professionals were knowledgeable enough and motivated to integrate cogent elements of sexual, marital, and familial relations into their work with clients when the need arises. For example, both professionals and para-professionals involved in providing human services are likely to confront various sexual, marital, and familial issues as they deal with their clients. If their training would encompass some of the possible approaches for dealing with these issues, they could more comfortably and competently serve their clients.

More important, it is crucial that the layman (and the professional as well) be familiar with professional helping for sexual, marital, and familial relations in such a manner that he can make an informed, reasonable application to his own life situation. Undoubtedly "self-counseling" is the primary source for behavioral and attitudinal change in everyone's life, and this can be best used when alternatives are evaluated intrapersonally against a backdrop of academic knowledge.

Basically, the material in this book is intended to provide professional helpers who deal primarily or secondarily with sexual, marital, and familial relations with an academic knowledge of relevant dimensions; as will be brought out subsequently, the emphasis is on developing a personalized approach to clients via integration of different theories and explication of techniques that can be used. The material is intended to provide a general orientation to the professional helping procedures that are used for understanding and improving sexual, marital, and familial relations. At the same time, details and specifics of actual practice process are included.

While there is probably some safety in hiding behind the shield of a discrete theoretical approach, there is reason to believe that adherence to a single theory greatly restricts helping efficiency and effectiveness. Throughout this book, the underlying assumption is that no one theory with its inherent set of techniques will be adequate for all persons and that the most comprehensive approach (and the one that will assure a maximum degree of professional effectiveness) is to develop an eclectic posture (particularly integrating behavioral and insight approaches) that permits each individual helper to tailor his services to the needs and characteristics of each given helpee. This focus on integration is summarized in the so-called *Psychobehavioral* frame of reference, as presented in Chapter 7.

From both personal experience and research, we believe that there is an important relationship between the professional self and the personal self identities. Consequently, we have tried always to keep the personal qualities of the professional helper present in presentations of helping techniques. The "self" factors can be powerful adjuncts to the helping processes. The important goal is, of course, to assure that they are positive adjuncts, since they obviously hold negative potential as well. Thus the development of a healthy synthesis of professional and personal self constructs is prerequisite for effective professional helping, and we serve notice that this "personalized filter" must be applied from the onset of both studying and practicing professional helping.

Related to the proselytizing that occurs so often in published treatises, we have aimed for the goal of objectivity. To be certain, we are vulnerable to allowing our personal biases to overtly or covertly influence, but we have striven to present diverse theoretical and technical parameters in an objective manner. To do this, we have attempted to base discussions and assertions on more than personal-professional opinion, relying instead on clinical and experimental research. Although it is always necessary to make use of clinical expertise (which automatically introduces subjectivity and opens the door to possible bias), we have tried to view sexual, marital, and familial relations from the vantage point of the applied behavioral scientist. Since a readable, practical style was desirable, we have not made this a compendium of published research studies; nonetheless, documentation is offered for important points—with a reference source that exemplifies clinical aspects, provides empirical evidence, or more extensively covers the subject.

Another goal was practicality. Since our approach to documentation provides sources for more thorough coverage (this is particularly true for the theoretical issues), we have directed the material toward a reality-orientation for day-to-day practice. As might be expected, this has led us (and Drs. L'Abate and Schauble) to offer accounts from our own clinical activities; we hope that our failures and successes in professional helping can help the reader minimize the former and maximize the latter. Moreover, we have tried to translate a seemingly vast amount of published material into a relatively brief synopsis (i.e. this book) and to do so in a style that avoids extensive intellectualizations and gets right to the information that will help the practitioner in his own functioning as a helper.

Writing this book has led us to apply the various principles to our own lives. This procedure introduced many new dynamics to our relationship, and the outcome has been a beneficial increased understanding of the material academically and increased understanding of ourselves (both individually and as spouses-parents). Although not intended to be a "self-help" book *per se,* we hope that the book will provide the reader with the same kind of stimulation for self-growth (and sexual, marital, and familial understanding) that it had for us.

We wish to express our appreciation to Luciano L'Abate, Ph.D., and Paul G. Schauble, Ph.D., each of whom has attained distinction for their clinical research and was willing to contribute a chapter to this book; from our viewpoint, their contributions definitely enhance the coverage. We would also like to thank our professional colleagues, friends, and members of our own families who have offered information, exchanged ideas, and provided examples that have helped us in our formulations. Our parents and children have, of course, given incomparably to our knowledge of and appreciation for interpersonal relations.

ROBERT H. WOODY
JANE D. WOODY

CONTENTS

xi

Sexual, Marital
and Familial Relations

CHAPTER ONE

CONTEMPORARY PERSPECTIVES OF SEX, MARRIAGE, AND THE FAMILY

E VERYONE IS AWARE that living in today's society presents many formidable challenges. More specifically, of concern to the field of mental health is the increasing difficulty people seem to have in creating and maintaining fulfilling, meaningful interpersonal relationships. Authorities are careful to explain that no one factor makes this so; rather a variety of factors are involved. The one factor that seems to pervade all considerations is that of significant and rapid social and cultural change. As we look around us, the tried, traditional ways and ideas are being challenged and are seemingly being changed almost overnight. The communications media are constantly barraging audiences with indisputable facts that people are relating to each other in other than the traditionally accepted ways. Perhaps the single most powerful example is what might be called "the hippie movement." At first, what was happening in the movement was something that one watched on television, read about in magazines, joked about and denounced loudly. Then it was everywhere and every family had at least one real hippie or hippie-imitator. The so-called hippie movement is only one of many contemporary socio-cultural phenomena that are exerting a powerful influence on the nature of relationships. It is reasonable to assume that difficulties in relationships will multiply in the future, in view of the rapidly changing cultural scene.

The chapters in this text deal with various therapeutic approaches to sexual, marital and familial relationship problems. But in order to provide a broader perspective, the nature of relationship problems must be placed in the context of contemporary life. Some important questions are: What is the input of current changes in norms and values to relationship problems? How do the value systems underlying the various therapies compare with the emerging values in the contemporary scene? To what extent do the therapeutic approaches and individual therapists take into account the input of contemporary socio-cultural conditions to the problems that clients present? The chapters on therapy herein may not deal with these specific questions, but the following discussions will enable the readers to scrutinize the impact of socio-cultural factors in therapeutic activities.

Classification of the socio-cultural changes can be an endless task. It would be useful, however, to begin with the broadest factors as a way of viewing people in the real social environment in which they function; then can come a focus on specific changes that impinge directly on relationships.

One can link together three important factors at once: rapid urbanization, rapid economic growth, and an ever expanding technology. These produce a lifestyle that forces us into many contacts with a number of different people, that surrounds us with an endless variety of goods and services, and that confounds us with the ever present paradox of poverty and plenty. Thus, the overall tenor of modern life exerts a great influence on personal living, but for the most part it seems beyond anyone's personal control (Toffler, 1970).

Two other factors contribute to the rapid socio-cultural change with which we live and these are much closer to individuals and to their relationships. The first has to do with *knowledge,* and the second has to do with the *flow of situations.*

In today's world, knowledge and ideas spread like wildfire. If we limit our consideration for the moment to knowledge that has a directly discernible impact on human life and relationships, the result can be overwhelming. For example, medical knowledge confronts us with the reality of organ transplants and of contraception; the physical sciences warn of population and pollution problems; and the social and behavioral sciences offer an impressive body of information regarding racism, women's liberation, and human sexuality (to mention but a few topics). The results of both *hard research* and *speculative thought* get transmitted to the public in a short period of time. And often along with the transmission of the information comes the creation of an image for emulation and ultimately a social movement of sorts. This is what has happened with the hippie movement, the peace movement, the sexual revolution, the women's liberation movement, and the black power movement. Thus information about socio-cultural changes comes quickly and may begin to influence the way individuals handle themselves in relationships.

The other factor is what Toffler calls the "flow of situations." Simply explained, it means that the acceleration of change in society has altered the flow of situations within the individual's life experience: more and more situations now pass through man's experiential channel, and they are of shorter duration. They vastly complicate our lives by multiplying the number of roles we must play and the number of choices we must make, and by presenting us with more and more novelty with which we must cope.

The overall tenor of modern life suggests that individuals need to develop greater adaptive capacities; this should be a basic goal of preventive mental health. Yet it does not seem that the helping professions are (at least as of yet) adequately tuned in to the reality of rapid socio-cultural change with which their helpers are forced to live and cope.

The situation is complicated by the fact that a debate still rages about the extent of influence of the external environment on individual behavior. One can review the two extreme positions and conclude that: since we do not really know the exact nature and extent of the influence, we cannot do anything about it. This is probably the justification for the contemporary "do nothing" position in mental health. Therefore, one camp believes that major determinants of individual behavior originate from within the individual personality; and the other extreme camp sees a normative social press acting similarly on all individuals. Given these extreme positions, it is not surprising that few are willing to confront the inevitable links between therapeutic activities and the impact of socio-cultural conditions and behavior.

To further clarify the issue, let it be acknowledged that value systems relating specifically to some of today's social and political issues are, in fact, embedded in certain therapeutic approaches. To consider extremes once again, the position set forth in *The Radical Therapist* (Agel, 1971) holds as a basic principle that therapy is a social and political event. That is, therapy must not only acknowledge the impact of social and political factors on people's problems, but it must also work to change the status quo. Thus "a *strug-*

gle for mental health is bullshit unless it involves changing this society which turns us into machines, alienates us from one another and our work, and binds us into racist, sexist, and imperialist practices" (Agel, 1971, p. xi). The radicalism of this position may cause some readers to dismiss it easily, but there are also representatives at the other end of the continuum who foster strong support of traditional norms and values. In a recent book on family and marriage counseling, value judgments pervade both the introduction to the contemporary family and the discussion of techniques throughout. The writer is especially negative toward permissiveness in general and toward colleges' capitulating to the demands of students: "They have allegedly decided that it is the faculty that should change, admit them with few restrictions, accept their licentious indulgences on campus, eliminate examinations, and graduate all who desire a degree" (Stein, 1969, p. 14). Trends such as this are "causing a progressive breakdown of hard-won standards and values of freedom, fair play and democracy. All these are inevitably reflected in the average home" (p. 15). Stein further attacks the liberalizing of state hospital regulations, and notes that "we seem to have forgotten that overpermissiveness and solicitude for the unfit members of the group was also a luxury that could endanger an entire community" (p. 16).

Both this view and that set forth in *The Radical Therapist* certainly encompass social and political values; both are extreme. Somewhere in between is the majority of therapists (espousing different approaches to therapy); the majority generally regards socio-cultural factors as irrelevant to their treatment of helpees. Such an unrealistic "no-man's land" position is no longer tenable.

Debating extreme positions is useless. It is obvious that a number of societal conditions do exert an influence on the nature of relationships, and it is up to the professional helper to be able to discern the nature and extent of such an influence. But what happens once he does discern it? A number of specific cases come to mind which pose important questions. For example, an older couple is having difficulty with their eighteen- and nineteen-year-old daughters about their late hours. Another of their daughters had an illegitimate child the previous year. The parents express concern about what their neighbors will think if they see the girls coming in at two and three o'clock in the morning. The father hates the girls' long-haired boyfriends and seldom communicates with the girls. The parents' greatest source of pride comes from getting the whole family together in church on Sunday. This is not an unusual case, but it should be obvious that this is no one individual's problem; it should be obvious that various changing socio-cultural norms are involved in the parent-children difficulties; it should be obvious that the situation is loaded with value issues.

What are some meaningful guidelines for the professional helper as he confronts such clinical situations that are complicated by socio-cultural factors, especially the rapid shifts in ideas and values that influence interpersonal relationships? This is an issue that merits special consideration aside from clinical specialties and different approaches to therapy. The suggestions that follow are offered in order to provide some stimulation to helpers to face up to the impact that social change can exert on helpees (be they termed "clients" or "patients").

First, *there is a need for the professional helper to be aware of the variety of social phenomena that might be operating in clinical situations.* He needs to be able to discern whether the presenting problem involves currently "hot" social issues. For example, role definitions and responsibilities within marital relationships may be getting an indirect or direct input from current ideas espoused by the women's liberation movement. Or the sexual difficulties presented by both the married and the unmarried may be related to what is often termed the sexual revolution, which includes everything from the scientific study of Masters and Johnson (1966, 1970), the explicit nature of sexual acts in all the entertainment media, free teenage contraceptive clinics, official endorsement of coeducational housing (as well as "shacking up"), the unisex fashion, the gay liberation movement, etc. The list could go on and on. Then there is another stratum of issues, e.g. the culture of minorities and the culture of poverty. The people who find themselves in these categories suffer from the same individual and interpersonal crises of the middle class, but their problems are further complicated by health, economic, housing, and discrimination problems. In addition, the sources from which they seek help usually operate on the basis of white, middle class assumptions and values. Thus the professional helper needs to cultivate an awareness of the variety of socio-cultural factors that may be contributing to the helpees' problems, and he needs to develop a sensitivity to the unique culture and subcultures in which people function. Awareness and sensitivity, however, are not enough.

Second, *the professional helper needs to recognize the many value implications involved in the social changes that are engulfing society.* In the past five years, it is acknowledged that American society has become more and more polarized in more and more different areas. There is less and less consensus about anything, and many theorists believe that this trend will increase in the future. There is extreme division about international affairs, about domestic issues (such as welfare reform and economic controls), and about local issues (such as integration, busing, and community control of schools). Activism among minority groups has further splintered society into a variety of opposing camps. Women's rights groups, homosexual groups, abortion-reform groups and groups to oppose these keep multiplying. And the age-old opposition between the young and the old continues and intensifies with the eighteen-year-old age of majority. All of the different groups have their own ideas about how things should be conducted, and these ideas usually involve diverse values. The professional helper cannot approach issues such as these lightly and assume that he will maintain objectivity. The individuals, the married couples, and the families that the professional helper sees are likely to be intimately involved in some of these very value struggles. He must come to know what the opposing camps are, what their ideas are, what their values are and exactly how they impinge upon the intrapersonal and interpersonal lives of their followers and fellow-travelers.

Third, *the professional helper must recognize that he himself is very personally caught up in many of these same socio-cultural changes.* He, just as his helpees, lives in a world of interpersonal relationships with his spouse, children, friends, and colleagues. It is foolish to assume that he is somehow free of all the many pressures stemming from family and job responsibilities and from general environmental press. He must explore what personal feelings, experiences, and acts are being influenced by his society and culture and how he deals with this influence. He must evaluate his value system in comparison to some of the contemporary shifts in values and concomitant behaviors. Very simply, he must continually explore himself. With this knowledge of the self, then he can begin to see where the personal self merges into the professional self–either consciously or unconsciously. He can begin to distinguish which values serve personal needs and which have some scientific validity for use in the helping professions.

Much of the writing about the need for the therapist to cultivate the "examined life" centers on highly personal concepts of self-understanding and mental health, e.g. on personality variables or the ability to establish an empathic relationship or correlations of self-actualization with quality of clinical service, or on self concept.

Discussions of the therapist's responsibility are similarly quite limited. Generally, responsibility is defined differently by the various therapeutic approaches, e.g. responsibility to create a therapeutic atmosphere, responsibility to implement certain techniques, or responsibility to construct and execute a technical program. One concept of responsibility, called "facilitative responsibility," is based on flexibility in the treatment approach and is somewhat broader than other concepts mentioned above. Facilitative responsibility is:

> the communication by the counselor of an awareness that his behavior
> has major consequences for the client and the therapeutic process.
> The counselor then discharges this responsibility in an appropriate
> manner (Pierce and Schauble, 1969, p. 71).

This definition of therapeutic responsibility might readily be extended to include the therapist's examination of his particular social, cultural and political values and his assessment of how and if they should carry over into therapeutic activity. Specifically, the competent and responsible therapist or helper is aware of changing norms and values in contemporary life, explores their impact on his personal life, assesses their validity and usefulness according to the best knowledge available, studies their relationship to therapeutic approaches and human relationship problems, and strives for conscious awareness of their place in his professional person and in therapeutic practice.

Let us consider for a moment how this enlarged concept of therapeutic responsibility might work with regard to sexual problems that helpees bring to the helper. One of the most important facts of life in our pluralist society is the legitimacy of diverse subculture norms and values. For example, a helper in a given day might counsel with a twenty-year-old college student who presents her problem as failure to achieve orgasm with her boyfriend with whom she lives; he then might see a twenty-year-old secretary who presents a history of fear of any kind of sexual involvement. In these situations the helper must recognize the totally different subcultures in which the two girls are living; he should have examined carefully the reality of the so-called sexual revolution; he should know his personal value system on sexual matters; he should have assessed the most recent empirical studies on sexuality and its relationship of concepts of mental health; he should know of the various therapeutic approaches to dealing with sexual problems and their underlying theoretical and value orientations; he should be personally and professionally secure in his competence to assess each unique problem situation and to tailor therapy to the helpee's individual situation and needs, including dealing openly with the helpee's values when necessary.

The last point leads to the fourth and final suggestion: *the professional helper should recognize that values do get transmitted in therapy, and that this transmission must become an open and conscious process.* All therapeutic approaches are founded upon various "behavioral science concepts" possessing varying degrees of empirical validation; these concepts impinge in diverse ways upon human relationships and they reflect socio-cultural and political value. Such concepts are continually emerging and giving birth to new ways of living and new approaches to therapy. Some of the most recent therapeutic approaches are sensitivity and/or human potential training, behavior modification, effective communication training, reality therapy, etc. Training in these various approaches to living is often given via special workshops where goals and values are clearly labeled and dealt with. At the same time, however, many of these concepts are taken into therapeutic activities without careful evaluation and without clear recognition of the values involved. For example, the approach to childrearing espoused in *Parent Effectiveness Training* (Gordon, 1970) applies proven principles of effective communication to childrearing practice; the method is also based on a value abdicating the whole concept of parental "power" over children. This latter value is apt to conflict with the value of parental authority and responsibility held by large segments of our population. Can the professional helper espouse this approach and incorporate it into his dealings with helpees, as representative of the best behavioral science can offer—without dealing in an open and conscious manner with the potential value conflicts and necessary value changes required of the helpees?

This question points to the issue of education for mental health or preventive mental health. Everyone acknowledges that preventive mental health necessitates the learning of new values. Certain values related to accepted public health practice are now widespread, e.g. immunization and vaccination; others have less acceptance, e.g. prevention of venereal disease, birth control, pre-natal care, etc. The field of preventive mental health is just beginning to witness the various and widespread resistances to value changes that relate to mental health. For example, all the controversy surrounding sex education stems from this issue. In other words, if one is going to accept some of the most recent scientific findings about human sexuality, he will likely have to discard some traditional values and assumptions.

But the important point to this discussion is that preventive mental health concepts cannot be kept in a totally different compartment from what goes on in therapy. To be specific, a good deal of sex education takes place in therapy, regardless of the therapeutic approach; moreover, helpees' values about sexuality change, and these value shifts do not simply evolve from the helpee's own insights and decisions. Recent research has indicated that unconscious selective verbal conditioning by the therapist operates in even the most "client-centered" therapies (Truax, 1966). In summary, it seems best to acknowledge that a certain amount of "education for mental health" takes place in therapy, that some of this will necessitate dealing with values, that the therapist has the responsibility to select consciously the direct or indirect methods for dealing with the educational aspects of mental health, and that the professional helper has the obligation to openly explore with the helpee his feelings, values, and preferences regarding these educative aspects of therapy.

It seems that another legitimate therapeutic approach might be titled "education therapy" and that the helper could employ this in either direct or indirect ways, either alone or in combination with other therapeutic techniques. Education therapy would be much different from the "educational and supportive counseling" that is typically indicated today, e.g. for parents having problems with children. Unfortunately, the attention given to education in these situations is usually small. Parents are usually counseled to work through conflicting feelings they have about themselves as parents; this is another way of saying that the problem is simply an individual's problem and that it probably stems from a weak ego. In view of the contributions from family therapy, such an assessment seems oversimplified. There may be a total family relationship problem, a communication problem, a childrearing practice problem, a value-conflict problem, an economic problem, and/ or a school problem. There may be a need for some education therapy; and if there is, the helper should know what is available, the values that underpin it, its usefulness for this unique family, and the need for preparing the family to deal with any resulting conflicts it might provoke.

The main point is that we get nowhere in counseling with sexual, marital, and familial problems (in other words, with relationship problems) by retreating into the long outmoded role of the objective, detached, value-free helper.

The idea mentioned previously in the discussion of *The Radical Therapist*–that therapy is a social and political event–may indeed seem radical to some persons. But similar ideas were set forth by Hobbs (1964); his title too was radical: "Mental Health's Third Revolution." His awareness of the powerful impact of the societal factors on mental health is clearly demonstrated:

> The changing conception of the nature of mental illness and mental retardation will require that the mental health specialist be a person of broad scientific and humanistic education, a person prepared to help make decisions not only about the welfare of an individual but also about the kind of society that must be developed to nurture the greatest human fulfillment (p. 826).

CONTEMPORARY SEXUAL ATTITUDES AND BEHAVIOR

Writers in the 1970's are no longer denying the presence of a sexual revolution in America. Rather, efforts now are aimed at squarely facing the question of evolving rational and humane ethics in a sexually liberated society. Naturally, not all people are equally affected by changing norms and values regarding sexual matters, but it is safe to assume that many of those who seek help for interpersonal problems have been affected in some way by these changes.

Trends Toward Permissiveness

Sexual behavior is largely the result of the attitudes one learns about sexuality. Sex education, it is acknowledged, begins in infancy, and is greatly influenced by parent-child interactions. Other factors, however, obviously also affect the development of sexual attitudes, for example, broad cultural expectations and specific cultural factors (such as one's religious affiliation, sex, age, education, and socio-economic status). Many contemporary sexologists believe that human sexual behavior is much more a product of learning than of instinct. Interaction within the family and with peers, plus the broad sexual assumptions of the culture, insure that the majority of people learn and adopt the expected sexual behavior.

In modern society we must not discount the influence of the increasing permissiveness toward sexual attitudes and behavior. Whether or not one is willing to call the phenomenon a "revolution," the reality of an overall greater permissiveness cannot be denied, and it is having an impact regardless of the fact that the impact has not yet been empirically documented. It is usually argued that widespread cultural change takes place only very slowly, but the speed with which images are created, mass produced, and adopted should make us aware that the sexual revolution is having an effect on the lives of individuals and on their relationships.

In the face of greater openness and permissiveness about sexual matters, concern runs high among parents, educators, and professional helpers. Many applaud the demise of some of the prudery and taboos, but a growing issue is whether people will be able to maintain a perspective of sexual relationships within a human and humane context.

Defining what is meant by human and humane context is no easy matter. For centuries, most people depended upon religious teachings to provide the guidelines, and they tacitly accepted that certain persons and groups were exempt from these guidelines, namely men, prostitutes, the lower socio-economic classes, etc. As society has become more secularized and more permissive, the traditional religious guidelines have become more blurred.

It is obvious that sexual codes are no longer as simple as "no premarital sex," or "no premarital sex for girls," or "no premarital sex for girls unless they are in love with the partner," or "no extramarital sex." Since sexual codes based on "thou shall not . . ." are no longer the basis for social consensus, there is a need for a serious reexamination of viable standards for sexual behavior. This is a difficult task since it requires first an admission that increasing numbers of people are in actuality ignoring traditional sexual ethics. The problem is further complicated by several related but unpredicted phenomena: (1) attacks upon the institution of marriage; (2) the concerted pursuit of full female equality; (3) the gay liberation movement; and (4) the power of communication media to disseminate information about these phenomena.

The attacks upon marriage and women's liberation movement are intricately related. In 1960, Reiss, in trying to evolve a theory about increasing sexual permissiveness remarked:

> In short, there has been a gradually increasing acceptance of and overtness about sexuality. The basic change is toward greater equalitarianism, greater female acceptance of permissiveness, and more open discussion. In the next decade, we can expect a step-up in the pace of this change (Reiss, 1970, p. 208).

Although Reiss stated at that time that he did not expect to see full male-female equality, a powerful thrust for female equality is, in fact, upon us now; and with it has come criticism of marriage and of the nuclear family. In other words, these two factors, the institution of marriage and female subordination, have been at the center of all traditional codes of sexual morality, and these two factors are now at the center of the sexual revolution. Discussions of sexual values and ethics can no longer overlook this fact.

The various issues surrounding the whole question of homosexuality are openly discussed today and serve to accentuate the changing sexual codes. There is a variety of responses toward homosexuality which the public is now aware of, including open proselytizing, dialogues to foster understanding, legal reform to guarantee civil rights, scientific debate about etiology, and both a humorous and sensitive treatment of the topic in the entertainment and communication media.

There is no question but that the communication media have had a tremendous impact in disseminating information about changing sexual attitudes and behavior. The stories carried by popular magazines on college living arrangements, current films and books, communes, and changes in male-female roles are household passwords. The explicitness of sexual matters in both films and television shocks very few people today (even those who are "shocked" continue to watch). And the presence of "adult" bookstores and cinemas is by no means limited to major cities (and, more importantly, their patrons can scarcely be all categorized as being "dirty old men," since a variety of citizens, including women, frequent the premises). The exact impact of all the sexual stimuli remains an unknown, though this matter is beginning to be investigated. Eysenck (1972) deals with this topic in a recent issue of a British men's magazine and notes that both the desensitization and modeling principles are involved in the effect produced by violence and "pornography" in the communication media:

> . . . it cannot any longer be argued with any degree of conviction that pornography, or the portrayal of violence, have no effect on the behavior of the people who see these things on the screen, or read about them in books and magazines (pp. 101-102).

Sexual Needs

The pervasiveness and continuity of human sexual needs have by now been well-established. Since the Kinsey studies (Kinsey, Pomeroy, and Martin, 1948; Kinsey, Pomeroy, Martin, and Gebhard, 1953), the concept of the sexual latency period in childhood has been nearly dispelled. Childhood masturbation and sexual exploration are seen as normal developmental milestones, and with the onset of puberty and adolescence comes an expected increase in sexual tension.

The sex drive is usually considered to be somewhat greater in men than in women, especially during the teenage years and early in marriage. But it is no longer accepted that the nature of the female sex drive is an innate or fixed characteristic. Current research and speculation on the matter emphasize the influence of culture in conditioning women to repress or sublimate sexual drive. Sherman (1971) mentions that Masters and Johnson have suggested that "because of the greater female sexual-response capacity, cultural restraints on women arose in order to provide a better balance between the sexes" (p. 150). Regardless of the reason, women at the present time seem to have less sex drive than men but have a greater capacity for sexual response in the form of multiple orgasm.

In speculating about the future, it may be that as sexual mores change regarding the propriety of female sexual rights, society will come to accept more direct manifestations of the female sex drive. In the past, females have had a blurred and confused image of their sexual selves, because female sexuality was beclouded by most of the mores. For example, young girls learned that they were supposed to look sexy but were to ward off all sexual advances until marriage. But with the advent of marriage, they were to be totally responsive to their husband's sexual desires. The difficulties evolving from lack of female responsiveness in marriage was noted by Thorne (1965). However, he totally overlooks the fact that female difficulties with sexuality are linked to prescribed cultural norms and that this situation need not continue in the face of a changing society. According to Thorne:

> The problem becomes one of how to condition, or recondition, young women so that they accept their biologic roles, look forward positively to sex life, are able to cooperate flexibly in achieving a mutually compatible sexuality, and can approach marriage and family life without disabling frigidity and conflict (p. 122).

This statement seems extremely dated and short-sighted.

The problem of frigidity is related to the double standard which leaves many women in a state of debilitating confusion about their sexuality, and it is precisely a change in the double standard that is at the core of the sexual revolution. As young females gain control over their reproductive processes and as society comes to accept that males must share equally in the responsibility to prevent unwanted pregnancy, there need not be so much hypocrisy and gamesmanship surrounding female sexuality. If these conditions ever obtain, we can expect that females will come to accept their sexuality as naturally and smoothly as most males. Contrary to Thorne's remedial approach to the problem, there should be no necessity to *recondition* females into sexual beings after marriage. The 1972 appearance of the first male nude "fold-out" in a woman's magazine (i.e. actor Burt Reynolds in *Cosmopolitan*) suggests that contemporary society is beginning to provide some cultural support to the reality of female interest in sex.

One other fact about sexual drive merits attention: the nature of its demise in later years. There is considerable evidence that men and women can engage in regular and pleasurable sex activity long past middle age. The male sex drive typically declines somewhat from its intense peak of the twenties, but this is no deterrent to sexual activity. And it has been demonstrated that once a woman reaches the peak of her sexual drive (today it is usually in the late twenties), it remains at that plateau until she is sixty or even older. The sexual drive of older people usually reflects their overall pattern of health and physical performance; and given good health, the more sexually active men and women are in youth and middle age, the more active they are likely to be in old age. Misinformation regarding sexual needs in later years and guilt for these often cause older people needless psychological discomfort and a loss of interest in sex and ability to perform sexually.

Sex and Morality

The actual reasons as to why people engage in given sexual acts and relationships constitute a complicated situation, since they are tied with the overall fulfillment of needs. Because of the greater openness about sexuality, the ideal goal is that people will honestly explore the needs that they expect to fulfill in a sexual relationship. Openness and self-exploration are, in fact, necessary if modern men and women are to evolve viable standards of sexual behavior to replace the faltering traditional ones.

Let us consider the typical sexual behavior of teenagers of several years ago (and to some extent today) as reflected in dating patterns. In a recent text, Saxton (1968) states:

Dating does not (or is not supposed to) provide socially acceptable experience in expected patterns of primary sexual behavior. There is no socially recognized provision for premarital sexual experience in our society, although half of the females and most of the males do utilize dating for this purpose (p. 187).

Despite its relative recency, this is a position precisely reflecting traditional sexual mores. Specifically, sexual behavior in teenagers is not acknowledged, and sexual needs are supposed to remain unconscious or disguised. If teenagers act upon them, then this act is regarded as something that just happened or got out of control. According to this pattern, it is widely, though tacitly, accepted that the male might use a variety of verbal persuasions for attempting sexual intercourse; these range from a profession of love to appeal to the girl's sense of adventure, curiosity, loneliness and insecurity, pity, logic, shame, or her female biological needs (Saxton, 1968, p. 185). And these techniques are effective, especially if safety from discovery and from pregnancy are also available. In other words, there is involved in this pattern of sexual strategy an inordinate amount of disguising of real needs and motives from oneself and the partner. It is thus not surprising that this same pattern gets carried over into marriage and affects all aspects of marital life—not just the sexual aspects. Yet it is again part of society's "doublethink" approach to sexuality to endorse all variety of sexual gamesmanship before marriage and then to boast of the values of open and honest communication in marriage.

According to today's most responsible authorities on sex education, the emphasis should be on learning how to live with and manage one's sexuality and reproductivity in modern society. Many educators as well as many young people are coming to recognize that traditional patterns of sexual-dating strategy are fraught with dishonesty. The ideal is more openness and more dialogue between young people, their parents, educators, and professional helpers to encourage people to learn how to face up to their sexual needs openly, evaluate these according to overall needs and goals, and act in a responsive and responsible manner toward those with whom they engage in sexual relationships. Achieving this goal will require considerable learning and relearning for most people.

In further exploring the human needs associated with sexual behavior, today's experts on sex can note the variety of reasons people have for engaging in sexual relationships–without condemning all but one or two of the acceptable reasons. They simply acknowledge the facts of the matter and attempt to work from that point. For example, Berne's (1970) classification of the reasons for engaging in sex is fairly comprehensive:

1. Impregnation;
2. Procreation;
3. Duty;
4. Ritual;
5. Relief;
6. Physiological readjustment—giving a feeling of well-being;
7. Pleasure—seeking the pleasure of orgasm;
8. Mutual pastime;
9. Play of seduction and retreat—all the psychological games possible between a man and woman;
10. A medium for union and understanding—for approaching ever closer to a meeting of two souls;
11. Intimacy and attachment; and
12. Expression of love.

In analyzing this list, one must acknowledge that traditional social mores *openly* endorse sex only for the purpose of expression of love and for the purpose of procreation.

Underlying Berne's classification is a moral position in which sexual relationships are categorized according to the broad transactional dichotomy of "straight" and "crooked." Straight sexual relationships exist when the partners involved have a clear understanding between them and act upon it. Crooked relationships exist when corruption, exploitation, deception, or ulterior motives are operating. In other words, the morality is based not on a prescribed or forbidden act but on the honesty and responsibility involved in the relationship. This classification represents a rational approach to developing viable sexual ethics for today's society.

With the increase in openness about sexual matters, traditional sexual mores are being analyzed and questioned. Their roots in the double standard, in all manner of hypocrisy and gamesmanship, and in the denial of the reality of human sexual needs and actual behavior have been uncovered. It is, therefore, no longer rational to deny the implications of these social facts. But for many people denial is easier than facing the complexities involved in sexual values.

The question of values and morality is at the center of the controversy surrounding sex education in the schools. It is obvious that sexual information cannot be conveyed without values and ethics also being conveyed–no matter how subtle, disguised, or peripheral they might be. The professional helper needs to be aware that specific values are evolving from contemporary trends in sex education and from the growing reality of the sexual revolution. Those who deal with sexual problems should become comfortable in exploring values relating to sex with their helpees, become aware of their own values and the basis for them, and understand what values are implied in various therapeutic approaches.

MARRIAGE IN CONTEMPORARY SOCIETY

Anthropological accounts of the evolution of marriage usually describe the earliest forms of marriage as coming into existence to fulfill very concrete needs. In civilized and highly sophisticated societies, however, the marriage relationship serves a wide variety of more abstract purposes.

In the most primitive societies, the male-female relationship gradually evolved for the practical reason of physical survival. Later this survival function came to be labeled as economic survival. During the Middle Ages, another dimension was added–that of romantic love–although its impact on the formation of marriages was not felt until much later. The concept of romantic love has had greatest influence probably in American society where most young men and women presumably are free to make their own choices of marital partners, and they rely heavily on romantic love as the primary determinant for their choice.

Economic security and romantic love are obviously involved as major motivations for most contemporary marriages, but there are doubtless other important, though subtle reasons that merit exploration. More specifically, people marry to fulfill a variety of emotional needs. Taking account of this factor is crucial today, since many authorities believe that the major task we face in the age of automation is emotional or psychological survival. Some feel that through marriage and the family, human beings can derive the intimacy and intensity of relationships that will sustain them, yet others question the viability of these institutions.

Rationally, it seems that the success of modern marriage will depend upon three major factors: developing a clear understanding of the emotional needs that partners expect to be met in marriage, maintaining an understanding of how the complexities of modern life influence need fulfillment in marriage, and evolving ways of dealing with and acting upon these understandings.

These factors suggest an attitude of consciousness and flexibility in dealing with marriage that has not been widespread in the past. In fulfilling needs, it is necessary to understand that as our world and situation change, needs may change and we are required to learn and relearn how to fulfill needs under different conditions and stresses. This is the situation in contemporary life that will require consciousness and flexibility from those who look to marriage as an avenue to human fulfillment. In other words, concepts of marriage must be brought into line with contemporary reality.

There are several new facts to take into account. Perhaps the most important one is the growing equality of women, which requires marriage to be a more cooperative and conscious venture than it was in the past. Then there is the fact of the increase in choices relating to marriage. As the institution of marriage comes under even more intense scrutiny in the future, people will realize that they have several options. Some may choose not to marry at all. Another possibility is the evolution of different types of marriage, for example, the childless trial marriage, the more permanent marriage with or without children, and perhaps group marriage. The range of choice is also increased today with regard to marital partners, as a result of high mobility and extensive communication and contact between the various social, racial, and economic groupings. Thus the reality of the growing equality of women and of greater choice points to the need for greater awareness of self and motivations for entering a marital relationship.

Consciousness about embarking upon marriage has not been the custom of the past. Our society typically has been satisfied to shield the reasons for marriage under the giant umbrella called love, but it was tacitly understood that love might cover a multitude of unspoken reasons: discovery of pregnancy, obtaining an approved

outlet for sexual tension, fulfilling parental or societal expectations, economic security, compensation for loneliness or insecurity,
etc. The complexities of modern life and the toll that it takes on
marriage in the form of divorce rates and marital dissatisfaction
suggest that a lack of consciousness about marriage is a hazardous
business. In view of the fact that most people have such great expectations of the marital relationship, it is unwise to remain un-
aware of its nature and the basis of these expectations.

Conceptualizing About Marriage

Several behavioral science concepts recently applied to marriage
have considerable relevance to marriage in contemporary and future society. One of these is the application of systems theory to
marriage; the other is the application of human growth potential
theory, which has given rise to the concept of open marriage.

Systems theory as applied to marriage by Lederer and Jackson
(1968) emphasizes that the interrelationship between spouses is the
crucial factor; i.e. there is a constant action-reaction taking place.
Another dimension is that changeability must be accepted as a part
of the interrelationship. It is also important to know that the relationship can be affected by factors outside as well as within the
relationship. Recognizing the fact that there is a state of constant
flux in the marriage relationship does not mean, however, that
there must be constant turmoil. There will evolve a predictable pattern of events.

The system of predictable behavioral responses is called the
quid pro quo, which means literally something for something.
Much of the reciprocal behavior in a marriage is conscious; in
other words, it is essentially a technique by which partners assure
themselves that they are equal. Once the pattern has been established, partners can live with some degree of security because they
can predict each other's behavior. Such patterns can be either destructive or healthy. Generally speaking, however, more consciousness about role expectations and values, and greater openness and
communication about changes in these will lead to healthy, workable *quid pro quo* arrangements.

In looking at marriage from this perspective, it becomes obvious
why long and intimate courtship and engagement are advisable and

why patterns of openness and honesty should be encouraged in pre-marital relationships.

Lederer and Jackson (1968) see the abstraction "love" as much too vague to serve as the basis for marriage. Instead, they list three characteristics of a *workable* marriage: (1) the spouses respect each other for one or several qualities or abilities; (2) the spouses are tolerant of each other; and (3) the spouses make the most of their marital assets and minimize their liabilities. For this last characteristic to be meaningful, spouses must learn to communicate and continually and consciously negotiate the *quid pro quo's* of the relationship.

This analysis may leave one wondering about the place of love in marriage. It may very well be that the meaning of love in the marital relationship needs reassessment. Authorities have pointed out for a long time that much of what is called love is a sexual attraction, coupled with the partners' willingness to fulfill sexual needs and other psychological needs. A more specific and therefore more demanding definition of love is that proposed by Harry Stack Sullivan: "When the satisfaction or the security of another person becomes as significant to one as is one's own satisfaction or security, then the state of love exists" (Lederer and Jackson, 1968, p. 42). This definition of love implies the requirement of knowing one's own needs for satisfaction and security as well as knowing the needs of the partner. The definition also implies that considerable exploration is necessary to see if the two sets of needs are compatible, i.e. such that each partner could work toward the security and satisfaction of his mate as well as toward his own security and satisfaction. Finally, the definition implies the actual work and compromise necessary for evolving a love relationship. Overall, such a love relationship can develop during a marriage, but it is unlikely that it exists in a very realistic form before marriage.

The application of systems theory to marriage requires openness, honesty, and intimacy between marital partners. Yet our typical social conditioning does not inculcate these behaviors or teach us how to relate to people in an intimate way. By and large we learn how to keep people at a distance and how to camouflage feelings. Therefore, considerable effort is usually required in learning how to communicate openly and honestly in an intimate relationship.

Recently, humanistic theory, associated with the human potential movement, has been applied to marriage. The most comprehensive treatment of the subject is O'Neil and O'Neil's *Open Marriage* (1972).

The basic premise is that traditional marriage stifles the human growth and potential of both partners and that open marriage can optimally foster such growth. In many ways the couple who subscribes to an open marriage must have already achieved the workability and functionality described in the systems approach to marriage. Open marriage, however, is purported to provide greater benefits than workability and respect for partners. These benefits go beyond the practical into the realm of individual fulfillment or self-actualization that are associated with humanistic philosophies.

The basic guidelines for open marriage are:

1. Living for now and realistic expectations;
2. Privacy;
3. Open and honest communication;
4. Flexibility in roles;
5. Open companionship;
6. Equality;
7. Identity; and
8. Trust.

Several points about the guidelines bear emphasis. In open marriage the couple writes their own contract, instead of blindly or tacitly accepting all of the written and unwritten conditions of the traditional closed marriage. Specific goals include the separate and individual growth of each partner, thus doing away with the "tight-couple front" that calls for partners to do all things together, be all things to each other, fulfill all of each other's needs—emotional, intellectual, psychological, and physical. Moreover, role flexibility is suggested with the objective being to avoid being controlled by the role. The final point is that the honesty and freedom attained through this kind of relationship constitute the bond that holds the couple together and compensates for the risks involved. It is described as a strong, positive, fulfilling bond that is much different from negative bonds stemming from jealousy or fear. The O'Neils caution that for open marriage to work, the husband and wife must already have attained a high degree of emotional security and selfhood; it should not, therefore, be viewed as a therapeutic model for a "sick" or weak marriage.

It seems reasonable to assume that some of the concepts of open marriage may well become part of the marital value system in varying degrees for different subcultures in our society. Certainly the idea of open marriage is valuable for encouraging scrutiny of some of the hidden values and assumptions involved in marriage. Helpers engaged in marital therapy must be aware of this idea and the values underlying it. Generally speaking, however, most couples seeking therapy have probably never attained even the stage of having a workable or functional marriage; many will have entered unconsciously and mechanically into marriage as the expected thing to do, without clear realization of even the most basic factors involved in the marriage relationship in modern life.

THE FAMILY IN CONTEMPORARY SOCIETY

There are some avante garde ideas that the traditional concept of the family should be discarded. Nonetheless, it is more than likely that the majority of Americans will continue to marry and to rear children in the nuclear family structure for a long time to come, although concepts of marriage and the family will continue to change in accord with changing values. It is also clear that family interactions will continue as one of the most important influences on the shaping of personalities, attitudes, behavior norms, and values. Professional helpers are aware that many mental health and social welfare problems are directly related to inadequate family functioning. Problems range from severely disruptive (e.g. divorce, desertion, child neglect) to mildly disruptive (e.g. marital and family disharmony, and behavior and learning problems in children). The variety of possible problems related to family functioning is due to the many influences, responsibilities, and functions assigned to the family.

Conceptualizing About the Family

It is necessary to have some conceptual framework of the family, if one is to work with families who have problems. Several conceptual explanations of the family have been offered by sociologists, anthropologists, child development specialists, psychiatrists, and related professionals. Typically, any single framework usually has shortcomings since each of the different ones tends to draw heavily upon a particular specialized theory, discipline, or function of the family. Some frameworks focus on the family as a social institution, others on the dynamic interaction of family members. There is as yet no comprehensive theory of the family, but it is possible to combine certain existing frameworks in order to obtain a broad base for understanding family functioning, particularly as it impinges upon mental health and social welfare problems.

There are two recent conceptual frameworks of the family that have special relevance to a wide variety of disturbances related to family functioning–these include problems affecting both individuals and the whole family. These two frameworks are: the psychosocial framework and the family development framework. As a preface to discussing them, mention should be made of the variety of processes involved in family functioning. The family is viewed as a *biological unit,* which defines the family through birth, as a *social unit,* which refers to the family household and its social functions, and as a *psychological unit,* which refers to the emotional relatedness of the members. In other words, "The family may be seen as a collection of individuals who have separate and joint goals and problems and whose individual identity is maintained but also develops as an integral part of the family" (Feldman and Scherz, 1968, p. 64).

The psychosocial framework of family functioning, as set forth by Hess and Handel (1967), emphasizes the internal aspects of the family. Five family processes are identified:

1. Establishing a pattern of separateness and connectedness.
2. Establishing a satisfactory congruence of images through the exchange of suitable testimony, e.g. of self, of others, of the family.
3. Evolving modes of interaction in central family concerns or themes.
4. Establishing the boundaries of the family's world of experience.
5. Dealing with significant biosocial issues of family life, as in defining male and female and old and young (p. 12).

Hess and Handel emphasize the importance of two of these processes for the professional helper: patterns of separateness and connectedness and the family theme. For example, failure to establish acceptable patterns of separateness and connectedness is nearly always involved in parent-adolescent difficulties. In addition, the family theme is an especially useful construct; it is described as a pattern that pervades nearly all family processes. Investigation of it allows the helper to assess the family in its own terms. The theme is a pattern of "feelings, motives, fantasies, and conventionalized understandings grouped about some locus of concern" (Hess and Handel, 1967, p. 18). All members are involved in the psychosocial processes which are involved in the theme–though perhaps in different ways. For example, an oversimplified summary of a family theme might be the pervasive pattern of secretiveness, lies, and non-communication; or a pattern of pursuit of achievement, success, dissatisfaction with success, and creation of new pursuits for achievement.

The internal family interaction on which the psychosocial

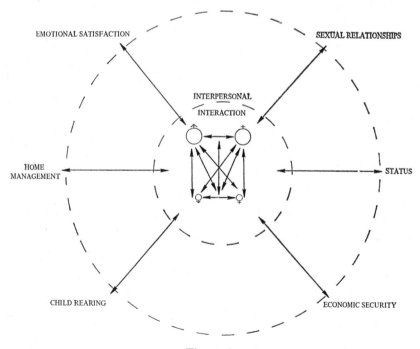

Figure 1.

framework focuses can be broken down into three systems: the marital, the parent-child, and the sibling systems. The following diagram suggests the complex interactions. (See Figure 1.)

The large outer circle represents the total family system, with the broken lines of the circle depicting it as an open system capable of interacting with the socio-cultural environment represented by the space outside of the circle. The carrying out of the family functions listed around the circle is a product of the interaction of the family with the socio-cultural environment. The arrows show this reciprocal interaction. The inner broken circle represents a system within the general family system performing the function of interpersonal interaction, which is likewise shown as interrelated with all the other family functions since it too is open. The symbols within this circle and the arrows depict the possible interactions of the three family systems–the marital, the parent-child, and the sibling. It is the system and the function depicted by the inner circle that constitute the focus of the psychosocial framework, i.e. the five major family processes listed above. Hess and Handel explain that the interaction that takes place within the family is a diffuse concept as yet insufficiently analyzed. It is used to refer to a variety of phenomena: physical contacts, cognitive interchanges leading to a definition of reality or to decision-making, behavior in which norms and roles are created and validated or in which *selves* are discovered, and affective behavior (exchanges and transmissions of feelings and emotions).

The psychosocial framework is useful for its emphasis on the interior of the family as a unique unit involved in functions required by the individuals within it. Perhaps two of the shortcomings of this framework might be mentioned: it assumes the nuclear family, and it overlooks the social system outside of the family within which the family must function–the socio-cultural environment represented by the space outside the large circle on the diagram.

The addition of the family development framework to the above concept of the family furnishes a broader perspective of the family within the context of the larger society. The family development framework focuses on family cycles or stages and posits certain individual and family tasks for the various stages (Duvall,

1962; Hill and Rodgers, 1964). It assumes the nuclear family and is structured around children. There are certain basic functional prerequisites necessary for the family's survival. These are: physical maintenance; allocation of resources; division of labor; socialization of family members; reproduction, recruitment, and release of family members; maintenance of order; placement of members in the larger society; and maintenance of motivation and morale.

Family development theorists are concerned with the family as it moves through time; this approach thus maintains the realistic perspective of the family as a constantly changing organization. Seven basic family phases are identified:

1. Families in the establishment phase;
2. Families in the childrearing stage;
3. Families with school age children;
4. Families with adolescents;
5. Families in the launching phase;
6. Families in post-parental phase; and
7. Aging families.

Obviously, families do not always fit neatly into these distinct stages, since family change is an ongoing process; however, the stages are useful in aiding analysis and diagnosis.

Each stage brings with it unique challenges and problems directly related to family and individual tasks; certain stages, however, seem to place greater demands than others, e.g. the adolescent stage. A family development task is defined as "a growth responsibility that arises at a certain stage in the life of the family, successful achievement of which leads to satisfaction and success with later tasks, while failure leads to unhappiness in the family, disapproval by society and difficulty with later development tasks" (Duvall, 1962, p. 95). Thus as the family in each stage must fulfill its tasks which relate to the functional requisites listed above, the various individuals within the family must also fulfill their own developmental tasks. For example, the children during the various stages of their development must:

1. Achieve an appropriate dependence-independence pattern;
2. Achieve an appropriate giving-receiving pattern of affection;
3. Relate to changing social groups;

4. Develop a conscience;
5. Learn one's psycho-socio-biological sex role;
6. Accept and adjust to a changing body;
7. Manage a changing body and learn new motor patterns;
8. Learn to understand and control the physical world;
9. Develop an appropriate symbol system and conceptual abilities; and
10. Relate oneself to the cosmos.

The adults within the family must fulfill general tasks similar to these, such as would be required by their age and role functions in the family and society. In other words, all of the family and individual tasks are constantly interacting, and from time to time may conflict:

> Each family is an arena of interacting personalities, each trying to achieve his own developmental tasks within the pattern of family life that in turn is evolving in interaction with the larger society of which it is a part (Duvall, 1962, p. 44).

A combination of the psychosocial and family development frameworks provides the professional helper with a broad overview of the complexities of family living. The interaction of individual and family needs and of individual and family patterns of behavior, both within the family and outside in the larger society, suggests the many possible sources of family problems. Any family treatment approach should take into account both internal family dynamics and the interdependence of the family with society. An inventory derived from these conceptual frameworks can often help pinpoint the extent to which an individual or a family owns the problem, its pervasiveness within the family, and its impact on the fulfillment of individual and/or family tasks.

THE FUTURE OF MARRIAGE AND THE FAMILY

There is considerable concern about the future of the American family, a concern which centers on the controversy about traditional values associated with marriage and the family. In the past the consensus regarding family values was considerably greater than it is today. The following are several major marriage and family values which have enjoyed wide acceptance and which have support in other societal structures; yet these are today being challenged:

1. Marriage is monogamic, with the legal structure being geared to this arrangement.
2. The family structure is nuclear and neolocal.
3. Cooperation and compromise are the desired modes of functioning between husband and wife.
4. The husband provides the major economic support, with the trend being for women to work at various stages.
5. The role of the wife is important for symbolizing the status of the family.
6. There are contradictory values and behaviors regarding sex.
7. There is the expectation to have children, to love them, and to support them until late adolescence (Lutz, 1964).
8. There are general expectations of children at various stages: to learn certain attitudes and values and act upon these, to meet certain emotional needs of parents, to cooperate, share, and show some degree of loyalty to the family.
9. The family is the major source for experiences of emotional support and release from tension (Kadushin, 1967).

It is important to be aware of the debate taking place today about some of these values. First the idea of monogamy is being questioned as a result of several factors: the reality of increasing divorce rates and of extra-marital involvements, and clinical evidence of widespread marital dissatisfaction. Various alternatives have been suggested, e.g. trial marriage with or without legal support, group marriage, "open marriage," and acknowledgement of serial marriage as an acceptable way of life, as well as acknowledgement of the value of no marriage for some of the population.

Another source of controversy centers on the ideal of the nuclear family. Some critics feel that this value overlooks the reality that a significant proportion of American families do not fit this classification at all, e.g. the lower socio-economic and minority groupings and the increasing number of families affected by divorce. Moreover, the effectiveness of the nuclear family in socializing children and in meeting the needs of all family members is questioned. Thus consideration is being given to the values of such alternatives as the extended family, communal living, and organized day care for children.

As a result of the women's liberation movement, nearly all of the values surrounding the role of wife and mother in the family are questioned. For example, regarding the value of cooperation and compromise between husband and wife, many women feel that this ideal can never be a reality until women share full equality with men. As long as the male enjoys all the status that accrues to holding a meaningful job, his needs and preferences tend to take precedence over the woman's. Traditionally, the work efforts of the wife outside the home have been sporadic, uncertain, and financially insignificant. The women's liberation movement emphasizes that the dilemma of many women is due to the traditional values associated with marriage and the family. It is a vicious circle: as long as women bear the major responsibility for childrearing, this function renders them insignificant in the economic and education marketplace, and this insignificance dictates the practicality of having the wife responsible for the childrearing. The growing number of women who wish to have both a career and family realize that unless they achieve equal job opportunity and remuneration, their husbands cannot afford to assume an equal share of the responsibility for childrearing; even though if they did, this would in turn allow women to make a greater commitment and contribution to their careers.

Historically, American family values regarding sex have encompassed all of the discrepancies and hypocrisies involved in sexual ethics and actual behaviors. A representative old saw is: "Don't do as I do but do as I say." This is part of almost everyone's upbringing. The challenge today to traditional sexual codes is to do away with the hypocrisy, that is, the tacit acceptance that stated standards of morality need not coincide with real behavior. Specifically, critics point out the illogicality of the double standard and the hypocrisy involved in the ideal of premarital chastity; they note that society's refusal to face up to the reality of sexual behavior in teenagers results in lack of parent-child communication, failure to provide sex education, and many of the teenage sexual problems, such as illegitimate pregnancy, venereal disease, and emotional disturbance.

The general expectation that married couples will have children is another value that is undergoing scrutiny. Both women's liberation and the ecology movements question the wisdom of this expectation. It is likely that more marriages in the future will be childless and that the average family size will continue to decline.

Moreover, there is today a trend toward emphasizing the rights of the child as an individual instead of the more traditional view of the child as the possession of his parents, who often feel they have the right to maintain control of his thinking and behavior well past adulthood. This trend will undoubtedly gain further support from the 18-year-old age of majority.

Controversy also surrounds the final value in the above list: the family as the major source of emotional support and release from tension. The criticism is usually aimed at the exclusivity and intensity of the nuclear family. As Sennett (1970) explains: ". . . the state of mind is that family members believe the actions and feelings that transpire in the family are in fact a microcosm of the whole range of 'meaningful' actions and feelings in the world at large" (p. 32). It is this kind of intensity that drains the energies of marital partners, parents, and children. If the emotional needs that each individual has can only be fulfilled by family, then husband and wife must be all things to each other, parents must be on 24-hour call to meet the needs of their children, and because of their great investment, parents feel they can dictate exactly what their children should be. Critics of the nuclear family support the more extensive contacts and exposure afforded by the extended family–whether based on kinship or other ties. While it is generally assumed that people will continue to need emotional support from each other and probably even more as the world becomes more complex, the question is whether emotional support and intimate relationships should be confined to the dwindling numbers of the nuclear family. Yet one theorist, Pollak (1969), predicts that the family will become even more a source of intimacy in the depersonalized world of the future, and thus he stresses the need for more and more competence in interpersonal dynamics.

Given the contemporary situation in which marriage and family values are in a noticeable state of flux, the task confronting the professional helper is formidable. With spouses and families beset by problems they do not understand, the helper has the double responsibility to diagnose and treat the here and now problems and to detect situations where problems are based on value conflicts. In the latter case, he has to prepare the spouses and family members to cope with future conflicts that might impinge on personal, marital, and familial functioning. An even more important task is that of preventing severely disruptive family problems. Any preventive program must be based on basic values of family life that are judged worth inculcating because of their contribution to individual and societal well-being. This means that program developers must face the current controversies about family life and support value goals based on both our scientific and humanistic traditions. Preventive programs must be thought out in such terms or they are doomed to failure before they begin.

REFERENCES

Agel, J. (Ed.): *The radical therapist*. New York, Ballantine Books, 1971.

Berne, E.: *Sex in human loving*. New York, Simon and Schuster, 1970.

Duvall, Evelyn: *Family development*. Philadelphia, Lippincott, 1962.

Eysenck, H. J.: A psychologist looks at pornography. *Penthouse, 8*:95-100, 102, 1972.

Feldman, Frances L. and Scherz, Frances H.: *Family social welfare*. New York, Atherton Press, 1968.

Gordon, T. L.: *Parent effectiveness training*. New York, Peter H. Wyden, 1970.

Hess, R. D. and Handel, G.: The family as a psychosocial organization. In G. Handel (Ed.), *The psychosocial interior of the family*. Chicago, Aldine, 10-24, 1967.

Hill, R. and Rodgers, R. H.: The developmental approach. In H. T. Christensen (Ed.), *Handbook of marriage and the family*. Chicago, Rand McNally, 171-211, 1964.

Hobbs, N.: Mental health's third revolution. *American Journal of Orthopsychiatry, 34*:822-833, 1964.

Kadushin, A.: *Child welfare services*. New York, Macmillan, 1967.

Kinsey, A. C., Pomeroy, W. B. and Martin, C. E.: *Sexual behavior in the human male*. Philadelphia, W. B. Saunders, 1948.

Kinsey, A. C., Pomeroy, W. B., Martin, C. E. and Gebhard, P. H.: *Sexual behavior in the human female*. Philadelphia, W. B. Saunders, 1953.

Lederer, W. J. and Jackson, D. D.: *The mirages of marriage*. New York, W. W. Norton, 1968.

Lutz, W.: Marital incompatibility. In N. Cohen (Ed.), *Social work and social problems*. New York, National Association of Social Workers, 1964.

Masters, W. H. and Johnson, Virginia E.: *Human sexual response*. Boston, Little, Brown, 1966.

Masters, W. H. and Johnson, Virginia E.: *Human sexual inadequacy.* Boston, Little, Brown, 1970.

O'Neill, Nena and O'Neill, G.: *Open marriage: a new life style for couples.* New York, M. Evans, 1972.

Pierce, R. M. and Schauble, P. G.: Responsibility for therapy: counselor, client, or who? *Counseling Psychologist, 1*:71-77, 1969.

Pollak, O.: The outlook for the American family. In E. C. McDonagh and J. E. Simpson (Eds.), *Social problems: persistent challenges.* New York, Holt, Rinehart, 1969.

Riess, I. L.: How and why America's sex standards are changing. In A. Shiloh (Ed.), *Studies in human sexual behavior: the American scene.* Springfield, Thomas, 200-209, 1970.

Saxton, L.: *The individual, marriage, and the family.* Belmont, Wadsworth, 1968.

Sennett, R.: The brutality of modern families. *Transaction, 7*:29-37, 1970.

Sherman, Julia A.: *On the psychology of women.* Springfield, Thomas, 1971.

Stein, C.: *Practical family and marriage counseling.* Springfield, Thomas, 1969.

Thorne, F. C.: *Tutorial counseling: how to be psychologically healthy.* Clinical Psychology Monograph No. 20. Brandon, Vt.: Clinical Psychology, 1965.

Toffler, A.: *Future shock.* New York, Random House, 1970.

Truax, C. B.: Reinforcement and nonreinforcement in Rogerian psychotherapy. *Journal of Abnormal Psychology, 71*:1-9, 1966.

CHAPTER TWO | INTERVENTION FORMAT

T HE PRECEDING CHAPTER presented a host of potential influences for sexual, marital, and familial relations. It is this set of influences that will necessarily be dealt with in professional helping, be it education, guidance, counseling, therapy, or consultation. This chapter is directed at casting a framework for the helping services; in other words, the focus is on creating an effective intervention format.

A one-to-one intervention format seems to predominate in most professional helping activities. The doctor/patient dyad has survived the years, and while unquestionably there is value to a close relationship between a single helper and a single helpee, there is increasing evidence to support that the involvement of others might best accomplish some intervention goals.

The issue of intervention format is particularly relevant to sexual, marital, and familial interventions, because functions under the rubric of each of these three terms are dependent upon more than one person. Thus, while there might be one person singled out as being the "patient," such as one spouse experiencing unpleasant reactions or demonstrating unacceptable behaviors toward the other or a child who engages in disruptive behavior within a family unit, inevitably any behavior change has direct bearing on both spouses and all members of the family. Therefore, there is reason to consider whether treatment of sexual, marital, and familial problems should go beyond the single "patient" or target person so as to involve all relevant persons—even though some may seemingly be well adjusted and not be experiencing emotional or behavioral difficulties.

This chapter will review critical factors that should be considered in the derivation of a treatment or intervention format. The underlying assumption is that no one treatment format is suitable for all "patients" or helpees and that the professional helper should give special consideration to the characteristics and needs of every individual seeking his services. He should not, therefore, simply employ his most used format or what has been done traditionally (such as doing one-to-one counseling because that is what is expected by helpees and colleagues alike and because it may be what would be the most rewarding psychologically or financially to him); rather he should tailor the intervention format to each individual. Critical format factors include: establishing the client system (the individual, the couple, and the family); the group as a treatment mode of choice; the shared helpee; the use of a co-helper; and follow-up.

ESTABLISHING THE CLIENT SYSTEM

When an individual seeks help, it is usually an acknowledgment of a deficit in emotional and/or behavioral adjustment that he wants to eliminate (or alleviate), or it is a rationale for placing the responsibility or "blame" on others (such as a spouse or family members) so that he can thereby absolve himself of a need to make commitment to alter the state of affairs. In either instance, there is a distinct insulating away from the real locus of the concern: the interpersonal communication and interaction.

What the foregoing two elements suggest is: *control in a relationship*. The term control could apply to control of one's own responses or control of the responses of others. As will be considered subsequently, the concept of control in a relationship is considered important in marriage and family interventions. The assumption is that the locus for all professional interventions (for marriage and family problems) is the relationship. Haley (1963) provides the following definition of relationship:

> When any two people meet for the first time and begin to establish a relationship, a wide range of behavior is potentially possible between them. They might exchange compliments or insults or sexual advances or statements that one is superior to the other, and so on. As the two people define their relationship with each other, they work out together what type of communicative behavior is to take place in this relationship. From all the possible messages they select certain kinds and reach agreement that these shall be included. This line they draw which separates what is and what is not to take place in this relationship can be called a mutual definition of the relationship. Every message they interchange by its very existence either

reinforces this line or suggests a shift in it to include a new kind of message (p. 6).

According to Haley, this mutually defined relationship is predicated on the interchanged messages, and logically the underlying dimension is communication. Any message carries other messages, i.e. other elements of the relationship, which add to the definition or meaning of the message at hand; qualification is given to messages by the context in which they occur, verbal messages, vocal and linguistic patterns, and bodily and non-verbal cues. And it is the dimension of communication that provides the mode for developing the important concept of *control in a relationship*. The importance of control is relevant to the therapeutic strategy used; i.e. the therapist must maintain control: "If the patient gains control in psychotherapy, he will perpetuate his difficulties since he will continue to govern by symptomatic methods" (Haley, 1963, p. 15). This leads Haley to support the use of directive therapy. The important point in this matter is that the relationship in general, and control and communication in specific, must receive therapeutic attention in sexual, marital, and familial professional helping; and it is only logical that the most efficacious approach would be to involve all relevant persons in some way.

As will be evident in the ensuing discussion, the most obvious approach to involving relevant others (in addition to the target helpee or "patient") would be to have them enter into the actual treatment sessions. This does, however, have concomitant problems. Foremost, perhaps, is the fact that while the target helpee or patient is motivated to seek some kind of resolution (even if it may be to absolve himself of responsibility), the other sexual partner or spouse or family members may not be motivated to make the personal commitment necessary for a therapeutic intervention to be effective. Thus a person might seek professional help for overcoming an unsatisfactory sexual response, such as a failure to reach orgasm during sexual intercourse, and it might be diagnostically clear that a suitable treatment approach would be systematic desensitization, a method that requires a cooperating sexual partner to help the target person progressively conquer the anxiety provoked by specific sexual acts or stimuli; but if the sexual partner is not motivated, i.e. unwilling to help, such a treatment approach will be of little or no consequence (unless arrangements are made for a surrogate sexual partner). Or if only one of the spouses is seeking professional help for altering unsatisfactory conditions within their marriage and the other spouse will not accommodate exploration and attempted changes, even on the part of the target person, then therapeutic change will be minimal, at least as compared to what might be possible if both spouses were actively working together to examine, change, and develop their marital relationship. Or if one family member is delineated as being the sole source of difficulty for a family, any change in him would have to be in the direction of accepting the family for what it is, rather than maximizing mutual contributions to each other, as would be possible if all (or at least most) of the family members were actively seeking an improved familial atmosphere. Therefore, when considering a treatment modality for sexual, marital, or familial problems, *the professional helper should analyze the possible benefits that could be derived from involving relevant others and should encourage these others to become involved as fully as their motivation and values will allow.*

One of the most favored formats for marriage interventions is the treatment of the two spouses together. Haley (1963) terms this Marriage Therapy:

> Marriage Therapy differs from individual therapy because the focus is upon the marital relationship rather than the intrapsychic forces within the individual. It also differs from Family Therapy where the emphasis is upon the total family unit with a child typically chosen to be the problem. Technically the term should be confined to the type of treatment where the therapist interviews the couple together. However, the variations are many: some therapists will see both marital partners separately, others will see one partner while occasionally seeing the spouse for an interview, and others will see one partner while referring the other elsewhere with collaboration between the two therapists. Actually the psychotherapist who only does individual psychotherapy and refuses to see the spouse of a married patient is involved in indirect marriage therapy. Not only is much of the time of individual treatment devoted to discussions of marital affairs, but if the individual changes the marital relationship will change—or terminate (p. 117).

A point to underscore is that when an individual is fixated, perhaps to the point of an "in-session therapeutic obsession," with the problems in the marital relationship, it is very difficult to move the person ahead in introspection about and behavioral changes aligned with intrapersonal factors. Therefore, there is reason to try to deal directly with the marital issues, and this creates a mandate: *for optimum success both spouses should be involved in the change efforts to the maximum extent that each can justify within their own set of values and motivational commitments.*

The obvious question is: When should Marriage Therapy be used? Haley's (1963) guidelines are that Marriage Therapy should be used when individual psychotherapy has failed and/or when methods of individual psychotherapy cannot be used, when the helpee experiences a sudden start of symptoms which coincide with marital conflicts, when a couple with conflict and distress (resistant to resolution) requests it, and when improvement in a helpee will apparently lead to a divorce or an eruption of symptoms in the spouse.

As was mentioned earlier, some persons enter into individual treatment presumably to deal with their intrapersonal difficulties but demonstrate the so-called "in-session therapeutic obsession," whereby they are unable to work on the psychodynamic aspects of their personality structure and behavioral repertoire. This circumstance might well contribute to Haley's guidelines that support the use of Marriage Therapy when individual psychotherapy has failed or cannot be used. In addition to therapeutically dealing with the marital problems in these instances, it is also beneficial to focus on why the person would allow or need an obsession-like response, as opposed to a strong commitment to intrapersonal foci. Haley's guideline regarding the possibility that improvement in the target person will result in a divorce or in the eruption of symptoms in the spouse should be considered from the philosophical position of "To whom is the therapist primarily responsible?" Stated differently, there are some professionals who would maintain that their commitment or responsibility is solely to their helpee, and they need not feel responsible for the spouse or family members; the helpee should, however, be aided in considering his responsibility to these others, such as what unpleasant conditions (e.g. divorce or other disrupting symptoms) might be created if he follows a particular emotional/behavioral track. On the other hand, it is clear that change in the target person will cast effects into the marriage and family relations, and it might well be in the best interest of the target person for the professional helper purposefully to orient the spouse or family members to the possibility of changes and to extend an opportunity for them to become involved in the change and in the course of events to be aided in their adjustment to the change. More consideration will be given to responsibility to spouses and family members in the section on follow-up.

As might be anticipated, the rationale for seeing both spouses, particularly seeing them together, creates the groundwork for involving all (or most) family members in efforts to improve familial conditions. There are two premises to this approach:

> Two premises are typically offered as reasons for bringing in all family members when one member is exhibiting symptoms. These reasons apply to treating couples when one spouse has symptoms or to treating the whole family when one child or parent is in distress. It is said that the person with symptoms is serving some family function by experiencing the psychopathology; he is satisfying the needs of relationships in the family by serving a scapegoat function, he is holding the family together, he is providing a focus for family discontent, and so on. It is also said that when the family member with the presenting problem improves, other family members exhibit distress, symptoms, or the dissolution of the family unit is threatened (Haley, 1963, p. 151).

In view of the possibility of the "sick" person's serving a family function, it is not uncommon to witness both subtle and blatant attempts by family members to sabotage constructive change on the part of the target person. This is because change in the target person automatically means that the need for a scapegoat is being upset and that another scapegoat or another means of placating the neurotic element within the family must be found, and this is disconcerting—the result: attempts to undermine or abort therapeutic efforts. Again it is evident that the cooperation and commitment of as many family members as possible is a prerequisite for optimal therapeutic success.

To approach Family Therapy, it is necessary to conceptualize both the global strategy of family interventions and the model for a family system. In regard to the former, Haley (1963) offers the following statement on the strategy for family interventions:

> It would appear that we need, at the very least, three classes of terms if we are to describe the repetitive exchanges people make in relationship with one another. We need terms for (a) the tactics, or behavior, of the single individual, (b) the exchange of tactics between people so that we can label the product or a set of tactics as a particular class of relationship, and (c) the total system which any set of relationships produces and therefore terms for classes of family systems (p. 158).

And this leads to the need for a model for conceptualizing the family system:

> As one observes that the behavior of one individual in a family exerts influence upon the others in the family, and as one further notes that a change in one person's behavior provokes responses in other family members, it becomes apparent that the theoretical conception being proposed is a cybernetic one. It follows that people associating together during long periods of time will not put up with any and all kinds of behavior from each other; they will set limits upon one another. Insofar as family members set limits for one another, it is possible to describe their interaction in terms of self-corrective processes in the total system. The family members respond in an error-activated way when any individual exceeds a certain limit. This process of mutually responsive behavior defines the "rules" of the family system. In this sense the family is a system which contains a governing process. However, there is not just a single governor for the system; each member functions as a governor of the others and thus the system is maintained (Haley, 1963, pp. 159-160).

In this conceptualization of the family system, there is a distinct conditioning flavor. The fact that members allow certain behaviors to occur but will not allow other behaviors to occur (at least not on a regular basis) reflects the principle of reinforcement. This means that much, if not all, of the family interactions, just like other interpersonal interactions (such as in the marital relationship), are dependent upon the contingencies that have received reinforcement. As will be brought out in the chapter on behavioral interventions, one of the basic therapeutic matters is the identification of reinforcement contingencies, i.e. what reinforces a given behavior. Then comes the mapping of a strategy to alter the contingencies, i.e. to start rewarding interactions that would be more preferable and eliminating the rewards incurred in the inter-actions that are less preferable or disrupting.

In the foregoing model for conceptualizing the family system, it is apparent that the concept of *governing* is critical. In families, governing seems to occur at two levels:

> (a) the error-activated response by a member if any member exceeds a certain range of behavior, and (b) the attempt by family members to be the metagovernor, i.e. the one who sets the limits of that range (Haley, 1963, p. 160).

This governing ties into the concept of *power,* which in turn ties into the concept of *control;* and it is a struggle for control within the relationship that the professional helper must deal with in or-der that mutual acceptance of influence, power, and control can be agreed upon, i.e. found acceptable, by all members of the family.

One of the seemingly best approaches for dealing with family problems is to bring the family members all together with the helper for exploration of the difficulties. It should be emphasized, however, that even with the entire (or most of the) family pres-ent, the tactics used have great similarity to those used in individu-al treatment:

> . . . in individual therapy the therapist usually indicates to the patient that the symptom is only a manifestation, not the real problem, and they must work upon what is behind it—the "roots" of the disturbance. In family therapy, the identified patient, usually a child, is offered as the problem and the therapist typically tells the family that the child is only a manifestation of the real problem and they must deal with what is behind it—the "roots" in the family disturbance (Haley, 1963, p. 167).

In practice (i.e. technically), individual and family treatments are quite similar; in theory, they have decidedly different rationales. It should be noted that, much like in group psychotherapy, the pro-fessional helper can:

1. treat the individual in the group or family context (that is, make therapeutic responses to each person as if doing individual treatment, but do so in the multi-person context, the family);
2. treat the collective (that is, make therapeutic responses designed to foster understanding of and change for the collective body, the family); and/or

3. treat both individually and collectively (that is, combine the tactics suggested in the first two points).

Thus, selection of a treatment format necessitates consideration of each of these three alternatives.

Network Therapy is an approach related to Family Therapy. In Network Therapy, the professional helper follows basically the same strategies as used with a family, but he brings in persons outside the primary family group. For example, if the focus was family, secondary family members (such as grandparents, aunts, uncles, cousins, etc.) and social contacts (such as friends, work colleagues, and casual acquaintances) might be brought in for at least one session. The "network" would be put under therapeutic scrutiny for purposes of clarifying all of the in-puts or influences and for developing plans for renovating the network, i.e. improving it. The size of the network, quite logically, could vary considerably, depending upon the breadth, depth, and number of contacts the target person or family has in their life space. It would not be surprising to have twenty or more persons present. The logistics alone of Network Therapy are difficult; it is hard enough to get all of the members of a family together, even if willing, because of work schedules and other commitments; and in Network Therapy schedule accommodation, space, and other extrapersonal factors require managerial expertise. Moreover, the size of the collective and the varying types of relationships (such as the differences in emotional proximity present in the collective) lead to potentially both benefits and liabilities. And finally, there is still but limited research to support that Network Therapy is more efficacious than other available approaches. However, there does seem to be theoretical support from the point of view of group dynamics and communications, but the professional helper should approach Network Therapy with the realization that there is not a clearcut scheme and that much of the success or failure will be dependent upon his clinical expertise.

GROUP INTERVENTIONS
AS THE TREATMENT MODE OF CHOICE

Group psychotherapy has evolved rapidly and has become one of the newly established yet reputable mainstays of mental health services. Sociological and psychological research into human behavior naturally led to consideration and investigation of interpersonal relations; and the logical extension was into collective behavior and group dynamics. As is true with most behavioral science activities that start as theoretical issues and move into laboratory and field research, it was only a matter of time until a translation was made to clinical applications.

Under the generic term of group therapy may be found a potpourri of *strange bedfellows*. Classic psychoanalysis has been altered to allow for the psychoanalyst to practice on several people at one time, thus doing individual psychoanalysis in a group setting. Neo-analysts have borrowed psychoanalytic principles and adapted them to techniques for many variations of psychoanalytically-oriented psychotherapy in groups. Behavior therapists have applied reinforcement contingencies and their related techniques in conditioning-oriented groups, such as providing systematic desensitization via a standardized hierarchy to a group of phobic persons. Indeed, throughout the array of theories of intervention there have been adaptations so that by now essentially every theory of counseling or psychotherapy has been successfully used in a group format.

Most recently, the trend has been toward so-called "Human Potential Growth Groups." Here again there is a variety of characteristics, with human potential growth groups encompassing many seemingly incompatible approaches. In general, the human potential movement emphasizes humanistic philosophy, but these humanistic principles often get transformed into intervention techniques that are more closely related to a quite different therapeutic change theory, such as using behavioral (i.e. conditioning) procedures to promote humanistic growth. Because of the special relevance of growth groups to the interactional or behavioral concomitants that occur between sexual partners, spouses, and family members, a separate chapter will be devoted to the human potential growth groups (see Chapter 6).

At this point, the key question is: Can a group intervention be the treatment mode of choice? The implication is that individual treatment, which has been so long maintained, is the superior intervention mode and that its efficacy must be surpassed or at least equated before a group intervention could be justified. Since the research is so vast and so contradictory and since the scope of this treatise prohibits a thorough review, it should be acknowledged that the following points represent a personalized summary statement. This statement, based on what the research has supported and contradicted, attempts to give a realistic perspective of the parameters of group interventions, and to retain, in keeping with the objectives of this book, a concern for practical matters.

As is true with other forms of interventions, group therapy has about as many definitions and perimeters as it has group leaders. Therefore, it must suffice to say that the global characteristics, based on a survey of members of the American Group Psychotherapy Association (Fidler and Waxenberg, 1971), are as follow:

> The profile indicates that the typical group therapist has two groups in treatment, each with an arithmetic mean of about seven patients, of whom six are likely to be present at any given meeting. Group membership varies, however, from two to 18 per group, with eight the most common number of members. The group sessions ordinarily run ninety minutes and are held once per week. Almost all (150 of 166) groups meet weekly; only 13 meet twice a week. The least frequent meet once every two weeks, and the most frequent meet five times per week. Length of sessions varies from thirty minutes to three hours, but 64 percent last ninety minutes and another 14 percent last sixty minutes. One group out of six holds an alternate meeting without the therapist. Most group sessions are held in private offices (56%) and in private clinics (13%), with the rest held in agencies or institutions. Only four groups of the 166 consisted of inpatients. The average total number of sessions attended by a cross-section of patients at a given point in time is fifty (p. 37).

In terms of type of person seen in group therapy, the survey indicated:

> Patients diagnosed as neurotic comprised 43 percent of all patients; another 30 percent were considered to have character disorders; 14 percent were labeled psychotic; and the remaining 13 percent were classified in a variety of other diagnostic categories (p. 37).

And regarding the use of concurrent therapeutic formats, Fidler and Waxenberg (1971) state:

> One-fourth of group therapy patients had had no prior psychiatric treatment, and one-half received no other treatment than group

therapy. One-third, however, concurrently received individual psycho-therapy, this treatment being conducted by the same person who was the group therapist in three-quarters of the instances and by another therapist in one-fourth. Patients in private therapy groups were more likely to receive concurrent individual treatment (p. 38).

It should be pointed out that this survey is based on information supplied by the membership of the American Group Psychotherapy Association, an organization that restricts its membership to professional mental health workers with specialized training and experience in group psychotherapy; therefore, the characteristics reflected in the foregoing descriptions can only be attributed to groups conducted by those sorts of professionals.

The total continuum of group experiences, some of which cannot justly be called *therapeutic* but are more *educational* or *self-growth* in objectives, encompasses, no doubt, types of groups that move far away from the psychotherapy groups described. Professionals with less or different kinds of training (who would not want, nor be able, to affiliate with an organization like the American Group Psychotherapy Association), community leaders, and lay persons lead all forms of group experiences, some of which are designed to deal with sexual, marital, and familial problems. The two most common types of groups are probably:

1. *Rap Groups,* where persons come together to *rap* (talk) about a given topic, the group leader facilitates verbal exchanges and explorations, and any attitudinal or behavioral change is left to be decided upon by the individual participant; and
2. *Self-Development Classes,* where again there is a specified topic and the group leader serves as an information-giver and the participants attempt to integrate academic knowledge about the topic into their personal lives.

There are, of course, many variations of these two types of groups.

While group experiences can be enriching, whether conducted by a professional mental health worker or a lay person with group skills, a critical concern for the professional helper must be whether to endorse or discourage a helpee's participation in one of these groups. The important questions to seek answers to are:

What does the helpee hope to accomplish by being in a group?
What are the objectives of the given group (being considered by the helpee)?

Is the group leader capable (in terms of personal characteristics and group skills) of effectively helping the group members achieve those objectives?

Have the group's objectives been clearly defined so that everyone in the group will understand its purposes, and have steps been taken to be sure that persons with incompatible objectives are not allowed in the group (e.g. some sort of screening procedure)?

And if this group experience is to be a supplement to another previously started form of therapeutic intervention, what will be the mutual effects of the initial therapeutic intervention and the group experience?

Finally, have arrangements been made that will accommodate a transmission of relevant information about the group experiences, particularly their ramifications for the helpee's life that should be dealt with by someone other than the group leader (e.g. have referral plans been arranged and an agreement by which the initial professional therapeutic helper can be kept informed of the developments fostered by the group experiences)?

It seems that positive answers to these questions can be much more valid for a given individual helpee than some predetermined set of values. For example, many professional helpers are prone to believe that a group experience can *best be accomplished* by a fellow professional, when in actuality, given fulfillment of the above guidelines, there are instances where a layman might be able to conduct a group that would be of even more help. Parenthetically, consider the situation in public health where it has been found that indigenous workers, such as laymen with special training in health practices, can win public acceptance for health ideas better than the professional; the premise being that the closer the communicators–the sender and the receiver–are to each other in socio-cultural characteristics, the more readily the message will be accepted; and when the layman has a professional consultant to work closely with, there is no reason why the service cannot be effective.

The nature of the qualities of a group leader is subject to individual opinion. As mentioned earlier, the emergence of Human Potential Growth Groups constitutes one of the major arenas for the issue of appropriate objectives and leadership competence. This will receive additional clarification in the subsequent chapter on Human Potential Growth Groups (see Chapter 6).

Underlying the entire consideration of the use of a group intervention as a treatment mode of choice is the comparative value,
particularly as compared to individual treatment. There is not total
accord among professionals about the efficacy of groups. However,
the position taken by those professionals who interpret the multitude of research studies as supporting group interventions is essentially that:

1. The power of peer identification and group pressure leads a person
   to accept a decision, such as for the need to alter one's behavior
   in a certain way, more thoroughly than if the decision is imposed
   or supported by only one other person, even if it is the high-
   status therapeutic helper.
2. Group process, with its combining of intellect and perceptual sets,
   opens the door to a more comprehensively explored and learned
   decision than if attempted by the single person.
3. The group can become a microcosm of the helpee's social world;
   and, since the therapeutic helper is involved, the participant or
   helpee can gain an accurate impression of his interactions with
   others (emphasis is on honesty and openness—even if it is unpleasant at the moment), can learn improved ways to cope with
   interactions, and can experience a new degree of affective intensity,
   as would be fostered by the reciprocal involvement, appreciation,
   and caring that would be elements of the group identity.

These global dimensions seem to cut-across all forms of groups,
and when placed in the therapeutic context become the structure
that can distinguish a group therapeutic intervention from an individual therapeutic intervention.

When comparing a group therapeutic intervention with the individual therapeutic intervention, it should be obvious that any
generalization is made with the full recognition that there will be
exceptions. In other words, generalizations about the effectiveness
of group interventions may be made only if it is acknowledged
that there will be some persons who will not benefit from a group
experience as much as they would from an individual experience.
This decision is, of course, why the group leader must be capable
of functioning as a diagnostician when screening participants for
a group intervention: *care should be exercised to assure that the
group intervention is the treatment mode of choice.*

There are, indeed, reasons why a group intervention would be the treatment mode of choice. All things being equal (meaning that idiosyncratic considerations for each helpee had been fulfilled), it can be asserted that:

1. The group, by virtue of being a microcosm of society, can provide a matchless laboratory society for prompting self-understanding and social-behavioral growth.
2. The group provides the helpee with a means for trying out behaviors and experiencing affective involvement that is not easily accomplished in one-to-one therapeutic interventions; likewise, the therapeutic helper is able actually to observe the helpee in action, rather than having to rely upon the highly subjective self reports made by a helpee in a therapeutic session.
3. The group allows for the experiencing of relationships, interactions, and emotions that cannot easily be attained in another context; for example, the concept of "sharing" is critical to relationships, and many spouses would not be able to create, encounter, and deal with the sharing of their spouse (in a psychological sense of the word) except via a group therapeutic experience.
4. Therapeutic economy, at least in many instances, seems greater for a group intervention than for an individual intervention. The economy is two-fold:
   A. The therapeutic helper is able to see more persons in the same amount of time, thereby allowing him to provide more helping interventions and thereby lowering the per capita cost; and
   B. The therapeutic progress appears to be accelerated (given certain prerequisites, such as readiness and motivation for a group experience) and thereby accomplishes relief from unpleasant conditions for the helpee in the least amount of time.

For a more thorough coverage of the theoretical, technical, and research materials and data intrinsic to the use of group interventions, the reader is referred to Bonner (1959), Cartwright and Zander (1960), Olmsted (1959), and Rosenbaum and Berger (1963).

In subsequent chapters, numerous techniques will be described. Almost without exception, each can be adapted for group use. Unless there are contraindications within a particular helpee's situation, there seems to be ample support for the belief that a group intervention could well be a treatment mode of choice for sexual, marital, and familial problems.

THE SHARED HELPEE

Mention was previously made about concurrent therapeutic interventions; this is quite common when one of the interventions is a group experience. One of the most obvious ways that "sharing" could occur in therapeutic helping is the involvement of a co-helper in the therapeutic sessions. Since this has many ramifications for the helper, helpee, and change process, a section will be devoted to this issue later. The major way that the sharing of a helpee occurs, and one which is quite different in effects from what is created when two helpers work together, is using two professional helpers to deal with the same helpee but in different intervention formats or from different theoretical stances.

In an analysis of separate therapists for group and individual psychotherapy, Roth and Stiglitz (1971) indicate:

> Concerns about sharing a patient (while additionally performing a different "technique" of treatment, individual versus group) seem to hover around the issues of transference and countertransference (p. 44).

Conflicting loyalties are seen as a possibility:

> when ambivalence toward primary objects is reflected onto the therapist, and much acting out of the transference may ensue, with seductions and manipulations geared at one to control the other. Material can be totally reserved for one therapist, making the other form of therapy flounder and perhaps fail . . . (pp. 44-45).

And the effects may also be revealed in the therapists' behavior, such as acting out or fantasies related to possible competition for the helpee's transference and relationship.

While the position maintained by Roth and Stiglitz (1971) could be labeled ambivalent at best (indeed, their major recommendation is that therapists and patients using this approach take an "unambivalent commitment to it"), there are also many potential benefits. For example, while a given format, such as one-to-one therapy may be achieving well, it is feasible that supplementation from another format, such as a group experience, could lead to even greater achievement in the same amount of time. Moreover, a commitment to and relationship with a second therapeutic helper could potentially enhance the work with the initial therapeutic helper. The important point is that the "sharing" of a helpee stimulates feelings within both the professional helper and the helpee, so that the decision to make use of a second helper or supplemental format should be made with the understanding that the initial helper and the helpee must confront their feelings continually and be prepared to deal with them therapeutically.

The sharing of a helpee has more than psychological factors; for the professional helper it introduces ethical factors. Specifically, professional ethics require that a therapeutic helper not accept a helpee that is presently receiving services from another therapeutic helper unless the initial helper has been informed, agrees that the second helper's involvement will be of potential value for the helpee, and arranges (with the helpee's knowledge, of course) for a coordinated exchange of information. For example, the Code of Ethics of the American Psychological Association states:

> *Principle 11. Interprofessional Relations.* A psychologist acts with integrity in regard to colleagues in psychology and in other professions.
> a. A psychologist does not normally offer professional services to a person receiving psychological assistance from another professional worker except by agreement with the other worker or after the termination of the client's relationship with the other professional worker.
> b. The welfare of clients and colleagues requires that psychologists in joint practice or corporate activities make an orderly and explicit arrangement regarding the conditions of their association and its possible termination. Psychologists who serve as employers of other psychologists have an obligation to make similar appropriate arrangements (American Psychological Association, 1969, p. xxiv).

Clearly, then, it is an ethical violation to begin to work with a helpee without communication with the professional helper already involved.

It must be acknowledged that some persons tend to seek out a second professional helper for less than honorable reasons. For example, it is not uncommon for a person in psychotherapy to become negative toward the therapist when therapeutic pressure to change is being exerted or when the psychic material being dealt with is disturbing. There may then be the tendency to flee, a tendency that needs to be confronted and explored in therapy to see its relevance to the person's general approach to problem solving and his life style. Therefore, a professional helper should be prepared to guard against the seductive, flattering overtures that some persons will present to him in hopes that they can justify leaving their previous or current therapeutic helper and finding a new one. One good rule of thumb is to always require a "transfer patient" of this nature to:

1. discuss the possibility of changing helpers with the initial helper,
2. contact the initial helper personally to ascertain a clear understanding of the potential second helper's position on the possibility of a transfer, and
3. only accept the person if the initial helper has had the opportunity of working with him on his termination plan.

Neglecting guidelines of this nature paves the way to potential violations of professional conduct and of optimum helping benefits for the would-be helpee.

Even with the ethical issue and the need to assure that any transfer is actually in the best interest of the person's therapeutic or growth objectives, there are some professional and lay helpers who are seemingly indiscriminate in accepting a person into their services. Often this seems to be motivated by a wish to build up a private practice or by a need for self-gratification or ego-enhancement on the part of the helper. Because of the nature of advanced professional training programs, which give intense attention to the development of a "professional person," these kinds of violations are less common among well-prepared professionals than among persons with lower levels of training, lay persons, and persons who (whether professional or not) are strong advocates of a specific approach to helping. In regard to the latter, there appear to be a number of instances involving leaders of human potential growth groups in which this sort of violation has occurred. Specifically, some growth/encounter group leaders (typically within the lower echelon of training) interpret their intervention as being "educational" or "self-growth," as opposed to "therapeutic" and therefore believe that they are exempt from ethical and therapeutic concern; in other words, they will allow anyone into their groups without screening and without communication with a professional helper already involved with the person. This is definitely not in accord with the high quality of functioning endorsed by relevant professional associations for the growth/encounter/sensitivity kinds of groups. One masters-level psychologist regularly violated these kinds of conditions, maintaining that even though he was professionally identified with a college psychology department and he used his departmental facilities to house his encounter groups, the fact that he was doing "self-growth" encounter groups rooted in education, not therapy, allowed him to disregard the clearcut guidelines in the American Psychological Association's Code of Ethics, such as the ethical obligation to communicate with the professionals involved with members of his encounter groups before accepting them as participants. This situation was not formally acted upon, but it seems that a professional judicial committee would quite likely label it unethical conduct. It should be reemphasized that the responsibility is far more than merely being observant of professional protocol, it is a matter of providing interventions in such a way that the recipient, the helpee, is assured of optimal opportunity for benefit.

Differing theoretical orientations constitute another way in which two or more professional helpers may be involved in "sharing" a helpee. It is unusual to find a psychotherapist referring a helpee to another psychotherapist, primarily because it is assumed that professional competencies are comparable and because all of the insight-oriented psychotherapies (i.e. those theoretical approaches that place emphasis on introspection and the development of insight in order to lead to resolution of an underlying emotional conflict and the acquisition of symptom-free behavior) support that transfer to another psychotherapist might just be postponing depth dynamics. An exception to this, however, might be the psychotherapist who does only individual treatment and wants one of the persons or helpees with whom he is involved to have a group intervention, and so he would refer him to a group therapist.

It is, however, both common (relatively speaking) and logical for an insight-oriented psychotherapist to refer a helpee to a behavior therapist for conditioning-based behavioral modification. In these instances, the referral is usually made for behavioral treatment of a specific symptom or behavior problem, one that may

have been seemingly immune to the psychotherapeutic intervention
or one that is so discomforting that it must receive specific attention for purely symptom-removal purposes, with the expectation
that further insight-oriented treatment will be provided for the
working-through and/or resolution of related emotional conflicts
(if any). In describing the behavior therapist as an adjunctive
source, Woody (1972) states:

> Professional protocol and ethics make it mandatory that the adjunct
> therapist always communicate relevant information to the referring
> primary therapist, particularly when his behavioristic intervention
> leads to recognition of, and therapeutic dealing with, psychodynamic
> factors. At no time should the adjunct therapist allow either himself
> or the patient to consider using their relationship evolving in
> behavior therapy as a total replacement for the relationship estab-
> lished with the initial psychotherapist, unless, of course, the initial
> psychotherapist and the adjunct therapist conclude, after consult-
> ing with the patient, that this would be in the best interest of the
> patient (p. 229).

While this discussion is focusing upon psychotherapy and behavior
therapy, it should be obvious that the principle–an insight-oriented helper making adjunctive use of a behaviorally-oriented helper
and vice versa–is applicable to all types of professional helping.

In an analysis of the use of a behavior therapist as an adjunct
to the efforts of a psychotherapist, Woody (1972) posits that there
are three unique types of effects. First, although behavior therapists
do not consider the therapeutic relationship *per se* to be of importance to promoting behavioral change, it appears that transference
does occur in behavior therapy (that is, for example, a patient reflects feelings about the behavior therapist that seem rooted in a
previous relationship, such as with a parent):

> Clinical experience, however, reveals that transference does enter
> into behavior therapy, often in a most pronounced manner; and this
> seems especially true with "shared patients." The term "especially"
> is used and seems justified, not because transference phenomena are
> not part of the behavior therapy relationship without psychotherapy
> (for the opposite seems true), but because they seem to be more
> readily recognized in situations where the patient is also receiving
> insight-oriented therapy. If this is so, it may be because the patient,
> as a result of previous psychotherapy, has already learned to allow
> transference reactions to occur unfettered and uncamouflaged,

whereas in pure behavior therapy neither the therapist nor the patient has typically been prepared even to recognize the occurrence of transference phenomena (p. 230).

And occasionally this transference seems to be presented as a reaction to a two-theory treatment approach, where the helpee "may reject or resist treatment by one theoretical approach on grounds that the other approach is superior, or he may try to manipulate by pitting one therapist against the other via pointing to the theoretical differences . . ." (p. 230). Second, again though neglected by behavior therapy, it appears that some degree of insight, well within the purview of psychotherapy, may occur during the course of behavioristic treatment, and the behavior therapist may find himself functioning, albeit to but a small degree, as an insight-oriented therapist. Relatedly, Woody (1972) states:

1. the acquisition of insight facilitates conditioning procedures;
2. behavioristic treatment of one symptom (e.g. by systematic desensitization) may result in generalization to other, perhaps psychodynamically related, symptoms (i.e. untreated symptoms are alleviated as a result of treating another symptom); and
3. elimination of behavior problems via conditioning techniques may produce increased self-understanding for the patient in his overall psychological structure (p. 231).

Third, the provision of behavior therapy along with psychotherapy seems to result, at least in many cases, in the total treatment program in general and the psychotherapy in specific being accelerated:

> As but one example, case studies suggest that a patient who is successfully treated by behavior therapy for a rather limited behavior problem will be favorably disposed toward entering into psychotherapy for more general personality problems; in other words, he will show less resistance to psychotherapeutic processes. Apparently this situation occurs because the patient's first-hand experience with behavior therapy convinces him that a therapist can help him; therefore, he is better able to accept the admittedly ambiguous parameters of insight-oriented psychotherapy (pp. 231-232).

Each of these three points gives support to the "shared helpee" concept, and particularly to the use of combined insight-oriented and behaviorally-oriented interventions. In regard to the integrated use of insight and behavioral techniques, the final chapter of this book will present a technical frame of reference for the so-called *Psychobehavioral Counseling and Therapy* approach. The *Psychobehavioral* frame of reference, elaborated upon elsewhere (Woody, 1971), maintains that professional helpers should adopt an eclectic theoretical stance, retain the potential for using either insight-oriented or behaviorally-oriented techniques (or both), and integrate behavioral or conditioning techniques into insight-oriented interventions whenever this combined format would best serve the helpee and his idiosyncratic psychological/problematic composite. As will be discussed in the final chapter, it would appear that an insight-oriented professional helper should turn to a behavioral technique and integrate it into his regularly espoused theoretical approach for: (1) facilitation and acceleration of his intervention; (2) elimination of uncomfortable symptoms; and (3) treatment of therapeutically unresponsive helpees.

To summarize the shared helpee concept, it is without question that involvement with more than one professional helper at the same time will lead to complex effects, both within the helpers and the helpee. However, since there are seemingly sound reasons for believing that multiple helpers, presenting differing intervention formats (e.g. individual treatment and a group experience) or presenting differing theoretical approaches (e.g. insight-oriented and behaviorally-oriented), can be of unique value at certain stages in the therapeutic progress of at least some helpees (and this may be understatement, since it is likely that every helpee could benefit to some degree from multiple helpers at some point), the possibility of implementing a shared helpee treatment format should not be underestimated.

USE OF A CO-HELPER

Involved in the "shared helpee" concept is the use of two or more helpers who work together. As contrasted to the situations presented in the previous discussion, the co-helper would work along with the initial helper, instead of being a relatively independent referral source.

The co-helper could see the helpee independent of the initial helper, but would consult (with the helpee's knowledge) with him regularly in order that their mutual in-puts would reciprocally contribute to the therapeutic change processes and goals. On the other hand, the co-helper could actually be in the sessions with the initial helper, so that the therapeutic effects would be manifestations, at least partially, of the fact that two different professional helpers were concurrently interacting with the helpee.

The use of co-helpers is supported by the contribution that it can potentially make to the helpee's progress. The old adage of "If one is good, two are better" seems to hold true for co-helpers for at least five reasons:

1. multiple helpers rely on more than one vantage point, thereby allowing for cross-validation of hypotheses and increased informational-gathering strength;
2. the general clinical expertise is increased;
3. the therapeutic power seems greater (whether this is additive or geometric remains for conjecture);
4. the helpee enjoys the benefits of having multiple models (i.e. behavioral examples for patterning); and
5. the transference effects seem to be enriched because of personal stimuli being emitted by the professional helpers.

The latter point is especially true if the helpee has both a male and a female helper; for example, he can conjure up transference reactions to both masculine and feminine figures, e.g. father and mother.

But the use of a co-helper is not a simple matter. While cognitively it is easy to recognize the potential benefits of a co-helper and it is relatively easy to accept the idea of another helper working with one's helpees, actual attempts at co-helping often introduce other highly personalized feelings, feelings that can, in turn, contribute to or detract from the therapeutic intervention.

One of the most basic issues is what will be the respective statuses of the helpers. If one of the helpers was initially involved alone, the introduction of a second helper tends to create questions of superiority: Is the initial helper displaced by the new second helper, i.e. his status lowered? Is the new second helper equal or subservient to the initial helper? These status questions seem to arise both overtly and covertly in the minds of the helpers and the helpees. It becomes especially pronounced when:

1. the helpers are from different professional disciplines and one of the disciplines has traditionally been accorded a higher status than the other (such as a physician-psychiatrist having a psychiatric nurse as a co-helper); and
2. one of the helpers is defined operationally or by labeling as an "assistant" or "adjunct" helper, with the connotation being that the other helper is the superior leader.

There may, of course, be instances where differing statuses are both necessary and of value to the treatment, but the status conflict, whether real or imaginary, can also be a deterrent to therapeutic progress unless confronted.

Another major issue is the quality of the relationship between the co-helpers. There seem to be three prerequisites that must be fulfilled in order to have a quality sufficient for unimpeded helping.

First, *knowledge of the professional functioning or style* is a definite prerequisite for co-helpers. Ideally this would mean a knowledge that was great enough to allow each to be able to almost subconsciously predict how the other would respond in a given interaction.

Professional respect is a second prerequisite. Each co-helper must be able to appreciate why and how the other will function and the justification (in academic terms) for their espoused treatment position.

But these two prerequisites are not enough. Several highly reputable psychotherapists have expressed surprise and dismay at the outcome of trying to work with a colleague for whom they possessed knowledge of their professional functioning or style and maintained professional respect. In some of these instances there was a distinctly positive personal bond, but even that did not circumvent disruptive and countereffective elements within their conjoint efforts.

What seems to be the third critical ingredient or prerequisite is a rather nebulous entity: a *high degree of intimacy* between the co-helpers. This means that mutual knowledge, acceptance, and appreciation of qualities must move beyond the academic and even beyond the professional. There must be honest personalized intimacy.

Personalized intimacy can take on many forms. There has to be an element of *caring*. Caring would mean that the co-helpers are aware of the other's needs and are concerned that their well-being (professional and personal) is honored. This does not mean that there cannot be hostile feelings or negative reactions toward each other; indeed, a relationship insulated from these kinds of feelings deprives the helpee of a very realistic aspect of human behavior that he could benefit from encountering within the helping context. But it does mean that the concern for each other is authentic and honest. Subsumed in this definition of caring is the implication that there must be the potential for affection and, theoretically, love. The affection need not be obtained at the beginning of the conjoint intervention, but the foundation must be laid, through appreciation and attraction, for it to evolve. Likewise, love–an intensive and extensive version of affection and caring and intimacy–need not be present, but again there must be the potential. The definition of love cannot be totally platonic; on the other hand, the sexualization of the relationship need not be acted out–indeed, because of the multiplicity of influences and responsibilities in the life space of each professional helper, there are many reasons why certain elements of numerous affective dimensions would not be acted out, but would be confronted and resolutions for defining the relationship would be accepted.

The provision of sexual, marital, and familial interventions, however, readily brings to the minds of both professionals and laymen the possibility of sexual intimacy between co-helpers. In one professional training workshop, a co-helping team of a male psychiatrist and a female psychiatric nurse, who were married but not to each other, found that the foremost question in their workshop-peers' minds was if they been involved sexually together; this was especially relevant in that the workshop was on sexual counseling and the co-helping team worked extensively with sexual response problems. To the surprise of many, the co-helping team answered that they had not been sexually intimate–they had sexual fantasies about each other, had encountered (via verbal sharing) each other's sexual self, and had discussed the ramifications of a potential sexual relationship in a therapeutic/supervisory manner. Moreover, they had concluded for both professional and personal reasons that to have sexual intimacy, in the sense of acting out, would not reflect respect for the professional and personal integrity of each other, such as their commitments to their respective spouses.

Husband-wife co-helping teams present another issue: Because of the day-to-day dynamics of being married to each other, is it possible for a husband-wife co-helping team consistently to be effective in their therapeutic interventions? As might be expected, there is no categorical answer. However, it seems logical that the shared intimacy and commitments create the potential for great contributions to helpees, and it seems that, because of the reality value of having both positive and negative affective encounters, disagreements between husband-wife co-helpers could be useful in treatment, just as would seem true for non-married co-helpers. Further, the key factor seems to be professional expertise. Just as a psychotherapist sets aside his personal problems, unless they are to be used in therapeutic service of his helpee, there is no reason why a well-trained husband-wife co-helping team could not set aside their personal lives to an appropriate extent when they engage in professional service. Of great significance is the fact that a husband-wife co-helping team provides a unique set of conditions for helpees, and in view of the rationale for co-helping in general and the relationship aspects of sexual/marital/familial problems in specific, it seems highly desirable to use this approach for sexual partners, married couples, and families.

FOLLOW-UP

Follow-up efforts are often forgotten or grossly neglected by professional helpers. Part of this is probably due to realistic factors like heavy case loads and time-drain (and possible lack of financial returns), but what might also be involved is a psychological reaction to having "lost" a helpee.

Professional helpers react quite differently to the termination of a helpee. Some profess no feelings. Some are openly glad, either because they feel good about having helped or because they are pleased at lightening their responsibilities (at least for the moment). Some feel frustrated and/or guilty because they do not know just how much they have or have not helped. Others feel like they have lost something, much like losing a loved one: one psychotherapist remarked that each time a helpee terminated, he felt that a part of his own life had finished or died. These are but a few of the reactions; undoubtedly there are as many reactions as there are professional helpers.

Conversely, the reactions on the part of helpees is comparably idiosyncratic. The most common concept is, of course, so-called "termination anxiety," and professional helpers typically attempt to deal with or resolve such anxiety, which is usually ambivalence about ending treatment, before the termination actually occurs. Some approaches to therapeutic intervention would maintain that treatment is incomplete until such time as the termination feelings on the parts of both the helper and the helpee had been encountered and resolved. Other approaches, such as those that are behavioral in orientation, would give little or no attention to such feelings, only to making sure that the helpee had reordered his life space in such a way that contradictory reinforcers would be eliminated or controlled.

Follow-up efforts are important, but they must be done in the interest of the helpee, not merely to resolve the anxiety or to satisfy the curiosity of the helper. However, it is quite appropriate for the helper to transmit his feelings of caring and responsibility via a follow-up, but care must be taken to be sure that the follow-up does not serve to reinforce the helpee back into treatment solely because of his feelings for the professional helper.

It is crucial that the helpee has reordered his life space or made behavioral adaption that will circumvent reinforcement of unacceptable or undesirable consequences. Despite this being a basic tenet of behaviorism, it is surprising how many behavior therapists do not give attention to follow-up. It may be asserted that every professional helper, regardless of theoretical orientation, should plan steps to assure that the post-treatment life space of the helpee will present minimal pressure to return to a previous unacceptable behavior or to create a new, equally unsatisfactory, behavior.

Implicit in the foregoing is the idea of follow-up efforts focusing on the period after the therapeutic intervention has been completed (and has presumably been successful). Follow-up may, however, be interpreted in a second manner: *The professional helper should take steps to prepare other persons primarily involved with the helpee for his improved, but different, functioning.*

It might seem that any concerned person would welcome behavioral improvement, especially in a spouse or family member. But such is not always the case. As was mentioned in the earlier description of family therapy, for example, many families use one member as a symptom-carrier; the same is true in sexual and marital relations. Therefore, there may be conscious or unconscious efforts by others to maneuver the helpee back into his pre-treatment functioning in order that their needs may be served by the helpee's having behavioral pathology.

Timing is a related factor. Behavioral techniques (to be described in detail in Chapter 5) promote rapid changes in behavioral responses. Therefore, to take but one example, a person who enters a hospital for intensive behavior therapy for a sexual problem may be expected to eliminate the disrupting sexual behavior in a matter of days or weeks. While his learning of new sexual behaviors will follow, he will be encountering his past sexual partner, but will do so as a person with a different set of sexual preferences. It is not uncommon in situations like this for a sexual partner to go to great lengths, partly because of the suddenness in the changing of sexual preferences, to reinforce the helpee back into the past sexual mode—one which satisfied both partners' needs at the time. Thus the professional helper must consider the preparation of relevant others to accept and support the helpee's post-treatment changes as a mandatory part of his therapeutic responsibility to the helpee.

SUMMARY

This chapter has presented five critical dimensions relevant to the intervention format for sexual, marital, and familial relations: establishing the client system, group interventions as the treatment mode of choice, the shared helpee, the co-helper, and follow-up. These issues in application provide the foundation for the theoretical and technical aspects of therapeutic interventions. The following chapters will, accordingly, provide theoretical and technical material for dealing with sexual, marital, and familial relations. Sequentially, the subsequent chapters will cover: facilitating conditions in helping relationships (with special reference to application to daily relationships), interpersonal interventions, behavioral interventions, human potential growth groups, and the psychobehavioral frame of reference (integrating behavioral and insight techniques).

REFERENCES

American Psychological Association: Ethical standards of psychologists. In J. A. Lazo (Ed.), *Directory: 1968*. Washington, D. C., American Psychological Association, xxi-xxvi, 1969.

Bonner, H.: *Group dynamics: principles and applications*. New York, Ronald Press, 1959.

Cartwright, D. and Zander, A. (Eds.): *Group dynamics: research and theory* (2nd ed.), Evanston, Row, Peterson and Co., 1960.

Fidler, J. W. and Waxenberg, S. E.: A profile of group psychotherapy practice among A.G.P.A. members. *International Journal of Group Psychotherapy, 21*:34-43, 1971.

Haley, J.: *Strategies of psychotherapy*. New York, Grune and Stratton, 1963.

Olmsted, M. S.: *The small group*. New York, Random House, 1959.

Rosenbaum, M. and Berger, M. (Eds.): *Group psychotherapy and group function*. New York, Basic Books, 1963.

Roth, S. and Stiglitz, M.: The shared patient: separate therapists for group and individual therapy. *International Journal of Group Psychotherapy, 21*:44-52, 1971.

Woody, R. H.: *Psychobehavioral counseling and therapy: integrating insight and behavioral techniques*. New York, Appleton-Century-Crofts, 1971.

Woody, R. H.: Conceptualizing the "shared patient": treatment orientations of multiple therapists. *International Journal of Group Psychotherapy, 22*:228-233, 1972.

| CHAPTER THREE | FACILITATING CONDITIONS: BASIC DIMENSIONS FOR PSYCHOLOGICAL GROWTH AND EFFECTIVE COMMUNICATION |

FACILITATING CONDITIONS: BASIC DIMENSIONS FOR PSYCHOLOGICAL GROWTH AND EFFECTIVE COMMUNICATION

CHAPTER THREE

PAUL G. SCHAUBLE, PH.D.
University of Florida

ONE OF THE MOST IMPORTANT advances for the helping professions has been the delineation of the so-called "facilitating conditions." Rogers (1961) set the foundation with the three major postulates of the client-centered approach, i.e. empathy, congruence, and positive regard. The theory behind the client-centered approach (i.e. the non-directive approach) was that if the helper could manifest these qualities in the therapeutic session and effectively communicate them to the helpee, the therapeutic relationship would facilitate psychological growth for the helpee. From this subjectively-derived, rather simplistic beginning came a plentitude of scientific research (much of which was empirical and highly respectable from the vantage point of research design). Further refinements and extensions have been made; and to date, there are several facilitating conditions, of which the main ones are presented herein.

This chapter has two objectives. First, the material is designed to introduce the professional helper to the facilitating conditions (or dimensions) of the helping relationship and to offer suggestions for implementing them in the helping services. Second, guidelines are offered for helping individuals cultivate facilitating qualities so that they can, in turn, promote psychological growth for themselves, their spouses, and their family members.

HELPING: PROCESS AND COMMUNICATION

When an individual requests professional help, such as counseling or psychotherapy, it is for seeking a means with which to facilitate adjustment to life. The person who is sought out to provide help is assumed to be competent in the business of adjusting his own life, and capable of providing direction and guidance to the seeker. When the person seeking help (i.e. the "helpee") finds a person whose assistance he desires (i.e. the "helper"), they become involved in a "helping relationship."

The degree of intensity of helping relationships varies considerably. The helpee may seek help from relatives, friends, teachers, or bartenders, but if he is unable to find a suitable helper, he may turn as a last resort to a professional helper, e.g. a counselor or therapist. By the time the helpee makes contact with the professional helper, he has typically experienced frustration and failure in his attempts to communicate himself and his problem in a satisfying manner. Because of his past contact with the potential "helpers" he has approached who have failed to respond to him in a facilitating manner, he is often conditioned into the expectation that he will not be heard or understood. Thus, the helpee often approaches the professional helping relationship with an understandably negative set. He feels unable to communicate himself in a satisfying manner; he has been unable to find helpers who can teach him how to improve his communications and he finds himself investing (perhaps desperately) in a complete stranger in hope that he finally can be understood and learn to understand himself.

The helper must try to understand, and must communicate his understanding to the helpee, if a helping relationship is to be established. *Understanding* is necessary, for without it any prescription or program would be premature and unreliable, and might be damaging. The *communication* of understanding is necessary, for unless the helpee experiences being understood (or experiences the efforts of the helper to *try* to understand) he will be unlikely to accept suggestions or prescriptions (even assuming their validity) from the helper until he believes that the helper does have an accurate understanding upon which to base his responses. If the helper is successful in communicating understanding, helping or therapy can proceed effectively into a variety of modes of treatment.

The helping relationship, then, consists of a helpee or person who seeks assistance because he has not been able to communicate satisfactorily in his previous contacts with people, and a helper or person who communicates understanding to the helpee, which enables the helpee to turn his energy toward understanding himself. It is at this point that the helper is able to suggest treatment or programs which will enable the helpee to become more effective.

In essence, *helping is the process whereby a helper understands a helpee, and the helpee comes to understand himself and learn new behavior*. It is no more, nor less, profound.

Communication, simply put, is the sending and receiving of messages. One party sends a message, or speaks, while another party receives the message, or listens. Successful communication is dependent first upon the ability of the sender to speak clearly and congruently, and second upon the ability of the receiver to listen sensitively and receive messages accurately.

The helping process is a sub-process of communication, and is necessary because the helpee is not functioning effectively as a speaker or communicator. He does not identify and project himself with clarity and congruence to other people in such a way that he is heard and understood. To be sure, whether or not the helpee is received and understood is dependent on the listening skills of the people around him. In fact, the manner in which the helpee speaks is, to a large extent, a reaction to the way he has been heard and responded to in the past. Nevertheless, the helpee is a helpee because he is dissatisfied with his ability to communicate with others, and is dissatisfied with himself (i.e. the qualitative aspects of his internal communication).

The helper, on the other hand, is a helper because he is a specially competent listener. Through his ability to hear and respond sensitively and accurately to the helpee, he enables the helpee to experience being understood. As the helpee experiences understanding, he learns new ways of communicating that increase his effectiveness to speak with his helper, and he gradually extends these beyond the individual helping relationship to speak and communicate with other people. When the helpee has become an effective speaker, he is no longer dependent on the helper for his communications, and at this point no longer *needs* to be "the helpee." Communication thus moves beyond the confines of the helping process, and helpee and helper are able to move more freely between the roles of speaker and listener.

The helping process, by focusing on either the speaker or listener role (in therapy or in training for therapy) is specifically designed to improve the level of overall communication. If we were all effective speakers or listeners, there would be no need for the helping process, but since most of us experience at least some difficulty in both speaking and listening, we are either helpees or helpers in most of our communications.

In order to conceptualize the potential outcomes in the interaction of sending and receiving messages, let us consider an analogy with two telegraph operators. Telegraph operator Oscar decides he wants to send a message to telegraph operator Edgar in a town 60 miles away. If we consider that Oscar's ability to send the message can range from 0 percent (absolutely ineffective) to 100 percent (absolutely effective), we can then identify three levels on which Oscar's message can be transmitted:

1. At *Level I* (corresponding to 0-33% effectiveness on our scale) Oscar's transmission is quite ineffective. Oscar may have neglected to turn on the current, there may be no understandable signals emanating from his transmitter, and/or when signals *are* sent out they are erratic and unclear.
2. At *Level II* (34-66% effectiveness) Oscar's transmission is partially effective. Now his current is on, there are definite signals emanating from his transmitter, and these signals are generally clear—although they may be somewhat erratic and inconsistent.
3. At *Level III* (67-100% effectiveness) Oscar is consistently communicating at a high level. Current is stable and a strong, clear message is transmitted in concise, understandable symbols.

Thus, when Oscar is functioning at *Level III,* he is an effective *speaker,* and his messages are transmitted competently in a productive communication process. When Oscar is functioning at *Level II,* he vacillates between the roles of *speaker* and *helper;* at times his messages are communicated competently, but at other times his messages are vague and non-productive. When Oscar is functioning at *Level I* he is definitely in trouble. He needs assistance in transmitting almost any understandable message, and often he is not even capable of communicating this need. Oscar must now function as a *helpee* if he is to communicate at all; in other words, he is dependent on contact with very competent receivers if he is to be understood.

Now that we can categorize the level at which Oscar transmits we can follow the message and see how Edgar receives it. Edgar's receiving skill can also be scaled from 0 percent (absolutely ineffective) to 100 percent (absolutely effective), and we can identify three levels at which the message may be received:

1. At *Level I* (0-33%) Edgar's reception is totally ineffective. He receives less of the message than Oscar originally transmitted and when signals are received, they either are not recorded or they are distorted and misrepresent the message that was sent.
2. When Edgar functions at *Level II* (34-66%) he experiences partially effective reception. He is capable of picking up and responding to most of the signals sent, but his understanding is dependent to some extent on a clear transmission from Oscar.
3. At *Level III* (67-100%) Edgar picks up all signals transmitted. He screens out unclear or unnecessary communications, and focuses on the *essence* of the sender's message—often arriving at a full understanding before the sender has completed his transmission.

Thus, when Edgar is functioning at *Level III,* he is an effective listener, able to hear and understand any intelligible messages Oscar may attempt. At this level, Edgar is able to function constructively as a helper, and his responses facilitate Oscar's development of transmitting skills. At *Level II,* Edgar generally receives Oscar's transmissions, and he can function as a listener if the message received is relatively clear. When Edgar functions at *Level I,* he is not receiving messages reliably, if at all, and he is not able to facilitate or even to continue productive communication. In fact, at this level Edgar's responses to messages transmitted produce a negative or deteriorative effect on most communication interactions.

Obviously, when Oscar and Edgar are both functioning at a *Level III,* their communication is direct, efficient, and reliable. This "model communication" is to be desired, although it is seldom reached or maintained. When both Oscar and Edgar function at a *Level II,* communication generally occurs, though the level of understanding may vacillate between poor and good. If both sender and receiver are functioning at *Level I,* virtually no communication is possible. The sender's messages are erratic and obscure, and if they are received at all they tend to be distorted or ignored. Of course, it is necessary both to send and receive messages if one is to be effective in communication; that is, it is known that speaking and listening skills are highly correlated. Thus it is rare to find someone functioning at Level I as a speaker who functions at a higher level as a listener, and vice versa. This being the case, inferences can be made about levels of functioning in the communication and/or helping process.

If Oscar is functioning at Level II, communication can occur only when Edgar is functioning at Level II or above. Stated differently:

1. Level II is the minimal level of functioning for both parties if an interaction is to be an efficient communication. If Oscar is functioning at Level I, Edgar must function at least at Level II (and preferably Level III) if he is to receive and understand Oscar's message at all;
2. Level II is the minimal level at which a person can function as a "helper," capable of facilitating communication; and
3. Communication cannot occur unless at least one of the participants functions at Level II or above.

FACILITATIVE CONDITIONS

In the previous discussion of the helpee and helper roles above, it was indicated that: the helpee is most concerned with learning and developing speaking skills (at least in the initial stages of the helping process); and the helper is involved in functioning in the listening role, offering listening skills that allow the helpee to experience understanding, thereby facilitating learning. In therapy and other helping relationships, there are a number of observable facilitative dimensions, many of which have been found to be necessary components of *successful* helping interactions.

Helpee Dimensions
Owning of Feeling

In order for a helpee to become a competent speaker, he must learn to express his reactions to himself and others. In other words, he must be able to *own his feelings*. When an individual is able to express his feelings spontaneously and congruently (he obviously is experiencing the feelings he is expressing), he is *speaking* or communicating himself at a high level. To the extent that his expressions deny, reject, or fail to identify his feelings, he is functioning at lower levels and needs help to tune in on and identify his feelings. The importance of the concept of owning feelings is apparent from the first moment in a helping relationship. For example, until the helpee has acknowledged that he has feelings about a marital conflict, he cannot explore or own the fact that a conflict exists. Consider the case in which a husband will approach a counselor or therapist requesting therapy to deal with the hostility and conflict that he is experiencing in his marriage; upon hearing a statement to this effect to the helper, the wife flies into a prolonged and agonized rage (or depression) because "There's *nothing* wrong with our marriage, how can you say we fight . . . you son-of-a-bitch!" In other words, until both spouses can accept the existence of a problem or conflict and begin to "own" and express their feelings about it, there is little chance for progress in therapy or marriage.

Commitment to Change

The second dimension influencing helpee growth is *commitment*. In the previous case of the married couple, both spouses may begin to own their feelings regarding their relationship, but further growth entails a degree of commitment. Commitment does not necessarily mean commitment to keeping the marriage intact. Rather commitment means working at changing and improving communication within the relationship. In fact, if it becomes clear that one spouse is committed to preserving the marriage at all costs, while the other is not so invested, progress within counseling or therapy may be very difficult. Once one member of the couple is unilaterally committed to ruling out a possible alternative (e.g. divorce) considerable energy is spent resisting any efforts for change that might move in that direction (including therapy itself).

Because of these factors, it is necessary for the helpee to establish his level of commitment (at any given time) to: himself, his spouse, and the change process. At low levels of commitment the helpee shows no motivation to change. He resists efforts by the helper and/or the spouse to accomplish change or even to explore the desirability of change. This may be acted out in the form of passivity (withdrawal), avoidance (breaking appointments or other commitments), or defensive, hostile behavior (often directed at the spouse). At higher levels of commitment the helpee actively cooperates with the change process and continually engages in confronting his problems and feelings directly.

Differentiation (of Stimuli)

When the helpee has owned his feelings and has decided to attempt to change, he must begin to identify and differentiate between the various stimuli or dynamics in his life so that he understands what changes he needs to make. For example, a married man was apparently unable to express any form of emotion to his wife. During the course of treatment it was learned that he had a domineering, punishing mother who preached that it was "wrong" to express anger towards his parents. As a consequence, the man, as a child, learned to contain his feelings, mainly via withdrawing from verbal communication. This may have been appropriate behavior *at the time,* if, as a child, this behavior enabled him to cope with feelings of guilt, fear of rejection, and even the basic fear of physical reprisal. As a child, however, he had learned suppression of *all* feeling, not just anger, and suppression of feeling with *all* people, not just with his mother. As treatment progressed, this man learned to differentiate between his difficulty in expressing anger and his difficulty in expressing other feelings, between his fear of rejection from his mother and fear of rejection from his wife, and between his feelings as a son and his feelings as a husband. Differentiation of stimuli, then, refers to the process of identifying various sources of affect and anxiety, and becoming aware of individual reactions they stimulate.

At lower levels of differentiation the helpee seems unable to discriminate between his problems, feelings, and concerns, and is unable (or unwilling) to move in that direction. At higher levels the helpee perceives the different stimuli in his world and reacts to them in a variety of differential ways. He shows awareness of his own individual characteristics and his impact on others.

Internalization

Once the helpee has identified and owned his feelings, decided to commit his energy to learning more satisfying behavior, and learned to differentiate the various dynamics and stimuli in his life, he has reached that point in the helping process where behavior change is possible. The manner in which a helpee approaches behavioral alternatives stems from the degree of control he feels over the events in his life. The helpee who sees his problems as situational and himself as a victim of circumstances is said to *externalize*. The person who sees his problems stemming from his own acts, feelings, and contributions *internalizes*. Thus an externalizer may ask the helper to intercede in his behalf: "If you could only explain to my husband how sensitive I am, and how upset I am when he gets angry with me. If he stopped pushing me all the time I would be able to get my work done." In this case the helpee sees relief for her problem only if the situation, the environment, or other people can be changed. An internalizer in the same situation would explore her own responsibility for the problem, and actively seek alternative actions by which she could decrease her discomfort: "I really get hurt and upset when my husband is angry at me, and I guess I withdraw . . . which gets him even madder. I suppose it would help if I could learn to tell him what I'm feeling . . . tell him to just 'back off' then I could get my work done and he'd have nothing to complain about."

The helpee at lower levels of internalization (in effect, an externalizer) simply describes situations and attitudes of people around him with very little awareness of control over alternatives. The individual functioning at higher levels deals with an immediate awareness of how he acts and feels, and recognizes the effects and impact of his behavior.

The Helpee's Facilitative Composite

These dimensions of helpee behavior often overlap to a considerable degree, especially at the higher degrees of functioning. In other words, a person who is owning his feelings and shows awareness that they are tied to his own specific behavior or to those of others is by definition differentiating and internalizing. At the same time, clinical experience indicates that there are situations in which individuals may function on high levels on a particular dimension but not on others. For example, a husband may own his feelings of marital dissatisfaction to an intense degree, and yet at the same time display low commitment to change and deny the responsibility he has for perpetuating conflicts in his relationship with his wife.

The dimensions of helpee behavior seem to appear in a progressive sequence; i.e. the helpee first learns to own his feelings, then becomes committed to changing, then begins to differentiate the sources of his feelings, and finally generates appropriate alternatives to action. This is not always the case, however. There are individuals who can communicate awareness of their responsibility for a conflicting relationship, and even see appropriate alternatives, but who cannot (or will not) make a commitment to change their behavior. For example, one wife stated: "Oh, I guess I do get back at George in my own way. When I withdraw he gets angrier, and then he feels guilty and tries to make up. It might make us both feel better if we talked it out . . . but I just can't seem to do it." In this case the wife's commitment to improving her relationship was marginal, so while she understood the dynamics in her arguments with her husband and even accepted that she deliberately stimulated his anger, she did not act to improve their communication. In a sense, her commitment in the relationship was not to changing her behavior, but rather to her *patterned behavior* of withdrawal, which had the value of "getting back" at George by increasing his anger. A further complication in this particular case was that George would ply his wife with flowers and other gifts when he was in the "making up" stage, an act which *reinforced* her withdrawing—or lack of commitment to change.

The helpee dimensions described here provide a useful conceptual framework for enhancing interpersonal communication; moreover, the importance of these dimensions to improve mental health (or progress in helping and therapy) has been demonstrated by empirical research. Such research indicates that clients who are successful in therapy function at high levels on these dimensions, while clients who are not successful function at lower levels (Pierce and Schauble, in press).

Helper Dimensions

Empathy

If an individual is to be a helper, he must be able to receive messages in such a way that he understands the helpee and shows the helpee that he understands. Once the message is sent (or spoken) the communication (or helping) process can continue only when the helpee is certain that he has been understood. When a person responds empathically, it means that he has heard and understood the speaker, and that his response demonstrates his understanding of what the speaker is really saying. When a helper responds clearly and directly to the helpee in such a way that none of the feeling or meaning in the speaker's statement is lost, or when the helper's responses are such that they convey *additional* feeling or meanings, he is communicating understanding at a high empathic level; this facilitates communication. For example, the following wife responds at a high level:

> Husband: There are times it upsets me when I don't know why you're being so distant, almost like nothing we have means anything to you any more.
>
> Wife: It's hard for you to figure out just where I am when I withdraw, and like . . . do I still love you?

When a helper responds in such a way that feeling or meaning is lost or distorted, he is functioning at a low level of empathy which detracts from communication. For example, the following wife responds at a low level:

> Husband: You know, I was really anxious about coming here today, because until Joyce told me she'd made the appointment, I hadn't realized how upset she was with our marriage. The fact that she thinks we need counseling shook me up.
>
> Wife: Frankly, that's par for the course. I half expected you not to keep the appointment anyway, and I don't care if you think we need counseling or not . . . I do!

In this last example, it is obvious that the wife has not accurately heard or understood the feelings which her husband was attempting to communicate. The extent to which she distorted what he had expressed makes it extremely unlikely that he will be able to continue his attempt to own and explore his own feelings about seeking help for the marriage. (Of interest, both of the last two examples are excerpts from counseling sessions with the *same* couple. The first excerpt was taken from the ninth session, the second excerpt was taken from the first session.)

Respect and Caring

In addition to understanding the helpee, the effective helper communicates that he respects and cares about who the helpee is. Regardless of how confused, pained, or inadequate the helpee feels or portrays himself, the helper communicates his regard for the helpee's value as a person, as well as the belief that the helpee has the ability to do something about changing his life. Unless such respect is communicated, it is unlikely that the helpee can begin to explore new behavior or that he can believe that he is capable of making any constructive behavior change. It is almost as if the person must know he is acceptable to the helper in his present condition before he can think about choosing to change his behavior. In a sense, the helper who responds empathically is already communicating caring, in that he cares sufficiently to let the helpee know he has been understood. In some cases, however, a "well-meaning" helper will attempt to convince the helpee that his feelings are inappropriate by suggesting a "solution" prematurely, explaining away the feelings being expressed. This can have the effect of communicating to the helpee that he is not competent enough even to describe his own feelings. Consider the following example:

> Wife: I just get so uptight when I think about having sex with Harry. I keep wondering if he is going to like it . . . and I get so nervous that I can't enjoy it at all.
>
> Husband: Oh brother, are you still feeling that way? I mean . . . I *tell* you you're attractive to me, so I can't see why you feel as you do. You should have more confidence in yourself, that's all.

The response indicates that the husband thinks his wife's feelings are illogical and dismisses them as being unimportant. While he is attending to her statement, he is clearly communicating that she should not have these feelings; and such a message makes further exploration difficult.

Concreteness

When the helper is concrete or specific, he enables the helpee to identify and discuss the particular feelings or concerns which are relevant to the helpee. Concreteness often has a funneling effect on helpee self-exploration. The helpee presents a variety of feelings related to a number of sources, and the helper's response tends to narrow the field, perhaps suggesting a connection between the helpee's feelings that was not expressed before. For example:

> Helpee: I'm feeling low today. I wasn't able to stick to my diet, for one thing, and I'm feeling fat, fat, fat! And I wasn't going to go out with Allan, remember? Well, he called, and the first thing I knew, I'd said yes. . . .
>
> Helper: You couldn't keep any of the limits you set for yourself— and you're feeling like you don't have *any* control over what you do.

In this example, the helpee began by describing the various reasons for feeling "low"; these were symptoms of her inability to commit herself to positive action. The helper's response guided the helpee to the focal point of her depression, her feelings of inadequacy in controlling her life.

In contrast, the helper who is not concrete in his response diffuses the attempts of the helpee to explore his specific and immediate feelings. At best, such a helper leads the helpee to an abstract, intellectualized discussion of feelings; at worst, the helper allows all helpee discussion to deal only with vague and anonymous generalities. For example, the following involves a therapist and his client:

> Helpee: I think I know why I've had such little success with therapy. I'm so afraid to contradict anyone—even when they are talking about me, that, well I'm afraid to tell any of my doctors he's wrong, and I think I am most afraid with you.
>
> Helper: Hmmm, tell me about your other therapists, what did they say that you thought was wrong?

In this example, the helpee is striving, albeit hesitantly, to discuss her feelings about confronting her therapist. Her communication shows a high level differentiation, and she is specific about identifying the source of her present feelings. The helper's response directs the discussion away from the helping relationship, out of concreteness and into the general, out of the present and into the past. The helper's response has a negative influence on the helpee's attempt to communicate. Thus at high levels of concreteness the helper's responses enable or guide the helpee to explore personally relevant material in specific or concrete terminology. At lower levels of concreteness the helper's responses lead the helpee into vague, confused, and at best intellectual discussion of helpee concerns.

Genuineness

The helper dimension of genuineness is similar to the helpee dimension of owning of feelings, in that when a helper is communicating genuineness his responses are congruent with his own feelings. While the helper at the higher levels of genuineness spontaneously acts on his feelings, positive or negative, he does so in a manner that is constructive for the helpee. The following interaction between a therapist and client illustrates:

> Helpee: You said that my not coming on time and missing appointments is a way I try to punish you. That doesn't bother you, does it?
>
> Helper: Yes, it bothers me. I get angry with you when you don't show for an appointment—because regardless of how legitimate your excuse is—the fact that you didn't call communicates a real lack of regard for my feelings. I think that it is important that we look at this, because whenever you get close to people and they start to care about you, you seem to fall into a habit of breaking commitments—until eventually they pull back thinking you don't care, and you're left feeling rejected again. I feel now that you're doing this with me.
>
> Helpee: I didn't want to hurt you or get you mad, but I guess what you say is true. I get anxious when I get close . . . and maybe I do push people away. I am afraid to be close to you, but I'm afraid not to, too.

The helper's response clearly expressed his feeling of displeasure with the helpee's behavior, but did so in a constructive, caring manner. Rather than "dumping" his feelings on the helpee, the helper expressed his feelings and the importance of working them out in the relationship. The helpee was able to benefit by the communication as he internalized what the helper had said, and he began to explore his fear of intimacy and his responsibility for isolating himself.

When a helper responds in a non-genuine way, the helpee is either misled or experiences the conflict between what the helper has said and what he feels. In either case, there is a negative effect on the helping process. The following is an example between a husband and a wife.

> Helpee: Janie, I'm awfully sorry that I missed dinner. I got so wrapped up in work at the lab that I forgot all about it. . . . I didn't even think to call you. I know you're hurt, but I'd like to talk about it.
> Helper: There's nothing to talk about! I know your work is important to you, and there will be times that this happens. It's only food, so forget it!

The helper's response in this example leaves the helpee little leeway in continuing communication. She has sidestepped expressing her feelings, and is ignoring his feelings. If she is upset, she has deliberately closed off any attempt to resolve the conflict and communicate with her husband. If she is not upset, she has still not given any cue to what her feelings really are, which leaves her husband with his unresolved guilt.

Another form of ungenuine behavior occurs when the helper responds in a "rehearsed" manner that fits the role that the helper "should" play. When a helper acts according to a prescribed role, he gives but few cues as to what he personally feels or who he really is. The importance of authenticity or "realness" is especially crucial to the communication of caring and respect, for the communication of caring in a "phony" manner is quite destructive to the development of communication. A husband and wife provided the following example:

> Helpee: In three years I can't remember a single time when you've said you love me. *Do* you love me?
> Helper: I think the answer to that is obvious. I *am* your husband, aren't I? And would I be here trying to keep our marriage together if I didn't love you?

In this example, there are no cues as to the husband's personal feelings or commitments. He responds to his wife's question by explaining his roles as husband and co-client (in therapy), but he does not commit himself to either a positive or negative statement of feelings.

At low levels of genuineness, then, the helper's responses appear unrelated to what he is feeling, or when feelings are expressed they are negative and have a destructive or delimiting effect on communication and on the helpee. At high levels of genuineness the helper's expressions are congruent with his feelings and are used in a beneficial, constructive manner.

Confrontation

The helper who is empathic, genuine, and caring in his relationship with the helpee is able to confront the helpee with the inconsistencies and conflicts experienced in their relationship. Confrontation with "what's really going on between us" contains high risk for both the helper and the helpee; hence, the establishment of a relationship containing the first three dimensions of effective helping is usually necessary before confrontations can be facilitative. At the same time, confrontation is the active outgrowth of the former dimensions, and maximizes the helper's potential for impact with the helpee by bringing the helpee in contact with the helper's "realness." The following illustration involves a therapist and his client:

> Helper: You keep talking about how Larry wants to keep the marriage together, and yet it sounds like everything he's done this past week indicates that just isn't true.
>
> Helpee: Larry's been under a lot of pressure lately. He's had to work and I can't ask him to make a choice between his work and the kids and I, can I?
>
> Helper: That's frightening to think about, isn't it? Because a part of you is feeling like Larry may already have made the choice. Much as it hurts, you feel like you've lost.
>
> Helpee: No, well, I feel like I'm losing, anyway. And I don't know what to do, and that depresses me.
>
> Helper: You're depressed, and you're angry, too.
>
> Helpee: I really don't think I'm angry at Larry.
>
> Helper: I think you're angry at yourself, Susan.
>
> Helpee: Because?
>
> Helper: Because you're not even trying to fight. You're not competing, and (cut-off).

In this example, the helper used his understanding of the helpee to confront her with her avoiding the painful feelings she was experiencing with her husband. In following through with the confrontation, the helper enabled the helpee to confront herself and gain awareness of her conflicting feelings.

When the helper does not confront with the inconsistencies and conflicts he experiences in the helpee, he denies the helpee the opportunity to become aware of the dynamics and choose more appropriate behavior. When this occurs, the helper might as well not even be there. Further, if the helper does confront the helpee, it is essential that the confrontation be *worked through* in the context of an understanding, caring relationship. Confrontation without resolution may be cathartic for the helper; but it can be destructive for the helpee and, moreover, it can seriously damage the communication process.

Immediacy

If the helper is to be maximally effective in his relationship with the helpee, he must be prepared to deal with the different feelings and experiences that "are happening now." In a sense, immediacy is: a confrontation with the present, and an awareness of the dynamics that are going on between helper and helpee at any point in the relationship. Often the helpee may express feelings about people outside the helping relationship that reflect the way he feels about the helper in the helping relationship. When this occurs, it may be due to the helpee's own anxiety about dealing with the immediate feelings, or it may be stimulated by anxiety that the helpee perceives in the helper.

In the situation where the helpee directs the feelings he is experiencing in the present (for the helper) towards others, he may be doing it with or without conscious awareness. In the previous discussion of confrontation, an example was given in which the helper was anxious about disagreeing with her therapist: she consciously introduced the feelings by attaching them to her previous therapists, and eventually brought them into the present therapy interaction; her therapist then led the helpee *out* of exploration in the immediate relationship and back into past encounters; this demonstrated the helper's own ambivalence about the relationship, and reinforced the helpee's ambivalence. In other cases, the helpee may not be conscious that the feelings he is expressing relate to the present interaction. The following example is an excerpt from a marital counseling session, with husband, wife, and counselor present:

> Helpee: It really pisses me off when Helen shares her feeling with anybody and everybody but me. I have to find out what she's thinking from a third party. Where does that leave me?
>
> Helper: It leaves you feeling left out and jealous. Like you feel left out and jealous here.
>
> Helpee: I wasn't talking about in here.
>
> Helper: But it happens in here too, Dave. You're feeling cut off from Helen and me right now. And I guess I'd be surprised if you weren't feeling jealous, because she is talking about feelings you haven't heard before.
>
> Helpee: I do resent you, you know that? Why should she talk to you when she doesn't to me?

In this example, the helpee was not at first aware that the feelings of hurt and jealousy he was experiencing were immediately stimulated in the counseling relationship itself. When the helper showed that he understood the connection between the feelings and the present interaction, the helpee was able to move back into the interaction and own his feelings. Thus, the extent to which the helpee is able to explore, to communicate, and to learn to deal with his life will be greatly influenced by helper's immediacy in the relationship. Helpers functioning at low levels of immediacy tend to disregard most helpee expressions which have the potential for relating to the helper, while high functioning helpers relate helpee feelings to themselves in a direct and explicit manner.

Like the helpee dimensions, the helper dimensions appear to be of conceptual value in understanding the helping or communication processes. These dimensions have been developed (and their importance in the helping process validated) through extensive research on helping relationships, notably by Carkhuff and his associates (Carkhuff, 1969).

Developmental Model

It was indicated that the helpee behavior dimensions seem to appear in a progressive sequence and that there is some overlap at the higher levels of functioning. This seems true for the helper dimensions as well. Combining the helpee and helper dimensions allows for the conceptualization of a developmental model for learning interpersonal communication in the helping relationship.

Stage I

At Stage I in the helping relationship it is necessary for the helpee to own his feelings. The helper contributes to the process initially by responding empathically and concretely, not only showing

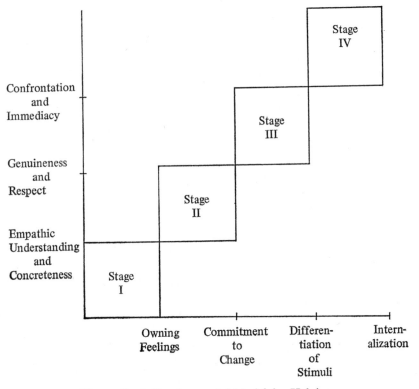

Figure 2. A Developmental Model for Helping

that he is listening to the helpee but understanding and suggesting identifying labels for the helpee's feelings. When the helpee is aware of and owns his feelings, i.e. he accurately assays his situations, he is ready for stage two, i.e. he decides what to do, or to what process he wants to commit himself.

Stage II

At Stage II the helper facilitates helpee commitment by genuinely communicating respect and caring for the helpee, even if the helpee decides to remain committed to his pain and distress producing behaviors. The nature of the commitment to the process of communication and/or change is such that it is very unlikely it can be made under coercion. Thus a helper cannot force assistance on a helpee, a therapist cannot "cure" a client, and a husband cannot "change" a wife. There must be an act of commitment by the helpee, and this requires that there be a "choice" involved, even if it is an apparently obvious choice between pain and suffering and relief and comfort. In many cases the coping behaviors learned by the helpee, however painful, are all he knows. It can be terribly frightening to think of abandoning these familiar behaviors for the nebulous goal of "feeling better" or "getting well."

In a recent therapy situation, I suggested to a chronic depressed client that we terminate therapy (after the third interview) for an undetermined period of time. I explained that I saw therapy as being a very painful, draining experience for him, and suggested that since he did not appear committed to changing his behavior, he was simply increasing his discomfort by continuing therapy. This client initially questioned my appraisal, suggesting that it was absurd to think that he would not want to change his behavior or life style, since he had experienced severe depression and had been in therapy (elsewhere) for six years. I explained that while I realized his depression was painful for him, I believed he had learned his depressed behavior as a means of coping with his environment at some previous point in his life, and that perhaps he was not so uncomfortable that he was prepared to risk the uncertainty and fear of changing behavior patterns that were once (and still might be) functional for him. I attempted to communicate that it would be entirely appropriate not to continue therapy if he could not feel committed to the change process. Three days later he phoned me and in a very businesslike manner stated that he had decided that he would like to try working toward change in some specific areas of concern for him, and requested that we try a trial contract for five weeks, reappraising the contract at that point in time. We are now in our sixth month of contact, the client has made remarkable progress (after two months he took himself off medication he had used for two years); he continues to demonstrate as high a commitment to growth as I have witnessed in several years. As he looked back on his therapy or helping process, he is clear that the "turning point" for his commitment came when he had to make a choice—a decision—as to whether he committed himself to working on attempting change, or consciously decided to remain committed to his depression. Until the point that he was confronted with that choice, he had not committed his energy to the change (or helping process).

While the commitment dynamic may not always be as clear as in this particular case, it seems obvious that each individual's behavior is a function of his personal commitment. Before behavior change can result there must be a corresponding commitment to change. Commitment to change (to a greater or lesser degree) is a choice: a conscious or unconscious decision to change or remain the same where one is (psychologically). The helper who communicates genuineness and respect to the helpee can contribute to the helpee's valuing his own uniqueness and potential, thereby freeing him to choose to attempt growth and change in whatever way he can.

Stage III

In the third stage of helping, the helpee is actively involved in identifying and gaining insight into his interpersonal relationships and feelings. As the helpee explores his feelings more fully, the helper provides constructive confrontation within the immediate helping relationship to aid the helpee in gaining increased insight into the sources of his feelings. It is important to note here that this third stage is instrumental to the next stage of generating alternatives to action, but that alternatives can be acted on only when a satisfactory level of commitment has been developed (as in Stage II). In this way, the stages can be seen as interrelating, for each stage incorporates and builds on the helpee and helper dimensions from the previous stage and the cycle of owning-commitment-understanding-action is repeated again and again.

Stage IV

In the fourth stage the generation of new behavioral alternatives–behavior change–is the ultimate goal of the helping process. When the helpee is well into Stage IV with consistently high functioning on all helpee dimensions he ceases to be a helpee and becomes a speaker. When the helpee becomes an effective speaker he no longer needs a helper, so the helper is free to become either a listener (if he is consistently high functioning on the helper dimensions) or a helpee (if he is less than effective on the helper dimensions). When both parties are functioning at high levels on all of the communication dimensions, their roles are complementary, and they are free to move between the roles of speaker and listener in an effective communication process. Whenever one party drops to lower levels of functioning, a helping relationship must be resumed and the cycle is set up again. The purpose of the helping relationship is to teach effective communication; the purpose of effective communication is to perpetuate itself; and effective communication results in the generation of new and more effective behavior.

INTERVENTION VIA THE FACILITATING DIMENSIONS

On the basis of research and clinical data available on the facilitative dimensions, there are a number of conclusions that can be made about their importance in communication and helping.

First, *the ability to communicate is learned.* We learn speaking and listening skills in much the same way that we learn various foreign languages. The extent to which we are successful in learning communication skills depends on our teacher models (beginning with parents and siblings) and on our experience of being "listened to" or heard. Generally speaking, we can predict that children with high functioning parents and family contacts will develop satisfactory communication skills, whereas children with parents who function at low levels will not. Clinical data often support this hypothesis, as interpersonal difficulty and emotional maladjustments seem to "run" in families. Empirical data on the communication dimensions also point to the influence of primary contacts on the functional level of children (Stover and Guerney, 1967).

Second, *more effective communication skills can be taught.* Once communication skills have been learned, they tend to perpetuate themselves. For example, the child who learns to suppress his feelings and withdraw from other people becomes increasingly uncomfortable in his daily contacts, since his peers are becoming more adept at their interpersonal communications. The child then tends to withdraw even more to avoid this discomfort, and so it goes. The cycle can be broken, however; for just as communication skills are learned, they can be *relearned* and more effective communication can result. Therapeutic interventions are based on this principle, and research data indicate that those people who are "successful" in therapy learn to function at higher levels on the facilitative dimensions (Pierce and Schauble, in press). In addition, what *the helper (or teacher) does* seems to be of less importance than the *level at which he functions in his own communication process* (Carkhuff, 1969; Pierce and Schauble, 1970). In other words, the helper (be it parent, therapist, or teacher) must function on a higher level than the helpee if growth is to occur. Otherwise, there is not a "helping" relationship. Finally, it has been found that the skills can be learned more effectively by direct teaching or training intervention than by traditional approaches to helping or therapy (Pierce, Schauble, and Farkas, 1971; Pierce and Drasgow, 1967; Pierce, Schauble, and Wilson, 1971). It is apparent that more effective communication can be learned at later stages in life, but it is necessary that the individual come in contact with high functioning or facilitative helpers if this is to occur.

Third, *most people in our society function at marginal levels of communication, with a significant proportion functioning at less than minimally facilitative levels.* Referring back to our discussion about Edgar and Oscar, this means that efficient *communication* between two people is more the exception than the rule; and where a *helping* relationship is required for communication to occur, it is difficult to find individuals who are functioning at a high enough level themselves to be facilitative helpers to others.

Thus, in many areas of our society the experience of an empathic response is so unusual that reasons are created for not even expecting it. The black man assumes the white man cannot understand what it is like to be black; women's liberationists assume that men are incapable of understanding women; and George is convinced that Martha cannot fathom the pressures of competing for a buck. These assumptions grow out of the experience of not being understood, and represent more the feelings of need and despair than conviction. Empathic behavior stems not so much from common experience, but from the active attempt to hear and understand the experience of the speaker.

The individual who has learned inefficient and unsatisfactory communication skills faces a slim probability that he will come in contact (on a strictly chance basis) with persons functioning at high enough levels to be capable of helping him learn more effective interpersonal behavior. Furthermore, the individual's selection process is based on his past experience, and if his experience is mostly with low functioning people, he is likely to choose from that population (for friends and mates) or be unable to discriminate successfully those people in his environment who might be functioning at higher levels. One method of intervening in this cyclical process is to teach people to communicate at more effective levels. Traditionally, counseling and therapy has been a method for accomplishing this purpose. Instruction (within or outside the context of therapy) on the dimensions of communications is another. When husband and wife can learn to communicate effectively, when they can establish a relationship wherein they are committed to help each other continue to communicate more clearly (especially during stress situations), then they will be capable of modeling and teaching effective communication to their children, thereby reversing the trend toward emotional distancing and disorder.

Teaching Effective Communication

There are three steps in teaching effective communication skills. In the first, the communication process must be defined and the dimensions of effective communication identified. In the second step, discrimination between effective and non-effective communication is learned. The third step involves practice in communicating what has been learned in the first two steps.

Identification

Teaching communication skills begins by defining interpersonal communication as: The process where one person speaks and another person listens. While this may appear a rather obvious definition, it is usually not considered in day-to-day interpersonal interactions (but it should be!). In communication training, it is important to make this definition and return to it frequently in order to provide a consistent and clear cognitive set within which to operate. As the definition is extended to "speaking is the sending of messages, listening is the receiving of messages," the elements of *speaker* and *listener* can be introduced.

In order to emphasize the importance of the two functions, it is often useful in this identification stage to have the "students" attempt a brief (perhaps ten minutes) communication, each attempting both roles for an equal period of time (perhaps five minutes). If this "role-playing" situation can be tape-recorded and played back to the participants, it can provide an immediate and personal experience with which to examine the process. In most cases, it provides a dramatic example of how the conditions of the definition of communication are not present. As a case in point, the example below is a recording of a first interaction between two individuals in a marital communication-skills training group. The instructions that were given to the two participants were:

> Communication, very simply, is the process wherein one person speaks and another person (or persons) listens. For the next few minutes, we are going to assume the roles of speaker and listener with one another:
> 1. to help us to focus on our process in communication and give

us an idea of how the roles can be differentiated; and
2. to give us the opportunity to introduce ourselves to the group and get some preliminary data on each other.

In the following, a transcription is presented in two sections; the first section contains a typescript of the role-played interactions, and the second section contains excerpts of the group discussion that took place when the interaction was played back via tape recording.

Speaker/Listner Interaction

Speaker: Well, my name is Helen, and I'm having trouble thinking of what to say.
Listener: Hi, Helen, my name is Joel. Why don't you talk about why you and your husband came into the group?

Playback Discussion

Leader: Helen, what were the feelings you were having here.
Helen: I was embarrassed and didn't know how to start. I really felt on the spot.
Leader: So the message you sent about "having trouble" was your feeling discomfort, not that you didn't have anything to say.
Helen: That's right, there was lots I could have said.

Speaker/Listner Interaction

Speaker: Well, we might have different ideas on that.
Listener: Oh, I don't know. I'll bet we all have pretty much the same reasons for being here.
Speaker: What do you mean?
Listener: Well, Fran and I want to improve our communication, we think it will help us to understand each other and the kids better.

Playback Discussion

Helen: I meant that my husband and I have different ideas on why we're here. I think the listener misunderstood.
Joel: Yeah, I did. I thought she meant each couple had different reasons.
Leader: Joel, are you speaking or listening here?
Joel: I was supposed to be listening, but I guess I was speaking.
Leader: O.K., I think that's something we need to be aware of. Often times we slip into being speakers when we want to be listeners, and the result can be a mass of messages that are transmitted, but no one's receiving.

Speaker/Listener Interaction

Speaker: You really think this group will help?
Listener: Oh yeah, I think it's going to be a big help.

Playback Discussion

Leader: O.K., Joel, what message was she sending?
Joel: Well, as I listen now. I think she was saying *she* doesn't think it will help.
Helen: You know, at this point I was really conscious of shifting roles . . . Joel was speaking now, and I was in the listening role.
Leader: So you were aware of deliberately shifting the speaker and listener roles. . . .
Helen: Well, it wasn't so much deliberately cause Joel really switched them, but then I kept my listener role, and that was easier.
Leader: This is another point we might try to remember. Helen is saying she wasn't comfortable as a speaker, so she shifted into listening, which didn't make her nearly as anxious. In this case, the opposite was true for Joel. When they got together then, the original purpose of this interaction (to speak and listen in assigned roles) was aborted. If this happens in a controlled situation, imagine how many times it happens in everyday interactions.

In this example, it was possible for the group members to observe and experience the importance of the speaking and listening functions in communication, and it was possible for the leader to begin to show how the process of *communication can be improved without emphasizing personal deficiencies of the participants.* Throughout the skills training it is important to emphasize a model for examining and *improving* the communication process rather than diagnosing and treating individual weaknesses.

Discrimination

Once the speaking and listening functions of communication have been established, the dimensions of speaking and listening can be introduced and the participants can be taught to discriminate between effective and noneffective behavior relating to each of the dimensions.

One approach to introducing discrimination training is for the trainer to explain that, since communication consists of speaking and listening, the success of an attempt to communicate depends first on the skill of the speaker to send a clear, accurate message and second on the ability of the listener to receive and understand the message. The example below is the typescript of one such introduction, taken from the first session of a communication skills training group for married couples. The leader is speaking:

> Whether or not you understand me depends firstly on whether I send a message that tells who I am at that moment. Now, when I send a message, three things may happen. First, my speaking can be inefficient, or the message I send may not represent me and the way that I experience myself at that moment. In this case it may be that I avoid communicating my feelings to you (perhaps to the point of misleading you), or I may be unable to identify my feelings for myself.
>
> Second, my communication may be partially efficient to the extent of cognitively identifying my feelings, but they seem distant and detached. In this case, my communication may seem incongruent with what I *appear* to be feeling. For example, if I speak of a series of recent tragic events in my life but do so in a matter-of-fact sort of way, my mode of communication might seem inconsistent with the content of my message, and you may be quite confused as to what I really am feeling. Third, my communication can be very efficient, in that I am identifying *and* experiencing my feelings; i.e. I have full access to my feelings, and they are clearly evident in my communication.

Such an explanation introduces the concept of different functioning levels for speaking.

The next stage involves training in discriminating between functioning levels, which typically involves the use of audio tape excerpts which have been specifically designed to represent the three levels of speaking. These tapes are usually prepared not only to demonstrate levels of functioning, but to suggest or model *content* that would be appropriate for the particular helpers. Thus, discrimination training tapes designed for training in marital therapy would portray content related to marriage situations; training tapes for family or child therapy would portray content related to typical familial and childhood conflicts, etc.

The taped excerpts are then played for the participants, and they are asked to rate each excerpt on a scale representing the particular dimension upon which training is focusing, e.g. owning feelings. Since each of the communication dimensions is a continuous variable, it is possible to create scales with a variety of different levels. While most of the empirical studies employing the scales as criteria for evaluation use scales with five levels, experience with training communication skills in marital therapy supports that a scale with three identified levels is most useful. The following is the *Owning of Feeling Scale* (created in conjunction with Richard M. Pierce, Ph.D.):

Level 1

The speaker avoids accepting any of his feelings or he expresses feelings vaguely. When feelings are expressed, they are always seen as belonging to others, or situational and outside of himself.

Example: The speaker avoids identifying or admitting to any feelings, or he discusses or intellectualizes about feeling in a detached, abstract manner and gives little evidence.

In summary, any expression of feeling appears intellectualized, distant and vague.

Level 2

The speaker can usually identify his specific feelings and their source, but tends to express what he feels in an intellectualized manner.

Example: The speaker seems to have an intellectual grasp of his feelings and their origin, but has little emotional proximity to them.

In summary, the speaker usually ties down and owns his feelings, but in an intellectual manner.

Level 3

The speaker almost always acknowledges his feeling and can express them with emotional proximity, and at the same time shows awareness that his feelings are tied to specific behavior of his own and others.

Example: The speaker shows immediate and free access to his feelings, expresses them in a genuine way, and is able to identify their origin.

In summary, the speaker clearly owns his feelings and accurately specifies their source.

After each taped excerpt is played, the trainees "rate" the level at which they hear the speaker "owning his feelings," and then discuss the reasons behind the particular rating. Each of the three excerpts listed below would be played for the participants, who would attempt then to assign a rating of one, two, or three:

Excerpt 1

My wife Barbara is heavily involved in community affairs. They're so important to her that sometimes she's out working when the kids and I get home. That leaves me to make the dinner, and, boy, I am a terrible cook. It would be easier if other people were more community minded, because then Barbara wouldn't always have to be doing all the work.

Excerpt 2

My wife Barbara is really into community affairs. She's so heavily involved that it gets inconvenient and upsetting for us at times. I come home from work and find I have to make dinner, and I get pretty sore that she's not able to be with me and the kids when we need her. I guess she has to work so hard because no one else does their share and she gets stuck with finishing things up. I wish she could learn to say "no" more often.

Excerpt 3

My wife Barbara is really into community activity. She really enjoys it, and I'm happy that she does, but it really burns me at times. I'm mad when I come from work and dinner's not made, and maybe she's not even there. I feel hurt, too, because sometimes she seems to choose her volunteer work over me and the kids. I resent all those damn committees, too, because *they* see her as a good-hearted sucker, and they exploit and overwork her.

After each excerpt is rated, the trainees' ratings are compared with the standardized ratings of professional experts. In the above example, *Excerpt 1* would be rated at level 1.0; that is, the speaker does not identify any of the feelings he has about the content in his statement. *Excerpt 2* would be rated at level 2.0; that is, the speaker introduces some of his feeling reactions but does so in a somewhat vague, cognitive manner. *Excerpt 3* would be rated at level 3.0; that is, the speaker clearly identifies and "owns" his feelings and is aware of their sources.

The three excerpts presented previously all concern the same person and situation; hence they provide a clear introductory illustration of the differences in the three levels of owning feelings. Subsequent excerpts deal with different people and situations. When the trainees have become familiar with the speaker dimensions and are able to discriminate reliably, similar training is conducted for the complementary listener dimension; in this case, empathy. The following is the *Empathy Scale:*

Level 1: Detracting Level

The verbal and behavioral expressions of the *listener* either do not attend to or communicate less of the speaker's feelings than the speaker has communicated himself.
Example:
  A. The listener may communicate little awareness of even the most obvious expressed surface feelings of the speaker.
  B. His communications drain off a level of affect and distort the level of meaning.
  C. He may communicate his own ideas of what may be going on but these are not congruent with expressions of the speaker.
In summary, the listener tends to detract from or respond to other than what the speaker is expressing or indicating.

Level 2: Equal Level

The expressions of the *listener* in response to the expressed feelings of the speaker are essentially *interchangeable* with those of the speaker in that they express the same affect and meaning.
In summary, the listener is responding so as to neither detract from nor add to the expressions of the speaker.

Level 3: Adding Level

The responses of the *listener* add to the expressions of the speaker in such a way as to express feelings *deeper* than the speaker was able to express himself.
Example: The listener communicates his understanding of the speaker's feelings at a level deeper than they were expressed, and thus enables the speaker to experience and/or express feelings which he was unable to express previously.

When tapes are made for training discrimination on listener dimensions (e.g. empathy), they can be made in response to speaker excerpts that trainees are already familiar with, as well as to new speaker responses. The following provides an example:

Speaker: My wife Barbara is really into community affairs. She's so heavily involved that it gets inconvenient and upsetting for us at times. I come home from work and find I have to make dinner, and I get pretty sore that she is not able to be with me and the kids when we need her. I guess she has to work so hard because no one else does their share and she gets stuck with finishing things up. I wish she could learn to say "no" more often.

Listener Responses:

1. What are these different groups your wife is involved with?
2. It bothers you that she's putting in all that time, if it means she can't be with you and the kids.
3. It sounds like you've got yourself a wonderful wife. You should be grateful you have a woman who's that civic minded.
4. You can understand how much it means to your wife to be able to do her volunteer work, but you still feel hurt and angry that her work sometimes comes between the two of you.

In this example, the first listener response would be rated at level 1.0; that is, it fails to attend to any of the feelings expressed by the speaker. Response 2 is rated at level 2.0; that is, it responds to the expressed feelings of the speaker. Response 3 is rated 1.0; that is, the listener is expressing his own opinion, and not reflecting the speaker's feelings. This response also has the effect of implying the speaker's feelings are invalid. The fourth response is rated at level 3.0; that is, it goes beyond the speaker's statement in identifying and clarifying his feelings.

While the listener responses demonstrate different levels of effectiveness, even the non-facilitative (or low level) responses are typical of commonplace interaction between two people. For example, listener response #1 above is the type of question that frequently occurs in interpersonal interaction, but which in this particular case detracts from the speaker's communication of feeling. One effect of the differentiation training, then, is that both effective and non-effective speaking and listening are "modeled" for the trainees.

The trainees rate and discuss the training tapes until they learn to discriminate between effective and non-effective levels of communication on the owning feelings and empathy dimensions. It generally takes from two to five hours for couples to learn to differentiate accurately and consistently between the three levels of effectiveness. When the trainees have achieved consistent agreement in rating, they are ready to begin to examine their own behavior in respect to the communication dimensions.

Communication

In order to begin the communication stage of training, two trainees are asked to assume the role of speaker and listener. These are "roles" only to the extent that the participants deliberately concentrate on either the speaking or listening function. The speaker has complete choice as to the contents of the message he attempts to send (although it is suggested that the contents have some degree of emotional value for the speaker), and thus it is an authentic sample of who the speaker is (or sees himself as being). Speaker and listener talk for about five minutes, after which the group assigns a rating to the speaker and listener on the Owning of Feeling and Empathy scales and then discusses the ratings and the interchange. The speaker/listener interchanges are short enough that a tape recorder is not essential, but it has been found that it greatly enhances the value of the practice if the speaker and listener can hear themselves and connect what they have said on tape to the group's rating of the way in which they functioned on the communication dimensions.

After one such "role-playing" session is completed and discussed, two different trainees repeat the process, and so on until all trainees have participated at least once in both the speaker and listener roles. In a group situation, it is advisable not to have a husband and wife team interact as speaker and listener until after they have experienced the roles with a non-spouse. It seems easier, initially, for most trainees to attend to the communication roles when not involved in an interaction that may have predetermined emotional content. Further, when husband and wife engage as speaker and listener, they sometimes feel their actual relationship is being examined and evaluated, rather than their individual functioning as speaker and listener in a role-playing situation, and this can cause considerable apprehension (perhaps leading to defending against any group feedback). The purpose of these initial practice sessions is to focus on the mechanics of the communication process, and not the underlying dynamics of the relationship. The more a rela-

tionship is "established" between the participants before the training interaction, the more difficult it is to accomplish this purpose.

One might question whether such "role-playing" might limit the
spontaneous and open expression of feelings by the participants.
Experience supports that much more intense and apparently honest expression of feelings is displayed in such structured interactions than occurs in early sessions of more traditional marriage
counseling. There seem to be a number of reasons for this phenomenon:

1. *The role interactions allow the speakers to talk about their feelings
   without being pressured to resolve them.* In a traditional group
   situation, when an individual expresses feelings or concerns there is
   often considerable energy devoted to "doing something about the
   situation," often before the speaker has clearly owned his feelings,
   and often before he's sure he's been heard (in fact, the premature
   proposition of a "solution"—however sensible—may be enough to
   convince the speaker he has not been heard). Instead, the speaker's
   purpose is solely to identify and communicate his feelings, and
   after a few minutes of so doing, he has a chance to stop and reflect
   on that experience as well as to observe how well he was heard.
   *For the listener, the task of "curing" the speaker is alleviated as
   well,* and he is able to experiment with responding to what he
   hears without the awesome responsibility of helping the speaker
   "work through" the feelings in a satisfactory manner.

2. *The structure allows each participant to experience both roles.*
   In every group, there are some people who find it difficult to
   "speak out," and "demand" group time for themselves as speakers.
   These same people often find it hard to be "aggressive" listeners
   and respond to other participants when they speak. In a traditional
   counseling group, such individuals might remain passive for several
   sessions, rather than compete for exposure in either role. In the
   communication skills training group, each member has a "turn" in
   which he can experience speaking and listening with less risk of
   competition.

3. *Feedback after each interaction focuses on communication skills
   instead of personal characteristics,* so that each participant receives
   critical input about specific interactive behavior. This reduces
   the threat of being evaluated (or devalued) as a person, and makes
   it easier for the individual to act on the feedback.

4. *Everyone in the group listens to the speaker.* While only one
   person is designated as the listener in the structured interaction,
   the rest of the group listens intently to the interaction so that

they can later rate and discuss the speaker and listener. This not only insures that the speaker experiences the attention of the group, but it serves to acquaint the group with personal content important to each individual for reference later on.

Once couples have become accustomed to the structured interactions, it is appropriate to introduce the remaining speaker and listener dimensions. Generally speaking, the addition of one dimension for both roles (speaker and listener) in successive sessions produces satisfying results. Since a format for considering a "continuum" for each communication skill has been introduced with training on the Owning of Feeling and Empathy scales, it is usually sufficient simply to introduce the new dimension and provide examples of extreme behaviors (in other words, the various stages of differentiation discussed above are usually not necessary once training moves beyond owning of feeling and empathy).

Thus, differentiation of stimuli might be introduced as follows (the leader is speaking):

A speaker who functions at a low level of differentiation seems unable to discriminate among his feelings or the people and events in his life; i.e. he seems to respond to everything in very much the same way. For example: "I just can't seem to do anything right. I try as hard as I can, but even when things seem to go well I wind up blowing it and everybody gets down on me."

A speaker who communicates at high levels perceives the different stimuli in his world and reacts to them in a variety of ways. He shows awareness of his own unique characteristics and the reactions he stimulates in others. For example: "I find I'm very dependent on the approval of other people. Even when I'm working well and doing a good job, if someone—especially someone I care about—criticizes me, I tend to get depressed and feel that nothing I've done is worthwhile, and that no one else cares about me."

These two statements represent low and high points on the differentiation of stimuli continuum. Both statements might be made by the same person, but the first statement shows very little discrimination ability—the message is general and vague. On the other hand, the second statement shows a high awareness of the specific stimuli which contribute to his feelings of self worthlessness. The latter communication is much more clear, and easier to understand.

As we speak and listen in our session tonight, try to attend to the degree to which each of us is differentiating in our speaking, in the same way we attended to the owning feelings dimension.

After the initial training for owning of feeling and for empathy has been accomplished, it is generally not necessary nor desirable to spend an entire session on the structured interactions. It is helpful to begin each session with *some* structured interaction, but then to move into a more flexible interaction based on the original concepts of speaking and listening. Thus the leader, in preparing to teach differentiation of stimuli, might instruct the group:

> Instead of maintaining our speaker/listener format for the entire session, let's begin that way and agree that anyone may become involved as speaker or listener whenever they choose. The only stipulation is that when a new person enters the interaction, he first communicates what he heard the previous speaker and listener saying before he begins a new communication.

This type of format encourages a more natural flow of communication, but it also builds in a framework for continuing to examine and evaluate the communication process.

Once each dimension of the communication skills has been incorporated into the training (and hopefully each couple's behavior) the purpose of the training is completed. The training method described in this section contains the basic approach to teaching communication skills. It can be conducted as an end in, and of, itself, as an introductory phase (or intervention) for marital therapy, as a component of parent-effectiveness training, and/or as both a para-professional and professional training procedure. The basic training as described above may also be implemented by various other methods of accelerating interpersonal growth, such as Interpersonal Process Recall (to be described subsequently) or a variety of the behavioral methods.

TRAINING IN THE FACILITATIVE CONDITIONS AS A PREFERRED MODE OF TREATMENT

As previously mentioned, the various dimensions of effective communication have been found to be related to success in counseling and therapy, and in fact are used as criteria for growth (or success) in counseling and psychotherapy research. There are also data to indicate that therapy which incorporates communication skills training is more productive than traditional therapy. One study which compared traditional group therapy with group therapy incorporating communication skills training (as described above) demonstrated that the group receiving "therapy *plus* communications training" showed more rapid growth than the "traditional therapy" group (Pierce, Schauble, and Wilson, 1971). Communication skills training has been examined in depth for two reasons: first, to introduce the concepts of the dimensions and their progression and interaction, and second, to introduce the position that communication skills training seems to be one of the most effective and economical means for accelerating behavioral growth on the dimensions.

It is important to note that training in the facilitative conditions is not restricted to the communication skills approach. Indeed, since successful therapy culminates in growth on the different dimensions, even traditional therapy can be viewed as a form of training in the facilitative dimensions. When reference is made to "training in the facilitative conditions as a preferred mode of treatment," what is meant is any approach to therapy that has a deliberate and explicit focus on one or more of the facilitative dimensions. Such approaches or treatment modes are interventions in the overall therapy or communication process, and should be viewed in light of the appropriate benefits and limitations inherent in the concept of intervention. It seems appropriate to assert that a therapy approach which incorporates interventions designed to bring about changed behavior–especially behavior central to more effective living–is a treatment mode preferable to an approach which neither identifies target behavior nor a means (or intervention) to accomplish change. The remainder of this section will present several modes of intervention in treatment that seem to have special value in accelerating growth on the facilitative dimensions.

Interpersonal Process Recall

The Interpersonal Process Recall (IPR) technique uses either audio or video tape to record any type of interpersonal interaction for subsequent playback and investigation by the participants. For example, if you (the reader) and I were in a room together now, and I was speaking the words on this page, we could videotape the interpersonal process of my speaking and your listening, and play the tape back when we were through. During the playback, or *recall,* we would then be able to use the tape of our interaction to stimulate exploration of the different reactions you, as the listener, had to what I had said (and vice versa). For example, at one point on the tape you might glance at your watch and yawn, at which point we might stop the tape and talk about the feelings either of us were having *at that point,* be they boredom, anxiety, embarrassment, etc. In this case, such exploration could have a twofold purpose. First, since I am attempting to communicate some rather abstract concepts to you, you could give me valuable feedback as to when I was clear and when my terminology became confusing. Second, it would help both of us gain a greater awareness and understanding of each other and our process than had been possible in the original interaction.

Although there are a number of variations for use with IPR, the basic procedure for counseling is for a helper (i.e. counselor) and a client to conduct and tape a therapy interview. Immediately after the interview is completed, the helper leaves the room and a second helper, the "Interpersonal Process Consultant" (or IPC) who has been trained in encouraging participant recall, enters the room and conducts a playback of the interview. The developers of this method identify two important ingredients for success in this basic procedure.

First, it is best if the recall worker (or IPC) is someone other than the original helper. When the purpose of the recall session is to explore the dynamics of the therapy relationship, the client seems better able to respond to a third person who was not a part of the original interaction. When the helper conducting the therapy session also conducts the recall session, it is likely that the client will tend to avoid the same areas of stress in the recall that he did in the therapy session *per se,* since the helper was, and still is, the focus of many of the client's feelings. Since the IPC functions as a "consultant" and deliberately avoids establishing a second counseling relationship with the client, the client can investigate his feelings and reactions in the "there-and-then" of the taped interaction without having to confront the helper's immediate reaction.

While it is desirable to begin IPR with a "third person" IPC (especially in the initial stages of therapy), it is possible for a skilled clinician who is thoroughly familiar and comfortable with IPR to conduct productive recall sessions with his own clients, but the interpersonal complications are still present and are taxing on the helper's expertise.

Second, it is essential that the helper directly observe (through a one-way mirror or via a tape of the recall session) the recall if there is to be meaningful therapeutic use made of the dynamics derived in the recall session. By observing the client's projections, fears, and aspirations about him (the helper), the helper can more clearly understand the client's interpersonal relationships. The client also can gain greater understanding of his own reactions to people by observing the way he interacts with the helper (Kagan, Schauble, Resnikoff, Danish, and Krathwohl, 1969).

When IPR is used as an intervention in marriage counseling, a similar format can be applied. After a therapy session including husband, wife, and helper (or a husband/wife interaction) is conducted and taped, either husband or wife can be asked to leave the room and the helper and the remaining spouse can conduct a recall session. After some proportion of the taped interview has been recalled (perhaps 20 minutes of a 60 minute segment), the spouses change places and the helper conducts a recall with the spouse who originally left the room. Since many practicing professional helpers do not have access to one-way mirrors or elaborate sound facilities, an acceptable variation of this approach is to have the spouse who is not participating in the recall session remain in the room, but move to some part of the room where he can be out of sight. It is imperative that this spouse not become involved in the recall and not have an influence on the other spouse's recall process (either verbally or non-verbally). This may require firm structuring by the helper initially, but husband and wife generally become quite comfortable with the passive role rather quickly. It has been found, however, that it is much harder for the spouse who is actively involved in the recall to confine his activity to the taped session and the IPC (in this case, the sole helper); i.e., he will attempt to engage his spouse in the recall session by turning physically and directing comments at the non-participant. This seems to support the concept that, whatever the relationship being explored, the participants have learned to interact in a conditioned manner, and will find it difficult to examine and improve their process of relating unless they can (temporarily) extract themselves from the interaction. Parenthetically, if a husband is frustrated and angry with his wife in everyday life because she cannot understand him and he tries to approach her with this problem, the chances are that she will not (initially) understand what he is attempting to communicate (by definition). Her lack of understanding will increase his frustration and anger, which will contribute more to her non-understanding, and so it can go until one or the other leaves (physically or emotionally) and sufficient distance is accomplished to allow objective understanding of the other person (or the relationship is terminated). Hence a dysfunctional system of communication is learned; yet when the system leads to conflict and husband and wife decide to change the system, they are locked into depending on the very system they want to change as the instrument for accomplishing that change.

The conditioned interaction phenomenon is illustrated in the typescript below. The therapy interview between husband, wife, and therapist is indicated as "Therapy Session" and the corresponding recall of the audio tape recording is indicated as "Recall Session." During the recall session with the husband, the wife had moved to a chair out of her husband's line of vision. Both spouses received the same introduction to the recall session, which was (according to the therapist):

> Now that we've completed our therapy session, we're going to listen to parts of the tape in order to recall some of the thoughts and feelings we didn't get a chance to express, or maybe chose not to express because they were uncomfortable. It's important in the beginning to concentrate on what we hear being communicated *in the session*. In order to give each of you a chance to express what you felt was going on—and hear what your spouse felt was going on—*back then*, I'm going to ask one of you to sit over on the side and not respond verbally to the tape or the recall of the other. We'll do this for about 15 minutes with each of you, and then we'll have a chance to discuss our reactions to the tape. Janet, let's do the

first recall session with Ted, and have you move to that chair (to the rear of the room).

Ted, during our therapy session you and Janet both had a great many thoughts and feelings, only some of which were expressed. As we listen to the tape, try to remember *any* feelings you had which you didn't get to talk about. Any time you're confused about what Janet's feelings are, or when you think she had feelings that didn't come out, let's stop the tape and discuss those as well. Remember, you and I will be talking about the tape—try not to attend to Janet for these few minutes.

The therapist then selected a spot about ten minutes into the tape and, after instructing Ted in how to operate the recorder, started the tape and began the recall session.

Therapy Session

Wife: . . . so I really don't think things are getting any better, and I see Ted getting more and more uptight. . . .

Husband: It's just this damn promotion that has me worried. Nothing else has been on my mind, and I guess I've been asking for more than I'm giving. If I only knew, one way or another. . . .

Recall Session

Therapist: Ted, what were you feeling at this point?

Husband: Well, just that I'd like to know if I was going to get the promotion or not.

Therapy Session

Therapist: Ted, I hear you focusing on the promotion as the cause of your hassles, but it sounds like Janet feels like it goes deeper than that.

Recall Session

Therapist: How did you feel about what I said right then?

Husband: About it going deeper? For Janet? Well, Janet said she agreed with me, didn't you honey? (At this point, Ted turned in his chair and directed his question to his wife.)

Therapist: Ted, we'll find out if Janet agreed with you when we talk with her later. Let's concentrate on what *you* think and feel now.

Therapy Session

Wife: Well, he has been preoccupied with the promotion . . . and if he should get it I guess he'd feel a lot better.

Therapist: *Ted* would feel better?

Wife: Well, sure he would. The promotion means a lot to him.

Recall Session

Therapist: I hear you saying you think she *agrees* with you, but how did you *feel* about my comment?

Husband: Well, I wasn't sure just what to think. I wondered a little if she maybe agreed with what you were saying.

Therapist: So you felt like maybe it did go deeper. That it wasn't just the promotion for Janet.

Husband: I don't know, I'm not sure. (Again Ted turns to his wife) Do you feel it goes deeper, Janet?

Therapist: Ted . . . it's important that we identify how *you* feel about it now. Let's try to leave Janet out of it for a few more minutes.

Husband: I don't *know* what I feel. How do you know I'm feeling anything?

Therapist: I'm picking up a lot of ambivalence. Like there's a lot of feeling there, but you're not sure if you can or even if you *want* to explore it . . . and that's O.K.—we don't have to—but it might be easier if you made a decision not to talk about it instead of playing hide-and-seek.

Husband: You think I'm avoiding my feelings?

Therapist: I think you're having a tough time coming to grips with them.

Husband: O.K., let's start over. Can I listen to that spot on the tape again?

(The tape was rewound, and the segment played over again.)

Husband: I felt uncomfortable with your remark. As I think about it, I guess I believe Janet does think it goes deeper, and I was trying to convince myself that it's just the promotion. If it wasn't the promotion, it would be something else—there always has been.

Therapist: So you were trying not to hear the other message, 'cause that makes you feel (cut-off)

Husband: Weak, afraid, hurt.

Therapist: Did you see Janet's agreeing with you as supportive?

Husband: Sort of, but I think she may have been building me up too . . . so if I do get the promotion I'm strong and "together."

Therapist: And if you're strong, you're not dependent on her and (cut-off)

Husband: And then she's free to leave without worrying about me coming apart. I think she's wanted to leave for a long time, but she didn't think I could handle it.

At this point, Ted has moved into a much greater awareness of his feelings, and he is able to "own" and communicate them much more clearly. In this case, the husband and wife had established clearly defined roles relating to dependency. When they began to explore these roles, both in the therapy session and the initial stage of the IPR session, the husband became caught up in his role and sought cues and support from his wife (despite the structure which was designed to prevent such an occurrence). With support and some firm direction from the therapist/IPC, the husband was able to distance himself from the ongoing husband-wife process, and explore his behavior in the there-and-then of the tape.

The IPR approach seems to have a direct and positive influence on most of the facilitative dimensions. By providing the client with firsthand information about his own behavior through audio or video tape, he is able to experience, to identify, and to own feelings that had previously escaped his awareness. *The IPC models the task of searching and differentiating feelings,* and the client typically carries the behavior learned in IPR back to the therapy and marital situations. The IPR procedure also has a significant influence on the development of empathy and concreteness, for it reveals the identification of the spouses' specific feelings at various points in the interview and, through spouse recall, provides the opportunity to validate the accuracy of the feelings that have been identified.

For further clarity, let us consider the same wife's (Janet) recall session:

Therapy Session

> Therapist: Ted, I hear you focusing on the promotion as the cause of the hassles, but it sounds like Janet feels like it goes deeper than that.

Recall Session

> Wife: You were right, of course, but even though I was upset with Ted for pushing it off (on to the promotion), I felt badly when you said it.
> Therapist: You felt like that was going to hurt him?

Wife: Yes . . . so that's when I made my famous response . . . which we all know by now.

Therapy Session

Wife: Well, he has been preoccupied with the promotion . . . and if he should get it I guess he'd feel a lot better.
Therapist: *Ted* would feel better?

Recall Session

Wife: I didn't know what you meant for a minute.

Therapy Session

Wife: Well, sure he would. The promotion means a lot to him.

Therapy Session

Therapist: What meaning does it have for you?
Wife: I'll be real happy, too.

Recall Session

Wife: But here it came clear . . . and I really evaded the question.
Therapist: You evaded it?
Wife: Well, in a way. Right then I wasn't thinking about what the promotion would mean, but about what his *not* getting it would mean.
Therapist: So you were afraid of Ted's reaction if he failed?
Wife: Uh-huh!
Therapist: How does this fit in to Ted's recall session, and the discussion we had about his dependency feelings?
Wife: I knew you'd ask that. First, let me say that until Ted mentioned it, I hadn't thought of leaving if he got the promotion. However, I did think about what would happen if he *didn't* get it.
Therapist: Then you'd feel trapped?
Wife: Yeah, he'd be devastated if he failed, and I didn't know how I could handle his being devastated and weak again; and I'd rather leave than go through all that—but that would really kill him. I thought!
Therapist: And now?
Wife: Now I don't know. I never heard him talk like he did before about the weakness, and he sounded really mad at me. Maybe he's not so weak!
Therapist: So you really didn't think he was aware of your feelings, and you're surprised that he doesn't like the dependency either?

Wife: Yeah, and maybe we've wasted a lot of time not talking about that before.

Since the husband was listening to his wife's recall, he was able to judge from direct feedback how accurate his appraisal of her feelings and motives were. In this case, the IPR procedure helped both husband and wife gain insight into their own feelings and the feelings of their spouse.

After both spouses have participated in a recall session, it is advisable to return to the traditional therapy format and discuss the material disclosed through IPR. Experience supports that when such an integrative (or "summary") session is not conducted, there is a tendency for the couple to repress insights and suppress new behaviors which are still different enough from their established way of relating as to cause dissonance and anxiety. Discussion of the IPR material in the presence of the therapist provides an immediate and relatively safe reinforcement for acquiring and continuing these new modes of communication.

The IPR procedure, then, typically involves the following format: a therapy session with the couple, individual IPR sessions with each spouse (with the remaining spouse a non-participatory observer), and a summary therapy session. The time allocated to each phase of the treatment is the prerogative of the therapist, although the typical format is to allow 30 to 45 minutes for the therapy session, 45 to 60 minutes for the IPR sessions, and 30 minutes for the summary session. This can mean an investment of time of from two to three hours, but the impact of the intervention makes it seem a valuable (and ultimately economical) use of time. Research data has consistently shown that IPR accelerates client movement in a variety of settings (Kagen, 1972; Schauble, 1967; Schauble, Kagan, Pierce, and Resnikoff, in press).

While the IPR procedure can be used profitably with an audio tape recording, there are distinct advantages to using a video tape recording whenever it is available. Some of the advantages of a video tape recording are:

1. It maximizes the stimulation value of the recall session, especially by providing non-verbal cues not available on audio tape.
2. It tends to generate more involvement through the novelty of the

medium, i.e. there is a distinct "halo" effect.

3. It provides complete data for each spouse to communicate, verify, and/or change their perceptions of their mate's behavior.
4. It allows the individual to confront himself as he is seen by others.

While many professional helpers are affiliated with facilities where video tape is (or could be) available, technological advances have reduced the cost and complexity of equipment on the market to a point where complete units (camera, recorder, and monitor) are available for even the private practitioner. Some of the newer units are portable enough that they can be taken into the home environment as well, and present a virtually untapped resource for family therapy. Chapter Five presents additional behavioral views on the use of recordings.

Contractual Training

Accomplishing positive change on the facilitative dimensions assumes that the couple will practice what they are learning in training between the therapy or training sessions. This is not always the case, however, especially when the new behavior being learned is dissonant with the process of relating that is already established. One means of assuring some degree of continued activity outside the therapy contact is to have the couple contract to spend a certain amount of time during the week practicing the communication skills they are learning. Since it is important that the new skills be learned correctly, it is advisable for the professional helper to monitor the contracted activity. One of the most efficient ways of monitoring is the audio recorder or cassette. An example of such a contract based on the communication skills training would be to have a couple contract to speak and listen to each other for one half-hour each day. They would take turns being speaker and listener for 15 minutes each, concentrating initially on the dimensions of owning feelings and of empathy. They would tape the interaction on a cassette or other audio recorder, and spend the next half-hour listening to the tape of their interaction and rating it on the Owning of Feeling and Empathy scales, and discussing the bases for their ratings. At the end of the week (perhaps more frequently initially, e.g. every other day), they would drop off the recordings and the ratings to their helper-trainer, who would check the taped interactions and ratings and provide suggestions (in the next regular session) as to how the interaction and ratings could be improved. As ratings of the daily interactions consistently approached acceptable levels of facilitation, a new communication dimension could be introduced.

There are several benefits to this type of contract. The following are five of the primary benefits.

First, it insures that the couple is sufficiently committed to improving their relationship that they will devote one hour a day to attempting to communicate with each other. Couples have reacted to the suggestion of such a contract with statements like: "It just wouldn't be natural to sit down for an hour each day and talk about our feelings. I'd feel too artificial; it's better to do that spontaneously!" In one particular case I agreed with the man speaking that spontaneous expression of feelings was to be desired, but I than asked him how often in the last week he and his wife had sat down with just each other and talked about their feelings. It turned out that this particular couple needed to go back *three weeks(!)* before they could remember having a conversation *alone* where they discussed their feelings with one another, and that instance had been an unresolved argument. This is a question you, the reader, might ask yourself. "When was the last time my spouse (or other primary relationship) and I sat down together *to really listen to each other* and share our feelings? Have we built into our relationship avenues for frequent and direct communications that extend beyond our everyday roles?" A startling number of married couples, especially those seeking help, have very little time during their daily schedules when they can count on direct and trusting communication with each other.

In many cases, couples will contract to spend one hour per day in structured communication, and then not fulfill the terms of the contract ("We had weekend guests, and they took all our time." "We were so busy during the week that we just were too tired to sit down at night and talk."). Such violations of contracts are an indication of commitment level, and can be discussed as such in the therapy session. If a couple is unwilling or unable to spend one hour a day with each other for even a trial period, it is only logical to question their commitment priority to therapy and improving their marriage.

Second, regular practice of the skills training where each person is intent on improving their speaking and listening with each other (i.e. *understanding* each other) increases the likelihood that matters and feelings of real concern will be shared.

Third, working by contract allows the couple to experience control over manageable units of their lives and relationship. It becomes less a matter of an unwieldy major problem ("What can we do to end the unhappiness in our marriage?") and more a matter of controllable actions ("Let's concentrate on learning from this next hour together."). By and large, this method also provides the opportunity to experience successful movement, since most couples who fulfill the terms of the contract notice immediate change in their ability to communicate.

Fourth, this method affords the opportunity for the therapist to hear how the couple interacts when outside the therapy session, and allows him to make constructive input into their daily communication process.

Fifth and finally, the contractual sessions encourage the couple to be "in-therapy" seven days a week, instead of one. The structure of the daily interaction encourages (and even increases) the feeling of being actively involved in the growth process. A consequent benefit is often a feeling of reduced dependency on the counselor, since the couple has the daily opportunity to "work-through" conflicts that might otherwise wait until the weekly therapy session.

The concept of contractual training can be extended to augment almost any therapy or intervention approach. The technique is especially valuable in improving parent-child relationships when combined with the IPR procedure (as discussed above). For example, one parent and a child can record a brief interaction or discussion, and then have the therapist or even the second parent conduct an IPR session with the tape and one or both participants. This approach seems especially suited for children, who often are not articulate (or confident) enough to discuss their feelings in the present. Listening to (or viewing) themselves in an interaction with the parent often stimulates fruitful discussion of "the feelings I was having back then," and it also gives the child (and parent) examples of his own behavior which stimulate various reactions in the parent.

One illustration of the initial impact this type of contractual arrangement can make is presented below. The typescript is from a tape made by husband (a physician) and wife during their third daily session of speaking and listening.

> Husband: I thought quite awhile before starting this tape tonight and that is because I was trying to figure out what to say on it. I was trying to collect my thoughts.
>
> Wife: There is a marvelous expression called "getting your shit together."
>
> Husband: Yeah. Yes, that is what I thought of. And so—not having anything else to think about, I started to think about: "why don't I have anything to say?" I thought of our talk two nights ago, when we talked about how we lived on a brain stem level a large part of the time. And then our talk last night that was just so lovely. No specifics, nothing deep, and yet it was really very deep. I thought about today, and I thought about dinner, and I thought about what we did *not* say at dinner, and how today is rather a typical day in our lives. I got up and left before you were up, and when I got home the kids were on me right away. Everyone wanted to do their things and so forth. I had work piled high on my desk which I went and took care of after dinner, and then I went back to the hospital. Now I'm home, late again, and I am glad that you could not get to sleep and stayed up to make a tape. Because you know, if it was not for the tape, I would not have any interpersonal contact with you at all today! Really!
>
> Wife: I know exactly what you mean.
>
> Husband: I guess a lot of days, though—*a lot* of days are "blanks." I wonder what we can do about it? Because I think if we are going to grow with each other, one of the things we are going to have to do is have daily contact. And we are going to have to make a real effort to do it.
>
> Wife: Well, there *are* a lot of days like today. I think today is a very good example of a "thing" day. You got caught up in things, you had things to do. They had to be done! Likewise with me. And here it is midnight before we can sit down with each other and look each other square in the eye and say "how are you"? And I haven't known the answer to that one in a long, long time.

This couple had been married eleven years, yet the introduction of a time for deliberate communication quickly brought home an awareness that their life style was making them strangers.

Another example illustrates control over manageable units and successful movement. The following two typescripts are of the first and second speaking and listening interactions with the same couple. The contract was established after the second regular therapy session. The husband and wife were given a brief explanation of the speaking and listening roles, and they agreed to spend forty minutes a day (taking turns speaking and listening for ten minutes each, and then listening to the tape for the remaining 20 minutes). The first such session, with wife beginning as speaker, went as follows:

Wife: Well, I feel embarrassed, as if somebody is in here.

Husband: You mean because of the tape recorder?

Wife: Yeah, because I know that he is going to listen to it. You know, like it is not—(Period of silence)

Husband: I guess I know what you mean. (Period of silence)

Wife: I am glad that you are going to get to go hunting tomorrow, but I guess that I am jealous of your hunting, in a way.

Husband: Why? What's wrong?

Wife: Because you are always running off and doing your little things. . . .

Husband: You mean like (cut-off)

Wife: Like I don't run off and do my little things. I guess sometimes it seems like I do, but you are always studying and you want me to go off anyway. You know!

Husband: What are you saying? I think you are saying (cut-off)

Wife: Do you think he can hear us, or do you think we should check it (the recorder)?

Husband: You think I am supposed to stay home or something?

Wife: No! I *don't* think you are supposed to stay home. It's just that when you go off like hunting and everything, I don't like it somehow.

Husband: Why?

Wife: But I do encourage you, and I am glad you have it, and I want you to get to do what you want to do. (Silence) I *think* I encourage you.

Husband: And yet you don't like it.

Wife: I really don't mind it so much. But, had you gone off and taken our car and left me here stuck without a car, plus all the laundry to do and the housework, *then* I would have been really *mad*. In fact, I would have suggested that you make other arrangements!

Wife: But I am really glad that you are going hunting, really. You have been wanting to go, and everything, and now you have finally gotten to go, and so now I can see your (cut-off)

Husband: Point of view?

Wife: No, not your point of view, I *have* seen that. It's just that now you won't be sad, and put on, and deprived.

Husband: Why do you say that? Deprived of what?

Wife: Of the great *pleasure*. Of hunting! I think that since you are going to get to go hunting you won't be sad anymore. Right? Correct? DEFINITELY. (with considerable sarcasm)!

Husband: That's a beginning, yeah,

Wife: I am also scared about it.

Husband: What are you scared of me going hunting for?

Wife: I am not worried about you going hunting!

Husband: I think I misunderstood what you said.

Wife: I actually said that I am *glad* you are going hunting. It's just that in a way sometimes I am not glad. I have not figured it out yet myself so I should not have brought it up.

Husband: Mmmm.

Wife: I am *scared* about this *infection*. I think I—I wish you would see another doctor.

Husband: Why? Because you don't care for that one?

Wife: No, because *you* indicated that you did not think much of him, so that make me ner—(cut-off)

Husband: *NO,* I didn't!

Wife: Well, I know that he gave you a "plastic" examination.

Husband: Yeah, he did, but he was in a hurry. I have made another appointment with him for next Friday.

Wife: I didn't know that you had another appointment.

Husband: Well, yeah, I do, and I did tell you about it. I have another appointment Friday, so stop worrying!

Wife: We have four minutes left, I know, and I haven't got anything to say. I'm getting irritated!

Giving consideration to the discussion of the facilitative dimensions, it is obvious that this couple was communicating at a very low level. When the husband and wife reversed the speaker/listener roles, the communication level deteriorated even further. Understandably upset, the couple contacted me to ask my reactions to the tape. After listening to the tape, I introduced the concepts of owning of feeling and empathy and suggested how they might try to incorporate these into their behavior in the next speaking/listening interaction (this "consultation" session took 30 minutes). Their next speaking/listening interaction (conducted the following day) went as follows:

Wife: I felt a little irritated when you started looking at that magazine when it came to be my turn—it hurt—it hurt my feelings.

Husband: So you were feeling kinda hurt because I picked up the magazine.

Wife: It's because—because you weren't very interested in anything in me, you know? It almost like, well—

Husband: So I seem not interested in (cut-off)

Wife: It's like you went to sleep or something—

Husband: It felt like I was wanting more to read the magazine than talk with you.

Wife: Yeah! (Silence) Now I've got distracted. (Silence) Sorta like I didn't count or something. Because I felt real close to you right there.

Husband: Hmm.

Wife: And then you picked up that magazine.

Husband: So you felt that my picking up the magazine was not listening, it just sorta made you draw away from me.

Wife: No. I feel like *you* were withdrawing from the closeness—I felt like you withdrew. Like you were pushing me away or pushing yourself away to your "sacred" place.

Husband: I see now. I see what you mean. In other words you feel like I was retreating into the magazine so I would not have to deal with listening to your problems or listening to you for ten minutes.

Wife: Yeah.

Husband: That's interesting. I mean, I wouldn't have expected that.

Wife: I also feel very guilty about what happened yesterday with the doctor. I feel a kind of shame. It was a chance to see if I was all right, and I guess that was the only way he could test it, but I almost wish something had been wrong with me so that hadn't happened. [Editor's note: She had been to a gynecologist, who had tested her sexual response ability by use of a vibrator; this produced an orgasm, which is referred to subsequently.]

Husband: Oh, well.

Wife: I mean—

Husband: Yes, what?

Wife: Because, if something was *physically* wrong, I would not have climaxed like that and embarrassed myself. It was the first time I ever did that, and it had to be in a *doctor's* office. I could have hit the ceiling.

Husband: Yeah. So you feel like it was embarrassing because you were in the doctor's office when that happened, and it was a mechanical thing and it did not even take love to bring it on. It was just some strange person.

Wife: Yes, and I feel ashamed. Like I should have been able to control it. And I know in my mind that it is not something that I have control over. (Wife begins to cry softly)

Husband: So you really felt ashamed and the need to control it.

Wife: I didn't even know what was happening! It dawned on me what must be happening—I mean that, it couldn't be anything else, well, it was something very strange and I could hear myself panting and making the terrible noises. I tried to stop it and you know—I wish that I hadn't tried to do *that*, too. I wish I hadn't had this pattern set—I mean the *very first time* to try and *stop* it. I just wish I had been with some man that I loved, like you.

Husband: Yeah, I know.

Wife: I feel gypped too, not by you, by me.

Husband: In other words, do you feel since it happened in this particular way—that it was not right and you tried to suppress it?

Wife: Mmmm.

Husband: And you feel guilty for that reason.

Wife: I feel guilty for trying to suppress it, and I feel more guilty for—(cut-off)

Husband: For having the feelings.

Wife: Yeah—I didn't have any feelings. I didn't—I wasn't aware of feeling sexual feelings—it was just this terrible thing taking over my body. I couldn't control it.

Husband: OK, I understand. I understand how you feel right now.

Wife: I feel like, well, you know—I have been superdehumanized.

Husband: This mechanical process makes you feel dehumanized, sorta like—

Wife: And empty! And I wonder what's *wrong* with me.

Husband: So you think there's something wrong, that you're insensitive?

Wife: Something like that.

Husband: If you can't experience that on your own.

Wife: *YEAH!*

Husband: Without having a doctor induce it.

Wife: Yeah. I feel like I'm a failure as a woman.

In this illustration, both parties are functioning considerably higher in their respective roles. It is interesting to note that the husband's reaction to this session was: ". . . she really was honest . . . made herself real clear. I just didn't know what to do though. I felt inadequate as a listener." The wife's reaction was: "I felt so close to Mike. I have never felt like he understood me so well–*or wanted to*–before. But he really did understand." In the space of two days, with a 30 minute consultation, this couple was able to improve their communication process significantly. Both felt an immediate positive effect, which gave them an increased sense of confidence and commitment.

Teaching Techniques

Since all therapeutic, intervention, and training techniques are (or should be) designed to result ultimately in the *learning* of new behavior, they can be classified as ways of *teaching*. It is possible, however, to apply more traditional or didactic teaching interventions to bring about change on the facilitative dimensions. One of the most critical areas of learning is the ability to distinguish affect from other psychological factors. Before an individual can begin to own his feelings more effectively, it usually may be necessary to be able to discriminate between feelings (or *affect*) and thoughts (or cognition). A variety of exercises can be developed which teach the difference between thoughts and feeling; after this, it is possible to teach helpees how to reward the expression of feeling.

In a family therapy situation, children and parents can receive the same instructions and participate in the same exercises together, with the objective being to learn the difference between thoughts and feelings. This builds a common frame of reference for the expression of feeling in later communications. This may be a necessary step for children in learning new behavior, but it can also be productive for their parents. Adults may know how to make an *intellectual* distinction between thoughts and feeling, but they often do not *operationalize* or *practice* the distinction in communication with their children.

Often the child who does venture a direct expression of his feelings is met by devastating and overwhelming adult logic; this can obscure the adult's feelings, devalue the child's feelings, and increase the psychological distance between the parent and child. Consider the following exchange:

Son: Daddy, I *hate* you for spanking me!

Father: I disciplined you because you woke your mother from her nap. I made it quite clear to you that you were *not* to disturb her. You broke a rule, and you were punished. What *you* did was inconsiderate, selfish, and wrong. What *I* did was quite correct. So there is really no reason for you to tell me you hate me.

If there are many such encounters, the child will indeed cease telling his father that "I hate you," but the suppressed feelings will have to be discharged elsewhere–and quite probably they will be expressed inappropriately.

Through a teaching intervention focusing on discriminating feelings from thoughts, spouses, parents, and children can begin to learn the common language of feelings. As they acquire knowledge and sensitivity to feelings, the probability is enhanced that they will be able to attend to each other more as individuals and to mutually benefit each other through facilitative interactions.

Research investigating the effect of this type of didactic intervention in therapeutic processes has found that client's internalization behavior can be significantly increased in a single session. In this case, the teaching intervention consisted of a straightforward (rather brief) explanation of what the concept of Internalization/Externalization is and how it furnishes a helpful way of looking at problems. For the next twenty minutes, the helper very directly made the client aware of when he was internalizing or externalizing and offered positive verbal reinforcement ("that's good," "you're doing better," etc.) for internalizing behavior. When the therapist ceased deliberately to reinforce internalizing behavior, the client continued to internalize at a higher level than he had before the intervention (Pierce, Schauble, and Wilson, 1971). As a facilitative dimension, the internalization/externalization variable is crucial in therapeutic growth. This research has exciting implications for such intervention approaches with the remaining dimensions as well.

CONCLUSION

It seems obvious that there are unlimited approaches to training or influencing psychological growth and communication via the facilitative dimensions. To the extent that professional helpers can communicate these dimensions and their importance in interpersonal interaction, they can then develop modes of influencing growth in therapeutic interventions. While most of the communication examples have related to marital counseling and therapy, each of the facilitating dimensions and the relevant techniques described are applicable to all helping relationships (including individual and family therapy, crisis intervention, teaching, etc.) and to "non-client" populations as well. Thus, as a preventive measure, there would be considerable value in providing training in the dimensions to *improve* communication in all families and marriages, even when there may not be evident or "declared" conflict.

REFERENCES

Carkhuff, R. R.: *Helping and human relations: a primer for lay and professional helpers. Volume I. Selection and training.* New York, Holt, Rinehart and Winston, 1969.

Carkhuff, R. R. and Bierman, R.: Training as a preferred mode of treatment of parents of emotionally disturbed children. *Journal of Counseling Psychology, 17*:157-161, 1970.

Kagan, N.: *Influencing human interaction.* East Lansing, College of Education, Michigan State University, 1972.

Kagan, N., Schauble, P. G., Resnikoff, A., Danish, S. J. and Krathwohl, D. R.: Interpersonal process recall. *Journal of Nervous and Mental Disease, 4*:365-370, 1969.

Pierce, R. and Drasgow, J.: Teaching facilitative interpersonal functioning to psychiatric patients. *Journal of Clinical Psychology, 23*:212-215, 1967.

Pierce, R. and Schauble, P. G.: Graduate training of facilitative counselors: the effects of individual supervision. *Journal of Counseling Psychology, 17*:210-215, 1970.

Pierce, R. and Schauble, P. G.: Client-in-therapy behavior: a therapist's guide to progress. *Psychotherapy: Theory, Research and Practice,* in press.

Pierce, R., Schauble, P. G. and Farkas, Andrea: Teaching internalization behavior to clients. *Psychotherapy: Theory, Research and Practice, 7*:217-220, 1971.

Pierce, R., Schauble, P. G. and Wilson, F. R.: Employing systematic human relations training for teaching constructive helper and helpee behavior in a group therapy situation. *Journal of Research and Development in Education, 4*:97-109, 1971.

Rogers, C. R.: *On becoming a person.* Boston, Houghton Mifflin, 1961.

Schauble, P. G.: Acceleration of client growth through interpersonal process recall. Paper presented at the American Psychological Association's Annual Convention, Washington, D. C., September 1967.

Schauble, P. G., Kagan, N., Pierce, R. and Resnikoff, A.: Accelerating client progress in counseling and psychotherapy through interpersonal process recall (IPR). *Psychiatry,* in press.

Stover, L. and Guerney, B. G.: The efficacy of training procedures for mothers in filial therapy. *Psychotherapy: Theory, Research and Practice,* 4:110-115, 1967.

CHAPTER
FOUR

PSYCHODYNAMIC INTERVENTIONS: A PERSONAL STATEMENT[1]

LUCIANO L'ABATE, PH.D.
Georgia State University

T HIS CHAPTER HAS BEEN WRITTEN from the viewpoint of a practicing clinical child psychologist. From this vantage point, the main focus of entry into a couple or a family is commonly the "imputed patient," a child or a teenager. After a thorough psychodiagnostic evaluation is administered, one or more of the following recommendations would be made, among others: (1) individual playtherapy;[2] (2) home management;[3] (3) marital therapy, if the conflict between parents is evident at intake, during the evaluation through the child's eyes, and on feedback of the evaluation to the parents and the child (when the parents are more likely to admit to some marital problems); and (4) family therapy, when the help of the whole family is asked in dealing with the child's problem. This chapter concerns itself with recommendations (3) and (4).

The reason for calling the present approach "personal" lies not

1. *Acknowledgment:* It is difficult to trace back all of the antecedents that make one become and be a family helper. I was personally and directly influenced by Virginia Satir, Albert Ellis, Haim Ginott, Robert Goulding, George Bach, Edward Duhl, Andrew Ferber, and James Framo, and by my students, particularly Roberta Golden, Katherine Harlan, and Valerie Marler. They have provided the stimulus for growth and change from individual to family orientation. However, they should not be held responsible for any shortcomings and weaknesses in the present statement. Books in and by themselves and this statement in particular will not teach anyone to become a family helper. Each of us must find his own way, borrowing, begging, or stealing, or directly experiencing from everyone else.

2. L'Abate, L. *Aggression and construction in children's play* (research in progress).

3. Rogers, Mary Brown. Home management: a personalized approach. Ditto, Child Development Laboratory, Georgia State University, 1970.

only in the personal experience of the writer but also in his philosophical assumptions specifically about himself and generally about behavior. It was during the course of writing this chapter that he became aware of how important the "self" is. Although he liked to view himself as an "empirical eclecticist," both philosophically and professionally, the importance of the self and the dysfunctionality that occurs from our inability to assert ourselves helpfully and hurtlessly came strongly to the fore. In addition, outside of playtherapy (L'Abate, 1971b), this writer has not, as yet, been able to clarify for himself and others his involvement and interest in the helping process. This chapter, then, represents what he currently believes and practices to the best of his ability. In other words, there is very little in this chapter (outside of the historical background) that does not represent what the author practices.

THEORETICAL ASSERTIONS

It would be helpful if the theoretical assertions of the helper were as simple and as clear as possible. The assertions he makes about himself and others should lead directly into the process of helping. There should be as much consistency as possible between his theoretical assertions and his practical applications. These assertions should lead him but should not interfere with or distort the process of helping. Each assertion should be continuously reevaluated and if invalid, discarded.

Assertion 1. A great many interpersonal dysfunctions result from the failure to assert ourselves helpfully and hurtlessly.

The terms "helpful" and "hurtlessly" represent the best and most humble way of expressing what we can do to help someone who hurts. Outside of encouraging recognition and expression of internal feelings of hurt[4] and helplessness, there is little that any-

---

4. As Ellis (undated) pointed out, from a rational viewpoint, the only way to "hurt" someone is to steal, cheat, or lie to him or hurt physically. Hurt, as a psychological reaction, is a selective choice we ourselves make, that is, we choose to be or become "hurt," just as we choose to be or become angry, furious, fearful, etc. We choose whatever feelings we emphasize because we have learned since childhood that these feelings bring us the greatest degree of pay-off. We choose to feel helpless and hurt just as we can choose anger and attack. Either choice is dysfunctional.

one can do about them, including the helper. Springing into action is the worst effort that the helper could exert (Szasz, 1959). Painful feelings deserve someone's being able to recognize them. Doing something about them is the helper's responsibility, if he wants and chooses to do so. Helpful, in this context, represents the opposite of "helpless" and the recognition that no one, unless severely crippled or handicapped, is objectively "helpless." However, some of us do feel helplessness at certain times, under certain conditions. The recognition of someone's helplessness is helpful. Hurtless is used within the present context as the opposite of "hurtful": that is, the reactions that follow one's direct or indirect experience of helplessness, anger, withdrawal, distracting, competing, blaming, etc. Silence or admission of one's helplessness may be helpful in and by itself. Of course, the helper would be sensitive to the manipulatory aspects of helplessness ("Mrs. Smith, it looks to me that with your helplessness you control the whole family, is that right?").

Interpersonal closeness is bound to produce reactions between the parties involved. Typically most reactions are helpful. Both parties can use and grow from their partner's reactions just as the child learns and grows from his parents' reactions. The most helpful reactions are those that come from our own sense of confidence, satisfaction, and self-contentment. At our best we can be helpful: that is, we can see to it that what we say can be helpful to our partner and, consequently, to ourselves. At our worst, under stress, the more helpless the communication we send or receive, the more helpless we may be or become. Yet, it is difficult to recognize, identify, and express our helplessness and hurt in our inability to help those we love.

Consequently, in response to the helpless and occasionally hurtful reactions of a partner we tend to respond in kind: helplessly, and in addition, hurtfully. This transaction, then, becomes a vicious circle that repeats itself like a broken record: helplessness producing more helplessness and adding greater and greater hurtfulness from our inner inability to be helpful.

Assertion 2. Helpless and hurtful assertions derive from reversals ⌐
of priorities in the family.

Instead of individual selves being given primacy over the marriage and the marriage being given primacy over the children, dysfunctionality occurs when these priorities are reversed or confused. Usually the children assume priority over the marriage and the marriage assumes priority over the individual selves of the parents. This reversal of priorities produces a dysfunctional child with an incomplete sense of self. This incompleteness may come out in grade school and/or acting out during adolescence. Once these priorities are adhered to and the parents dilute themselves for the love of their mates and their children, some degree of dysfunctionality is bound to come forth in one form or another and to a certain degree in the marriage or the children or both.

Satir (1965) touches upon the family system having rules about: (1) self and manifestation of self, or how each member may report about himself; (2) the self and expectations from others, or "what I may expect from you," and (3) the self and the use of the world outside of the family, or "how I may go outside the family." Family members, of course, may not be necessarily aware of these rules. However, the individual selves of a marital or parental dyad or family member cannot be understood without the presence of other selves which are part of the everyday transaction. The self in and by itself has little meaning unless it is related to the self or selves of other important and significant intimates in one's life. The individual self is discovered in terms of: (1) how uniquely and individually it manifests itself; (2) how it reacts to similarity and differentness in selves other than one's own, and (3) how it validates its own uniqueness and individuality without denying and invalidating the uniqueness and individuality of its loved ones.

In intimate and prolonged interactions, our sense of self may be diminished. This is the self we have surrendered at the altar or at the moment of courtship or at birth of the first child, when we subscribed to the romantic or religious myth that our inner happiness is bound and dependent to making our partner or child happy. This surrender may produce a reduction in self-identity, a lowering of self-boundaries, and an inevitable snowballing that may deteriorate into a dilution of self-identity, culminating in the extreme into a denial, a negation, and ultimate dissolution of the self. As a result we lose track of our priorities. We put marriage and the family ahead of ourselves. Our self-denial comes from our caring and wanting to care so much for those we love to the point of making them responsible for our happiness! And they fall into the same trap! Consequently, if they are responsible for our happiness, they become also responsible for our unhappiness or any unhappiness produced in the family. This process results in the externalization of responsibility that is so frequently seen between marriage partners, parents, and children. In all of the unhappiness and hurt, the self loses the ability to be helpful. Instead, it acquires characteristics of unspoken and unrecognized helplessness and hurtfulness. The hurt comes from seeing our dear ones hurt and from our feelings of failure to find ways of helping them.

Whatever we try to work out from our sense of failure and losing out, hurt and helplessness, is bound to fail. The self, our internal gyroscope for direction, selection, and problem-solution becomes lost, confused, and frustrated. Sometimes the hurt is so great that we are unable to get in touch with it. Sometimes it is so difficult to get in touch with our hurt and/or to let others help us that we go on the rest of our lives hurting ourselves and hurting those we love most. We build our own straightjackets, our own cages, and our own graves because we are unable to find ways to help ourselves and those close and dear to us.

It derives from this assertion that a great deal of helpless and hurtful behavior is the result of our inability to look into our very selves and to be clear about ourselves. If parents want to deal with how to feel about each other and their selves, then the psychodynamically-oriented helper can volunteer his services. Sometimes, of course, this line of distinction is thin and tenuous. The helper should be flexible and knowledgeable enough to give out a few occasional prescriptions that may help achieve the goal the family wants immediately.

Defenses against unpleasant feelings of helplessness, hurt, fear, grief, and low self-esteem are difficult to deal with intrapersonally and interpersonally. Their recognition, admission, and expression are beclouded by a variety of maneuvers designed to forget, deny, deflect, and distort them. We will go to great personal expense and to great lengths to avoid dealing with them. We are often personally, interpersonally, and culturally unprepared to deal with them appropriately. These feelings are hidden from ourselves and from the view of others. If and when they are expressed, their reception may become so distorted that whoever is half able to let them out needs to put them back in. They are unacceptable at a variety of levels, ranging from intrapsychic to the interpersonal and from the familial to the communal. No one is trained and knows how to deal with these feelings.

The continued helplessness and hurt of the couple and the family has the net effect of reducing self-boundaries (Satir, 1965) and of diminishing the ability to assert, be in touch with, express, and acknowledge the importance of one's self. The dysfunctional (helpless and hurtful) marital or familial system shows a pervasive absence of selves, in extreme, frightening cases behaving as if these selves did not exist. One family, with a teenager and school-age child in treatment with the writer, was unable to define (parents were college graduates) what "boyhood" meant for the child's benefit, what "adolescence" meant for the teenager's benefit, and what "adulthood" meant for the parent's benefit. This pervasive inability to recognize, be in touch with, and express and assert their own selves was accompanied by inertia, lack of initiative, passivity, withdrawal, and inability to take risks. The younger child, the imputed patient, suffered most from this pervasiveness and was unable to answer most questions except through assertion of ignorance ("I don't know.").

Assertion 3: Most dysfunctional (helpless and hurtful) marital, parental, and familial patterns can be summarized into four general categories.

Our inability to help and our feelings of helplessness and hurt are covered, hidden, and distorted by more external reactions: anger and blame, intellectualization and distancing, irrelevant and distracting behavior, overindulgence and placating. These in themselves are helpless attempts that hurt either ourselves or our partners, whether our mate or our child.

Here the influence of Virginia Satir has been paramount to an understanding of marital, parental, and familial dysfunctions. According to her, most interpersonal dysfunctions can be summarized into blaming, placating, distracting, and computing. Blaming represents disagreeable fault-finding externalization and displacement on an external target ("It's all your fault!" "You never . . ." "You always. . . ."). Placating represents the martyr-like, peace-making acceptance and agreement of one's weaknesses and faults ("Yes, dear." "You are right." "I'll do whatever you say."). Computing is the intellectualizing emphasis on cold logic and facts at the expense of any feelings. In this stance there is an over-reliance on self-help books, half-baked esoteric information, and a mask-like, tight-lipped, know-it-all attitude. Distracting represents hyperactive, irrelevant behavior which is neither here nor there. It is impulsive action as an escape from an inability to cope with an otherwise unbearable situation. These dysfunctions can give rise to typical characters like Casper Milquetoasts, and Red Cross nurses for male and female placators, Patriots and Amazons or Harpies for male and female blamers, Cowboys and Butterflies for male and female distractors, and Robots and Ann Landers for male and female intellectualizing computers.

In a further elaboration of this model,[5] each of these patterns sets itself up in an orthogonal paradigm, whereby blaming is more related (negatively) to placating and distracting correlates negatively with computing. This paradigm is useful in understanding most interpersonal dysfunctions and in relating theory to practice. It is a useful device to understand, summarize, and deal with, through instant recognition of dysfunctional patterns that hide an individual's helplessness and hurt. Although this model seems consistent with empirical as well as clinical observations, it is in the process of being tested (see last section on Research).

---

5. L'Abate, L., and Golden, Roberta. Satir's framework of family dysfunctions (research in progress).

FURTHER THEORETICAL ELABORATION:
THE DEFINITION OF SELF

How is the self defined? Structurally, we could talk of "ego-structure," "self-concept," "self-esteem," and equivalent terms. Within the context of levels of functioning in behavior (L'Abate, 1964), the self is here used synonymously with the term "genotype"; this is the ultimate, intrapsychic basis for one's identity, individuation, and identification. The self is a composite, more or less integrated or more or less differentiated, of past and present personal perceptions of one's physical and cultural heritage. In this respect then, *the self is a system developing from the interaction over time of the biological and the cultural systems* (L'Abate, 1969).

Functionally, the self is expressed in many ways and at different levels of functioning: self-presentationally, and phenotypically. At the conversational and interpersonal levels, the self is shown by one's expression of wants, desires, needs, likes, dislikes, preferences, and choices. Developmentally, the self finds its roots in the child's simple-minded voicing of "I want . . ." and "I don't want." Discrimination of relevant payoffs is one of the functions of the self.

Dysfunctionally, the self is expressed in the inability to express one's likes, dislikes, etc., adequately and appropriately at the proper time, in the proper place, and in the proper fashion. There may be extremes in this experience, too passively or too violently, too weakly or too strongly, too indirectly or too directly. It is important, then, to understand how the self may be defined helplessly and hurtfully, and how dysfunctionality could be changed to find helpful and hurtless expression. There are various stages and steps through which the self descends down to nothing.

Hurtful and Helpless Definitions of Self

Self-assertion is one avenue of expression of the self that derives from self-definition. The way I think and feel about myself determines how I express and assert myself. How I see myself is linked to how I show myself. Dysfunctionality in the self finds a variety of expressions outside of the self: i.e. (1) *Self-denial:* "It makes me happy to see you and make you happy." One's self is sub-ordinated, and, in some cases, completely denied for the impor-tance and ascendancy of another self, our spouse, our children, or our loved ones. This form of denial produces a distortion in ac-tion: (2) *Self-distortion:* In actions the self could be distorted in terms of upside-down priorities; emphasis on irrelevant goals and objects; over-reliance on blaming, placating, distracting, and com-puting behavior; and inconsistent or deceptive behavior. Thinking and thoughts, facts, objects, or phony behavior take priority over feelings.

The Dilution of Self

The continuous dysfunctionality (helplessness and hurt) of the marital and familial interactions produces a lowering of self-boundaries (Bowen, 1966) and an almost neglect of the self. The family and the mate are put ahead of one's happiness and fulfill-ment. Consequently, the result is an inability of the individual self to stand up, to define itself, and to decide for itself. This dilution and, in extreme cases, loss of self is visible through the process of mind-reading in which a mate guesses or outguesses the other mate, externalizing on the other responsibility for his own behavior, and making the other responsible for his own. This in-ability to be responsible for one's action and to be true to one's self is especially pronounced in couples and families of long standing. The dysfunctionality, the externalization of responsibili-ty, and the wanting to please, placate, and appease the other or others in the family makes it impossible to become aware of one's self-boundaries.

As a result of this dilution, self-boundaries (the ability to make decisions, choices, and alternatives) become restricted, limited, or unclear. The self sees and finds no options. Creative solutions are not considered. Overreliance on the same pattern becomes more and more of a dysfunction. Someone else in the family "pays" for the intermediate step. The self at this point is ill-defined, unclear, rigid, and vague and asserts itself in helpless and hurtful ways. Self-defeating behavior becomes reciprocal.

The Dissolution of Self

Self-dilution and self-dissolution are visible by asking anyone in the family, especially the parents: "Who is the most important person in the world to you?" In most cases this question is answered as a matter of course in terms of: "My wife." "My husband." or in cases of divorcees: "My children." Another way of getting at the same point is to check on what is the most important motivation in a person's life ("Whom do you want to make happy the most?"). Again the answer is usually in the direction of somebody else except the person who is asked, indicating how priorities in the parents and the family are reversed, sometimes children first, marriage second, and self third (other times, marriage may be first). Children as well, are unable to assert their own selves appropriately because no sense of clear self is experienced. Another way to put it is that: *they care so much for each other that they submerge their selves to the needs of their mate ("I want to make you happy, dear") or the needs of their children.* It is difficult to say whether this is the result of dysfunctionality after years of intimacy or whether the self-boundaries were weak at marriage to begin with. This would be an important research area to study if we were able to assess adequately self-perception, self-strength, and adequacy of self-boundaries. The ultimate outcome, the negation and denial of the individual self, could have existed already or could have been the result of the romantic or religious notion that it may be more blessed to give than to receive.

The ultimate outcome of this process lies in the inability to make decisions, make choices, or pursue wants. Apathy, withdrawal, giving up, and inability to make contact and share one's helplessness and hurt are prominent. Whereas in the preceding steps there is still the ability to seek and want help and to use it, at this stage the self is almost absent because the individual is unable to make decisions for himself and lets others (courts, hospitals, jails, etc.) make them for himself. What started as a process of giving up ends in a process of being given to. If we give up our self, the void will be filled by others who claim that right. Under these conditions the self has no choice and cannot make decisions. Surrender and abandonment of the self find expression in alcoholism, suicide, murder, or extreme withdrawal.

It is inevitable, then, that if the mate or the children are responsible for one's happiness, they are also responsible for one's feeling miserable. Hence, one may see the pronounced externalization of responsibility and blaming that are so prevalent in dysfunctional couples and families! Then, there is the feeling of let-down and of feeling cheated that occurs whenever the mate is not able to deliver the expected goods of happiness ("If you are responsible for my happiness, then you are responsible for my unhappiness."). In this way one's last vestige of self-esteem is protected, but then the individual is caught into the vicious trap of not being able to speak for himself. It is the mate or the children who is or are responsible if things do not work out! Consequently, energy is poured outside of the self and whatever is left of the self is precariously protected.

There are usually two indicators of self-dilution or dissolution in the family: (1) appearances before objects and facts; and (2) objects and facts before feelings. Appearances and conforming to superficial standards of conduct are required as a way of getting along. Heavy emphasis on conformities to external appearances is concomitant with emphasis on pseudo-logical grounds and with direct commands. Emphasis on substitutes for feelings is visible in the process of demands and fulfillments of needs through objects, things, gifts, and other forms of subtle bribery or blackmail. The objects are "supposed" to be the expressions of love that the parent may have for the child. He "buys" the child's love through the giving of objects. The same process occurs in marital relationships where one mate, usually the wife, demands and obtains things (house, car, clothes, etc.) that are supposedly expressions of the mate's love.

Hurtless and Helpful Definitions of Self

The first helpful decision the individual, couple, or family can make is to decide that he or they need help. *Asking for help is a positive affirmation of one's limitations.* It indicates the self's ability to discriminate properly and to choose adequately. Individuals, couples, or families that are unable to take this step hurt so much that the choice is made for them. Under these conditions, as seems to be the case in many mental health clinics and child guidance centers, motivation for wanting and using help is minimal. Help is accepted from the outside but the self remains unassertive and weak.

By asking for help, the self or selves are essentially disclosing themselves. This step, then, is the primary positive assertion that can be made. There is help in the process of asking for help and admitting one's helplessness and hurt. The professional helper, then, needs to recognize and capitalize on the beginning of the self-disclosure.

SELF-DISCLOSURE: To help increase the process of self-disclosure ("Is it correct for me to assume you came to see me because you hurt for each other?"), the professional helper should look at both the positive and negative aspects of the process ("You came to see me because you hurt, feel helpless, and you care for each other. Am I right?"). The process of self-disclosure brings about the next realization.

SELF-DISCOVERY: Once all of the helpless and hurtful ways of functioning within the marriage and the couple are dealt with, the self cannot help but rediscover itself since it discloses itself to others. The discovery of self-importance should bring about the ability to assert oneself more helpfully and hurtlessly. Self-discovery brings about self-delineation.

SELF-DELINEATION: If the helper has indeed helped the individual, couple, or family, he has helped them find their individual boundaries and clarified what choices they can or should make for themselves. These choices would be a compromise that allows everyone in the marriage and the family to win. The helpful and hurtless choice is the one that helps the individual first without denial of the importance of one's spouse or family.

These three steps are necessary for growth and change. Without adequate disclosure, discovery, and delineation, the self cannot develop properly.

SELF-DEVELOPMENT: The self that grows is the self that finds and creates options for himself. Differentiation of goals and choices permits an appropriate consideration of specific pay-offs for each option. The choice with the maximum pay-off for the individual and those connected with him is the helpful and hurtless indication of self-development because: (1) *Feelings are how the individual self is expressed.* How do we know one's specific individuality? There are many ways of expressing one's individuality, such as through clothes and conversation. Yet all of these means of expression can be similar to those of others. The peculiar nature of our feelings speaks for our self. Self-directed help does not mean that because help is directed toward the self it implies helping an individual separately from his loved ones. It does not. On the contrary the self cannot be understood without its impact on one's intimates. (2) *The self does not live in a vacuum.* To help a couple or a family, emphasis is directed toward the individual's self-assertion in a way which may be (as much as possible) congruent with the self-assertion of other members. In cases where the self-assertion is antagonistic to the assertion of others, it may produce sufficient conflict to provoke severe emotional upset.

In this regard, Mullan and Sangiuliano (1964) speak about the therapist's use of his integrated self-acceptance of himself as a necessary requirement for helpful change. Part and parcel of change is the helper's self-disclosure. What is the helper to disclose about himself that can be helpful to those who seek his help? He can tell what he wants and does not want, what he likes and does not like. He can affirm himself as an individual in his own right ("If you defeat me it will hurt, but I have other victories that keep me going." "If I lose with you, who is the real loser?").

Helpless versus Helpful Communication

As a result of the self-dilution and inability to deal with the hurt and helplessness of those for whom we care, our efforts at communicating become tinged with helplessness. Our communicative efforts become helpless, that is: they do not do any good, they do not help our hurting mate or child. The hurt and helplessness are covered by circular communications and stances that drive the parents and the children further apart. The ability to speak up for oneself, since speaking up for oneself would mean speaking about one's hurt and feelings of helplessness, is considerably diminished at this point. As a result, one mate cannot help the other and neither of them can help their hurting child. The couple and the family are trapped in a quagmire of helpless and hurtful communication. This process is seen in the repetitiveness of the behavior, the "broken record" quality of the complaints, and the anger and the frustrations of their everyday battles. Instead of working together, finding options and creative solutions, there is a restriction and a decrease in creative and helpful options. The whole system, then, comes to a screeching halt and the couple or the family are unable to go ahead and grow.

It is important, then, to consider that one's helplessness and futile efforts have come to naught when help is sought. *The seeking of help is the beginning of the establishment of an improved self.* ("You cared enough for each other or for this family to seek help.") Couples or families that cannot find or are unable to seek help or profit by it are probably unable to assert the helplessness of their situation. Other more destructive solutions are then sought (murder, divorce, withdrawal, suicide, alcohol, smoking, or drugs). Seeking help is an implicit admission of one's helpless position and as a rule is the first step toward the establishment of a self-identity, just as termination of help may be one way, at times premature and inappropriate, to assert one's self-importance.

Helpful Communication: The Search for Self

If the foregoing assumptions have some degree of validity then it becomes the task of the professional helper to provide the kind of climate in which the individual, a couple, and a family can learn to assert his and their own selves in ways which are going to pay off and help everybody. Instead of everybody losing with each other, *the task is to convert everybody into winning with each other.* This is perhaps one of the most difficult tasks known to professional helpers or individuals who want to become professional helpers. Education, books, and courses, formal or informal, may be irrelevant and in some cases become an obstacle to getting in touch with ourselves and with others. How can we help others find their own selves if our own self is still ill-defined, incomplete, and in some instances helpless and hurtful? Intellectual masturbation of the pseudo-psychoanalytic type may lead us into greater intellectualization, an extreme that takes us away further from our selves and from the very people we want to help. We may become lost in a half-baked system of intellectual insights making robots and computers of ourselves. Mere expression of anger and "truthfulness," the bag of "authenticity" through self-expression, may under certain conditions, transform us into righteous blamers in the guise of referees, umpires, and detectives–roles that some of us have allocated to ourselves in the name of professional guidance. Intentions to help, no matter how intense, may be perhaps the worst type of motivation for the professional helper. His "good" intentions may become so overwhelming that all he may want to do is to please, placate, and make his charges "feel good" without any consequence to their actual behavior outside of the office. In other instances, if we fail to understand and meet the hurt and helplessness of the couples and families that come to our offices, our actions in their regard may be completely irrelevant to them, distracting them from the purposes of finding help.

These arguments are another way to say that the professional helper cares about himself and needs to establish humbly the importance of his own self in helping others. If he cares for himself, his care of others should come out. If he takes care of himself well, then he can help others. He may need to live, relive, practice, and experience those very experiences that represent helplessness and hurtfulness. He may need to become convinced that dysfunctional reactions (like blaming, distracting, computing, and placating) result from a profound sense of helplessness and hurt, a loss of self, and lowering of self-boundaries, as well as from a great deal of care and love for one's partner and one's family. Once the helper becomes aware of what does not work, he can experience and practice for himself what works. He needs to: (1) become aware and recognize that the foregoing fourfold dysfunctional patterns (Assertion No. 3) do not work for himself as a human being as well as a professional; and (2) become aware of and practice helpful communication.

Where does helpful communication start? It is doubtful that helpfulness and hurtlessness can occur unless helplessness and hurt are dealt with. In addition to the hurt and to the helplessness, the *caring* needs to be brought into the foreground. The couple or the family may have become so hurt and so helpless that they may have forgotten that they still love each other and care for each other. If they did not, they would not be seeking professional help. They would have sought other avenues, such as divorce.

What Is Helpful Communication?

Communication is helpful and hurtless when words are congruent with feelings and when feelings are congruent with actions. Helpful and hurtless communication does not blame, does not placate, does not compute, and does not distract. It does not put down or put up. It does not deceive, distort, and deny one's feelings or those of others. It recognizes the importance of one's feelings and those of others.

The beginning of helpful and hurtless communication is "It." The "It" reduces the communication to a less personal level and stresses the process (Ginott, 1965) by beginning to define what starts one's reactions to somebody else's behavior ("It pains me to see such a well-meaning couple at each other's throat." "It grieves me to hear how much you are hurting each other." "It grieves me to see that you are unable to help each other." "It makes me very happy to know you love each other." "It saddens me to hear how helpless you all feel."). In other words, what is the essence of helpful communication? It is the communication that does not put down; it does not tend to please or placate; it does not tend to intellectualize or excuse; and it is relevant to the behavior at hand. It is the kind of communication that helps one to proclaim the importance of one's self, that helps to reestablish respect for oneself, and that helps the self assert its primary position and priority.

The beginning of self-assertion is the recognition and expression of our sense and feeling of helplessness and our hurt in not being able to be of help to those we love most. Self-assertion is established through an impersonal ("It") expression of what hurts, saddens, grieves, excites, and makes us feel good-bad, happy-unhappy, tense-relaxed, stupid-smart, etc.

The disclosure of our own self helps to facilitate disclosure and exploration of the self in others. It helps persons start to get in touch with themselves, and to assert their self-importance, first to themselves and then to others ("What hurts me about you is to see how you all seem to defeat and frustrate each other. Is that right?"). If we become aware of the hurt others produce in us, we may become aware of how we hurt ourselves and how we hurt others. The truisms "To thine own self be true," "Know thyself," "An unexplored life is not worth living," become valid within the context of how we establish our own selfhood and our self-identity.

Ideas and thinking, like "I think, therefore I am," have partial validity in the process of intellectualization as part of our selves. On the other hand, most of our thinking and ideas, no matter how original, overlap in part, with the ideas and thinking of others. What is uniquely and inalienably ours? What is it that establishes our sense of selfhood in a way which does not and cannot overlap with the self of others? It would seem that one way in which the self becomes established is to assert what one wants and does not want for oneself clearly. If we do not know what we want most for ourselves, how can we help others find what they want most for themselves? Wanting happiness for others becomes a phony chimera because it fails to recognize that to make others happy is an unreachable and usually impossible goal. How can we make others happy if we do not know how to make ourselves happy?

There are many ways to help reestablish one's self-importance. It would be very pretentious and presumptious to state one's way as being the only way. One's self-assertion may impinge on someone else's self-assertion. Consequently, *one's self-assertion needs to take into consideration the needs of others in a way which is congruent to everybody's needs in a couple or a family.* If a couple cannot recognize what they want from each other, how can they recognize reciprocal wants within their relationship with their own children? If we cannot recognize what we want for ourselves, how can we state it clearly for those around us? We need to respect their self-assertion in a way that allows a compromise and a negotiation with the ultimate goal of seeing that everybody gets recognition and fulfillment of his peculiarly unique wants and needs.

PRACTICAL APPLICATIONS

Most parents and families come to see professional helpers because they feel helpless and hurt, because they care about each other, and do not know how to assert themselves helpfully and hurtlessly. Unless this assertion is understood, the negative aspects of helpseeking may be emphasized at the cost of overlooking and minimizing positive aspects. Unfortunately we are so pathology oriented that we have forgotten as professionals that loving, caring, and concern are as powerful and important emotions as rejecting, blaming, etc. *Positives need affirmation from the very beginning of the helping process,* lest the negatives submerge, hide, and destroy the positives. In the over-concern for the hurtful behavior of one member, these positive feelings are forgotten and kept in the background. The helper needs to bring them back into perspective and in the foreground as soon as possible ("I may be mistaken, but I wonder if your coming here is also due to the possibility that you care for each other?" "I beg to disagree with you about Albert being bad; isn't your bringing him to me due also to the fact that you care for him?" "Why would you have come here if you didn't care for each other?" "If you didn't love him [or her] I doubt whether you would be here now; isn't that right?").

It *must* be acknowledged to *everybody* from the very beginning (be it a couple, a family, or parents with their child) that the reason for their seeking help is out of *concern, caring,* and *loving,* for each other and their individual hurt and pain. The consequences of the previous approach, emphasizing negatives are usually plain to see: the child sees himself as the *only* reason for his parents coming, or because he is in some way "bad" and fails them in their expectations of him. This unfortunate emphasis lengthens unduly the process of opening up and helping couples and families. For example, after the question "Why are you here?" or "What can I do for you?" or "What do you want from me?" has been answered as usual in terms of the inappropriate behavior that has brought them to a helper, the helper should make it clear that he disagrees with this negative emphasis. He should then proceed to see that positive (rather than negative) feelings are expressed freely and openly, between or among the members of the dyad, tryad, or group. Once the air is, so to speak, cleared, attention should be directed toward assessing the underlying reasons for their coming in terms of how they feel, e.g. helpless, lost, bad, hurt, sad, fearful, etc. Consequently, the opening introduction should deal with *positive* feelings of their coming and with the individual *underlying* pain, hurt, and grief. Unless this primary goal is achieved, it is doubtful whether successful helping can take place.

Of course, these goals at times cannot all be reached in the introductory hours. In spite of emphasis on the positive reasons for coming, the couple or family can and often does get bogged down in their dysfunctionality right from the beginning, demonstrating how they are unable to help each other. If a child is the "imputed patient," attention should be given to him and the emphasis on positive love and concern may help alleviate his already heavy burden. The reciprocal expression of positive feelings to and from his parents helps him be reassured that he is not as "bad" as he had been directly or indirectly led into believing.

This basic acknowledgement is an important clue to how much work needs to be done. If tears flow, if hurt is acknowledged and expressed appropriately, and if these feelings receive an adequate reception and are reciprocally expressed, an important goal has been achieved. *Acceptance of these feelings usually involves doing nothing!* That is, the best way to accept one's feelings is to see that these feelings are freely expressed with no unpleasant consequences. Instead of the uproar that has usually followed their expression in the past, calm and tranquility should ensue. Reinforcement theorists would probably say: by reducing the unpleasant consequences that follow the expression of unpleasant emotions, the helper is producing their extinction. Whatever the explanation, the best way of helping someone to rest assured that his feelings have been received is to acknowledge their reception. Acceptance of a person's feelings implies acceptance of the person.

The most difficult part of the opening introduction is not the initial expression of positive feelings but going from this goal to the second goal of finding underlying feelings of hurt, fear and grief. Part and parcel of dealing with underlying feelings is the conclusion that someone, the imputed patient as well as the couple or the family, is losing out and is therefore a "loser."

At this point it should be clarified what it means to win or lose from the viewpoint of a member of the dyad and the helper. Usually certain principles of winning and losing should be established clearly at the outset. First, the dyad or the family comes in because one of its members is losing out. Second, if one member loses everybody who is involved with him (or her) is losing too. This latter could be called the *principle of interdependence.* Either the couple or the family hang together or they "hang." Third, the helper becomes involved in this circle; and it should be established that if he were to lose (or win), whoever is associated with him will win or lose as well. However, if the helper loses out with one member, a pair, or the family, the loss is going to be incurred by them and not the helper. It will hurt him to see them lose, but unless they work with him and stick with him they may lose. Sticking it out, leveling with themselves, others, and the therapist should produce the ultimate victory. Fourth, battles may be won but the war may be lost. This principle deals with the shortcuts that have been attempted thus far to keep the marriage or the family going. This principle applies to the use of excessive punishment, marked inconsistency in disciplinary matters, over-reliance on dysfunctional patterns of blaming, computing, placating, and distracting. The immediate end may be achieved, but in the long run the desired outcome (i.e. better behavior, adequate scholastic achievement, or more harmonious marital relations) is not achieved. Fifth, if the system is not working it will show it by its repetitiveness in doing the same thing ("Losers have no options, winners do." By the same token: "Winners have choices, losers don't.").

Once it is established that the helper will essentially help the system win, it will be necessary to agree on the mechanics of what is necessary for him to do so: (1) adequate recognition of his importance for change; (2) appointments at mutually agreed times; and (3) emphasis that in this world almost anything (time, fees, clothes, objects, money) is negotiable *except one's feelings.* These are the only nonnegotiable commodity that each individual, including the helper, possesses. He can trade techniques, viewpoints, philosophies, opinions, etc., but he, like the people he is trying to help, can assert his individuality and his self through the proper and acceptable recognition and expression of feelings. This is the commodity he works with but which he cannot trade.

Other principles can be established through helpful and simple clichés like: "Losers collect brown stamps while winners collect gold stamps"; "Brown stamps cannot be cashed in because no one will buy them. Gold stamps can be traded in." The seeming simplicity of these clichés helps establish certain principles for most people of any age, sex, socioeconomic level, and education. It is important that both the college graduate father and his son in kindergarten understand certain basic maxims that guide our behavior and the behavior of others. There must be recognition and acceptance of these concepts as a form of universal agreement, with an explicit contract that everybody is interested in winning and no one likes to lose.

It should be clear that the helper is willing to take the risk of losing out with one couple or family, and it is important at this time for him to voice whatever reactions have been brought out by the foregoing negotiations ("I feel good about this family." "I think I can work with you." "I am not satisfied yet; I don't have a feeling of closure."). There may be hesitancy in both the system and the helper. For this reason, a short-term contract, usually three sessions, with negotiations on both sides at the end of the third session, should be made at the end of the first session. There is really nothing magic about this number of sessions except that this seems to be the number of sessions necessary to make a decision: "Yes, we want to go on"; "No, we have had enough and it's not necessary to go any further"; or "We/I don't know; let's take some time out and let's meet again in a month, two months, or at the end of summer."

Scheduling of frequency of sessions should be mutual and the helper should indicate how he likes to operate best ("I like two hour sessions, every two weeks." "If this is too expensive, we can schedule our meetings (conferences) every three or four weeks." "I personally have found that a one hour per week meeting is too short. It takes 30 minutes to come to my office and 30 more minutes to go back home; what for? One hour's time?" "I think we can get more accomplished in two hours and there is less time spent coming and going."). By indicating his preferences, the helper is also able to indicate his sensitivity to the family's needs (in travel, parking, distances, work, etc.). The family can appreciate his recognition of the efforts they are making.

Identifying Dysfunctional (Helpless and Hurtful) Patterns

Identifying the pattern should be done clearly ("This family is cancerous with blame." "You seem to have read a great deal and know all there is to be known." And at times forcefully: "If this family wants to continue blaming, it does not need me." "Apparently this family puts a great deal of emphasis on words and too little on feelings."). Identifying the pattern should be done by pointing out its basic incongruity with underlying feelings ("I see that this couple spends a great deal of time on . . . but I miss finding out how each of you feels about each other.").

After identifying the basic helplessness of the couple or family, *a variety of confrontations are necessary.* In the first place, the helper needs to confront the pattern in terms of its intensity and frequency ("It looks like this family has used blame for a long time; it will take some doing to get rid of it."). In the second place, the helper needs to establish the basic interpersonal aspect of the dysfunctionality ("It takes two people to make a liar, one to judge and someone to lie." "It takes two people to fight." "It takes two people for blame to occur."). In the third place, the helper needs to establish the lack of payoff for dysfunctional behavior ("What does . . . get you . . . , you . . . , and you?" "What has blame gotten this family?" "What is placating getting you?"). In some instances, one aspect of the lack of payoff may be brought about by the helper ("It looks like emphasis on words gets this family away from feelings."). In the fourth place, the helper needs to bring forward the incongruous nature of the helpless and hurtful pattern as one way of hiding, covering up, and distorting underlying feelings ("You may distract me and this family all you want, but in the meantime I wonder how you feel.").

However, haphazard emphasis on feelings may become inappropriate and too frequent. Blind, rigid, ritualistic, and repetitious questioning ("And how do you feel right now, Mr. Chips?") can be one way for the helper to fall into a rigid form of escape. It fails to help the helper's questioning of feelings at the opportune moment. To require people to expound on their feelings without a context or regard to anything else could become a safety valve, an escape hatch, or a cop-out, that does not help either the family or the helper. It may become a futile formula for emptiness.

The Musts of Helping

Orderly and constructive helping cannot occur unless some limits and structures are imposed strongly and clearly by the helper. Both parents must be protected by knowing that the helper already knows what is working and is not working in helping them. At times he may need to demonstrate it to them and to let dysfunctional patterns occur sufficiently enough to prove, for instance, that as long as they relate the same way in the office as they behave at home neither one of them needs his help ("If you want to do in my office what you do at home, you don't need me."). Unless the helper is able to be strong ("I am sorry but I don't think you'll need to see me if you continue blaming each other."), and keep the issues to the essential interaction, it is doubtful that he can be helpful.

However, "musts" should be invoked only under certain conditions: for instance, when the externalization of responsibility ("I did it because you did . . .") cannot be broken otherwise, when blaming and projection are rampant ("You are a bitch; I am the only good partner in this marriage."), when bickering and fighting has reached such proportions that nothing gets accomplished. On the other hand, other starting positions may be indicated at the beginning, for instance, in the case of a couple or family so apathetic and passive that they have not even reached the point of externalization and outward fighting, or in the case of the couple beyond the point of externalization who are ready to receive "real" help. Under these conditions, other directions may be necessary. However, under conditions of externalizations, three progressive limits may be established, either altogether or one at the time (as it may be relevant).

Must No. 1: "Speak about yourself." This is a must for parents whose interweaving of their own selves is such that no separation can occur. The selves have been submerged by external concerns that do not allow recognition and acknowledgement of the importance of self and self-esteem. Externalization of responsibility ("You did it, I didn't") is one way in which the self is submerged, forgotten, and in some cases seemingly absent. The individual is unable to speak about himself (or herself) because all of his or her energy is directed toward finding faults in the partner. The *only* way in which the helper can really help is to make his help conditional on their assuming responsibility for themselves, and if either one cannot yet assume such a responsibility, help them reach it. At times this directive may occur in the first session. At times, it may take a year before the helper can reach his goal. Oftentimes, the self is so submerged that it cannot appear and function by the helper's fiat.

In this writer's experience, one of his major failures as a helper has been not to enforce and keep this dictum on the forefront of the helping process often or forcefully enough. Sometimes, he may have been defeated in trying to uphold this dictum. More often than not, however, he may have been too weak, or too passive, or too inconsistent to enforce it. Yet it is a vital imperative that needs enforcement by the helper at the cost of interrupting the helping process, since no help can be given unless both parents can talk about their own selves.

MUST No. 2: "DON'T BRING UP THE PAST UNLESS IT REFERS TO YOUR OWN SELF." As part of the uproar and confusion that are characteristic of the parental inability to function as parents and partners is the ever present intrusion and rehashing of past events. This rehashing is a continuous evidence of particularly selective processes to the point that each parent may have forgotten what they had for breakfast that morning but cannot forget a hurt received many years ago. It is clear that this historical approach covers hurt, pain, and grief, and it should be dealt with accordingly ("If all these events are remembered so well, you are telling me that they still hurt you; is that correct?"). Consequently, past events that are relevant to the individual's past may be used and exploited to continue fighting, bickering, and blaming. This destructive aspect should be noted and stopped ("What have you learned about yourself by telling me what he [or she] did ten years ago?" "What does it get you to tell me how mean your partner has been since you got married?" "I am sorry, but I haven't learned a single thing about you by listening to everything that you told me about your wife.").

MUST NO. 3: "QUIT READING EACH OTHER'S MIND." This dictum is really part of Must No. 1. It provides another way of telling how each parent can really talk about himself. However, in order for the helper to keep these dicta enforced, he must be convinced of certain fundamental assumptions that govern the process of helping.

Dealing With Anger

Anger is an ever present emotion. It frequently seems to be the smokescreen of underlying helplessness, fear, and hurt. It is a form of coercive self-assertion that brings very little except temporary and questionable relief. It is usually present at the self-presentational and/or phenotypical levels, but is not part of our genotype. It colors most interpersonal relations and helps destroy a great many relationships. Its presence, expression, and damaging results on the angry person and on his targets should be dealt with. One way of dealing with it is for the helper to acknowledge freely under what conditions he becomes angry ("I found out that I become angry when I am helpless to do anything."). The link between anger and helplessness or whatever other feeling should be acknowledged and made clear. This discovery and admission on the helper's part usually brings about some degree of agreement on someone's part ("How does this couple [family] deal with anger?" "It looks like these fights expressed a lot of anger." "Apparently in this couple [family] the expression of anger is a taboo." "What do you do when he [she] gets angry at you?" "Who does the hollering in this family?"). These are all types of questions leading to an introduction of this topic and its subsequent solution ("As long as I'm angry, I know I'm helpless.").

What results from anger? Its destructive consequences and its repetitive features should be emphasized and a decision should be made about it ("What are you planning to do with your anger?" "Do you want my help with it?"). Incidentally, at no point should the helper assume that this (or any other problem) is his exclusive province of help. He should check as often as possible on whether help is needed, wanted, or desired. Permission to help should be asked and help should be given if permission is granted. This note, by itself, represents part of the contractual nature of the helping relationship ("I cannot help you if you don't want or ask for my help." "How can I help you if you cannot ask for my help?"). It is important for this process to occur as explicitly as possible, because without its acknowledgement it may rob our clients of the rights to privacy, decision-making, and independence. The helper should not assume that he has the right and privilege to break in, open up, and probe into anyone's feelings. The intimacy of these feelings is too precious, delicate, and important to be tampered with brutally, inappropriately, and prematurely.

Dealing With Guilt

Guilt may well be a phony emotion.[6] Guilt is what we are supposed to feel for wrongdoing. We are expected to feel guilty, otherwise we may give the impression of not caring or not loving. Consequently, this emotion is occasionally brought forth if and when a member of the family assumes responsibility ("It's my fault") for whatever is wrong with someone else in the family. The expression of such feelings should be encouraged, but their continuation should be discouraged in terms of results ("What does guilt get you?" "Would you be better off using your energies in solving the problem?" "You are welcome to tell me whenever again you feel guilty, I would like to know."). Guilt is present if and when there has been blaming. If the helper can convey through words and deeds the feeling that he is not there to blame, expressions of guilt may become minimal ("If you want to feel guilty, go ahead. I prefer to put my energies in seeing what works for this system."). Guilt helps assess how much blaming or self-blaming is present in the system; in other words, who brainwashed whom, either in the past ("My parents always found faults in

---

6. Emotions, incidentally, are self-presentational and phenotypical reactions, feelings are genotypical.

me") or the present ("My husband thinks it's my fault"). Guilt does not need to be dismissed, but it does not need to be encouraged. Energy should be freed for creative problem-solving.

Dealing With Sexuality

It follows from the assertions previously enunciated that each individual is firstly responsible for *his* happiness and secondly for the happiness of *others,* e.g. his spouse and children. Consequently it is important for the helper to become aware (in case he is not) that *each of us is responsible for his own sexuality!*

Unfortunately, we are perhaps brainwashed in assuming that the man is usually responsible for his wife's sexuality. There are a great many unhappy women and men whose frigidity and impotence are imbedded within a personal inability to get something they want. From this viewpoint, the woman's inability to achieve orgasm or to enjoy her sexuality has to be laid to rest on her shoulders and not her husband ("Mrs. Smith, you are responsible for your sexual enjoyment, just as Mr. Smith is responsible for his." "What has putting the responsibility on Mr. Smith gotten you thus far?").

It is very easy for the helper to get involved in matters of technique and mechanics. He may try to give some advice, if it works. Usually, however, he will find that the wife's inability to enjoy sex is part of an overall pattern of self-defeat, whereby anyone dealing with her is defeated, including the husband and eventually the helper. Before dealing with sexual matters *per se,* it is important for the helper to bring such a feeling of defeat into perspective ("If your husband is defeated in achieving sexual satisfaction, in the long run who is it that suffers?" "If I cannot win with you and you lose, who defeats whom?"). Men all too often defeat themselves by declining or denying need for help in sexual as well as in other matters.

It is important, therefore, to consider such self-defeating patterns and consider any sexual failure as another expression of the individual's inability to give and to get. There is no end to where such self-defeating patterns can reach. The more the helper can deal with self-defeat (personally and professionally) the better.

Often mechanical aspects of sexuality are used as an issue to cover up the couple's inability to be aware of and to express their own feelings. In a couple where the wife's dissatisfaction prompted a run to self-help books on sex to improve the husband's manual foreplay and mechanical performance, it was discovered that for nine years of marriage and intercourse the wife had never expressed overtly, even when present, any feelings of pleasure. The husband had to inquire after each orgasm was achieved as to whether his performance had been satisfactory. Eventually, under threat of divorce, the wife was able to express freely her feelings of pleasure which had been repressed "because the children may hear us."

For any case of premature ejaculation in the husband, the helper should be sensitive to his wife's attitudes and feelings. The specific nature of such a fear-provoking failure on the man's part can be glimpsed from his history, where he is likely to find certain conditions and women with whom his sexual performance was satisfactory. In sexuality, as in other behaviors, each individual member is out to assert his or her importance. It is unfortunate that many couples assert their individual importance in self-defeating ways. More often than not it is the woman who needs to be helped to struggle with her sexuality within the context of self-defeating patterns. Once the husband is assured or understands that he need not be anxious about first making himself happy and second making his wife happy, who herself is responsible for her getting what she wants sexually, a great deal of anxiety is diluted in the relationship.

Mind-Reading and Clichés in the Helping Process

It is relatively easy for the helper to subscribe to clichés or easy, uncritically accepted generalizations about a couple or a family. Helpers themselves fall prey to easy clichés that may represent how they think or the kind of assumptions they make about others or themselves. The helper should be aware of the clichés he uses and discriminate when and how they should be used: "I don't know whether this behavior is normal or abnormal. What does it get you?" "I am not interested in how other couples and families work. How does this couple or family work with each other?"

Clichés can be made about the helper himself and he should be able to assert his own individuality just as he should be able to help each member of a couple or family assert his individuality: "I appreciate what you heard about me, but if I cannot help this couple (family), my reputation isn't going to help, is it?"

It is just as difficult to get away from certain clichés. As indicated throughout this chapter, they are used to make helpers aware of certain realities external to them and present in the world around them. Consequently, certain clichés concerning the winning and losing conditions of the helper, *vis-à-vis* the family, are a way of clarifying the helper's position ("If I lose what will happen to this family?" "We will need to work together, because if one of us loses out who will win?"). These clichés about winning ("Winners choose, losers don't.") and losing ("Losers can't choose, winners do.") have been found helpful within the context of relating the patterns of losing to the process of helping and clarifying that if the helper loses with one member, the whole family loses.

There is a kind of mind-reading that may be hurtful to the helping process. This mind-reading concerns preconceived theoretical notions in the helper about each couple or family that deprive it of its individuality. These preconceived notions may be intellectualized, unproved generalities of how the helper should behave toward his helpees without questioning whether his generalization applies to a specific couple or family. Such assumptions could be made about the symbolic meaning of being late, missing appointments, patterns of interaction, etc. It is important for the helper to face each couple and family free from preconceived notions and generalizations, because all of those tend to deny the specific individuality of that couple.

If there are any preconceived notions, they should be checked out as much as possible ("I am assuming that you hurt so much and feel so helpless that it is difficult for you to talk, is that correct?" "I wonder whether your not paying the bill on time says something about you and your family. Could you explain?"). Another way of stating the same problem is that if the helper cannot help himself about coming to some conclusions or generalizations, he should check them out rather than accepting them as given or absolutes. In a way, such generalizations on our *modus operandi* say something about the helper's peculiar individuality. He should be able to assert his own self helpfully and hurtlessly without recourse to the uncritical acceptance of generalizations that may be valid to the *modus operandi* of another helper, but that may have a questionable validity for his own peculiar helping style.

Essentially mind-reading, as expressed through clichés, takes away from the individual the ability and responsibility to speak for himself ("I don't know how other doctors work; however, I can tell you how I work best." "One hour per week meetings may work well for others, but I have found it more helpful to meet for two hours every two or three weeks unless there is some urgency about the situation; how badly does each of you hurt?").

If the helper is able to assert his peculiar individuality through his style and *modus operandi,* perhaps he will be able to help each couple or family assert its peculiar individuality as well ("There are many couples [families] that hurt, but you are the only one in my office at this time." "I cannot help all the people who need help, I can only help those who come to my office and pay for my time." "There are some people I can help and there are some that I cannot.").

"I Never Ask Myself If A Child Is Suffering . . .
I Become That Child"
(Riccardo Santi).

One of the most direct, nonverbal ways of helping the child subjected to a barrage of negative, critical, and hurtful messages from members of his family, is to literally exchange places with him. Although this technique can be used with anyone under attack, this substitution seems to fulfill a variety of functions: (1) it gets the child off the hook and away from the emotional impact of verbal attack; (2) it puts him in a symbolically safe and supposedly more powerful position (the helper's chair); (3) it introduces the whole family to techniques of role-playing; and (4) it allows the helper to confront the attacker on the effect his attack may have on the child, even though he may not be able to express it properly, by rebutting and talking back ("Why don't you pick on grown-ups your own size?") or expressing how it feels to be under attack

("What you say makes me feel like a criminal in court." "What you say makes me feel like I cannot win; if I do what you tell me to do you are not satisfied and if I don't you are not satisfied either." "I feel like I'm damned if I do and damned if I don't." "What you say makes me feel very . . . sad, helpless, hopeless, etc.").

From his position the helper can gauge the impact of his responses on the attacker, who up to this point received either no or inappropriate responses to his or her harangues, and by the child, who by his smiling, laughing, or even cheering may indicate to the helper whether what he has said represents his own feelings. This reversal can be continued to the point that the child can play the helper's role ("What do you think about this, Dr. L.?").

At any time the helper needs to be able to identify himself with, ally himself with, change places with, and assume the role of the weakest component member of the family, whether it is one of the parents or one of the children. This technique keeps things in movement and is sometimes useful and a natural introduction to role-playing. This form of alliance is probably one of the few liaisons allowed and justified in and by the family. In a way, the family is paying for the helper to come to the support of who may be the identified patient or who may be the weakest family member. Furthermore, the same switch can be done with any member of the family at anytime to exaggerate or to downplay a particular role. Of course, the successfulness of this switch depends a great deal on the role-playing qualities of the helper.

Another way of stopping a verbal harangue is to question the attacker and to confront him about his feelings: "You appear very upset about this matter." "What is it about your son's behavior that gets you so uptight?" "Why is his flunking out such a big deal to you?" "It does not seem to mean a great deal to him, isn't that right?"

The First Three Conferences

After the initial interview, which may be actually a feedback session to discuss the results of psychological testing on the imputed patient, some options and courses of action with their specific effectiveness and costs (length and probability of success) should be discussed. Options such as behavior management techniques, parental counseling (if this is acknowledged as being necessary or because parents refer themselves as being in need of help), or family counseling should be considered. However, whenever necessary and appropriate, other techniques should be discussed as well, i.e. teaching machines and programmed instruction, therapeutic summer camps, general summer camps, perceptual-motor training, etc.

The purpose of such a limited contract are many. In the first place, the couple or family has no conception of how long any help would take. Oftentimes realistic financial limitations shorten their overall perspectives. In some cases, the couple or family may not have an awareness of how dysfunctional their relationships may be. Consequently, these three sessions are used for the helper to become more familiar with the couple or family and to judge and evaluate its particular strengths and liabilities. If he does the work right, three sessions (of two hours each) may be all that is necessary to teach a couple or family how to cope with its components and with its own feelings. In other words, these three sessions may be used to solve whatever problem is immediately present or to become more aware of whether a longer period of time or investment is necessary.

Another purpose of these initial sessions is to make the couple or family more amenable to more intensive confrontation. In other words, the couple or family may not be ready as yet to face itself, but it can be led into facing itself more squarely in terms of its unresolved issues and dysfunctionality. Furthermore, such a limited amount of time limits the helper's responsibility. It allows him to decide whether he wants to become more involved, whether a different form or type of treatment is more appropriate, and whether he feels certain reservations about it. It allows him to bring up any reservations, uncertainties, and questions that he feels are standing in the way of further and more prolonged commitment. His time and efforts should not be taken for granted by the system, just as he tries not to take the system for granted ("I see that this family still has a great deal of work to do." "I don't feel quite right about what has happened thus far." "I don't feel good about this couple. . . . Perhaps a different therapist may be more appropriate that I am. Why don't you call Dr. X?" "I feel very good about this family and I really wonder whether there is anything else that I can do." "You have gone a long way in the last three sessions. Where do you want to go from here?" "Have I been of help to you? Why?").

It is important at this junction (the third conference) for the helper to assess whether any changes have occurred in the system ("What have you found out about yourselves?" "How are you relating to each other in ways that are different from the way you related before you saw me?" "I appreciate your liking me, Mr. Jones, but how have you changed?" "Yes, I agree with you, Mrs. Smith, a great deal of progress has occurred." "I am sorry but I don't really see what you are talking about, Mr. White, I still see your wife as being very unhappy."). Sometimes a compromise solution may be feasible ("I tell you what. Since neither of us is sure as to what we should do today, why don't I see you in a month and see what happens?"). Perhaps at this time more specific prescriptions may be given, and further appointments be arranged after some prolonged period ("As long as this family is broken up for the summer, with Jimmy going to summer camp, Joan going to see her grandparents, and your wife and baby at the lake, why don't we schedule another appointment for as soon as school starts next fall?").

Essentially, the purpose of these three sessions is to help the process of decision-making by avoiding making it a unilateral process on the helper's side. It has to be reciprocal and involved with both parties ("If this family is apparently wanting to go on, why don't we schedule several more conferences?").

Of course, there is nothing sacred about either three, or any other number. The purpose is always to make fairly clear, concise and time-limited contracts that allow for renegotiation and that do not take anyone for granted. Working with and for a definite temporal goal in mind puts a little more pressure on the couple or family to change than lack of time limitations. The number of sessions should be manageable, both temporally and financially ("Mr. Jones, if coming here every two weeks puts a financial strain on your budget, perhaps we could schedule them further apart.").

The frequency of sessions should be a matter of the helper's expert opinion, the choice of the family, the time available on the helper's calendar ("If I cannot change this family in the next three months, I may need to find a ditch-digging job." "I really doubt whether this family needs more than this number of sessions to pull itself together." "Let's plan for seven sessions and then we will renegotiate on what to do." "What is it that we want to accomplish in the next three months?").

Why Feelings Are Important

The emphasis on the belief that individual feelings are important, a practice that is basic to the whole process of helping, can be stated in a variety of ways, e.g. "I can give you my time and thoughts, but I cannot trade in my own feelings." "You can give me all the money you want but no amount of money can buy how I feel about this marriage (or this family)." Feelings are important because they are one way of asserting one's self. This assertion must be translated and kept up by the helper in everything he does and says, e.g. "I feel helpless about this marriage as long as you keep blaming each other." "It frightens me to see you distort everything I (or your wife) say(s)." It may need practical translation into courses of action ("If you want a judge or a detective you better go and see a lawyer. If you want me to help you, we better stick to each of you speaking about your own self."). This conviction must be kept up by the therapist at all times ("I can trade everything I have except my feelings." "My feelings are my own self." "How I feel about you is more important than any amount of money you may be willing to pay me." "Your feelings are more important to me than whether it is right or wrong to do this or that.").

It becomes the goal of the helper, therefore, to assert for the members of the system their individual worth and the importance of their importance, showing always what the destructive results of their present approach may be ("What has putting your husband, wife, children, first, etc., gotten you and your family?" "Your putting yourselves second seems to have resulted in everybody in the family doing the same thing." "How can your children assert their importance if you deny yours?" "How are your children going to learn that they are important if you don't?" "How can a loser teach a child how to be a winner?").

Once this level of self-dilution or self-dissolution is established, it is the helper's task to lead toward considering its dysfunctionality, especially in regard to the children ("If you can't take care of your own self, how can you take care of others?" "How can these children know what they want for themselves if you don't?" "If you don't respect yourself, how can you expect your children to respect you?").

This process renders the helper's role difficult unless he becomes aware of this effect and is able to confront and face the parents and the family with such a dilution ("You care so much for each other that you seem unable to speak for yourselves." "You spend so much time and energy talking about your mate that you seem unable to speak up in your behalf.").

At this juncture, the helper needs to establish and realign priorities in a clear, forceful fashion ("Unless you take care of your own self, I can't see how you can take care of others in this family." "What has caring for others first gotten you and this marriage?" "If you don't care for yourself, who will?" "How can this family find what it wants if its members don't know for themselves?").

In the first place, the importance of the self needs to be reestablished, reinstating each individual's importance in the family. If the individual is too depressed or brainwashed to believe in his or in her own importance, the possible reasons for such a disbelief may need to be considered ("How come you can't believe that you are important?"). In the second place, the importance of the marriage as taking priority over children needs to be reestablished ("What is going to happen to this marriage once the children are grown and gone?" "If you plan to live your life through your children, it does not look like you have much going for yourself." "Do you want your children to care for you?"). In the third place, the needs of the children need to be viewed within the perspective of a compromise between the individual self, the marriage, and the family ("We'll have to find a solution in which everybody wins." "How can everybody win and still be a family?").

After asserting the importance of self, pointing out the debilitating effects that denial of one's self may have had, the helper's next step is to teach each family member to assert one's self-importance, equating self to one's innermost feelings ("My own self is how I feel underneath."). Assertion of the importance of one's feelings is equated then with being able to know your own self and to be able to express one's worth ("I count, you Mr. X count, you Mrs. X count, you Jimmy count, you Debbie count. You are all important and none of you can have second place in this family."). This assertion can range, technique-wise, from simply having each member state (sometimes holler) "I count" to teaching how to express one's feelings creatively, congruently, and constructively, demonstrating the difference between dysfunctional and functional expression ("What happens if I told you: you are no good?" "What would happen instead if I told you that it grieves me to see that you are not getting what you want?" "How would you feel if I blamed you, attacked you, criticized you, etc.?" "How would you feel instead if I started each sentence by expressing how what you do affects my feelings, i.e. it hurts me, it grieves me, it pains me, it makes me feel good, bad, indifferent to see that etc.?" "Mrs. X, you can say 'You never help me' which would be an accusation leading us nowhere, or you could also say 'what is it about myself that does not allow me to get what I want from you?' ").

Essentially, then, the task of the helper at this juncture is to teach each member to be and become in touch with his (her) feelings and to express them without blaming, placating, distracting, or intellectualizing. It means going below and beyond the phenotypical level of expression and reaching the genotypical level, one's self. Such teaching can be done by modeling; that is, the helper becomes the example of how to express one's feelings constructively, or by demonstration ("Let me show you, what would you say if I said . . ."), or by having each member practice with others within the family the processes of changing from dysfunctional to functional expression. Demonstration is perhaps the best way of conducting this teaching ("How would you feel if I called you names?" "If you then got angry, what would the anger do to both of us?" "It looks like if I called you names we would both lose, isn't that right?" "Let me show you what happens if, instead of calling you names, I speak about myself." "It seems that by talking about my feelings, I allow you to talk constructively about your feelings and to get in touch with your own self. Is that correct?" "Do others here see the difference?" "Who would like to try?"). Here the helper can proceed to have each member practice with the other members, praising when it is appropriate or correcting when it is necessary, but always showing how one's feelings have become lost in the mutual interdependence and dysfunctionality of the family.

Usually when negative feelings are inappropriately or inadequately expressed, turmoil, uproar and unpleasant consequences follow. Denial, rejections, belittlement, scorn, and refusal to deal with the feelings are some of the consequences. What is the helper to do if and when he is able to help their free and undistorted expression? In the first place, he needs to help in the recognition of these feelings. They need to be pinpointed in terms of the words that will express them. In the second place, he needs to help in the admission of these feelings. This process can be achieved by having these feelings worded loudly or by having the individual move from his seat and utter these feelings in front of other members of his system. In the third place, the helper needs to see that these feelings are expressed congruently; that is, if there is an incongruency between the verbal expression of these feelings and their context, like, for instance: sadness is suffered with a smile, anger expressed laughing, or helplessness announced boldly. This basic incongruency and denial in action or words needs to be brought to the attention of everybody involved. Corrective measures to deal with this incongruency may be like: "Wipe that smile off your face"; "You don't look so helpless to me"; "It does not sound true, you are saying one thing and doing another." Ask if anyone else shares the same feelings and sees that actions also in other members are congruent to their words. If the expression of these feelings is followed by continued incongruency outside of the individual, these feelings will continue to be distorted.

After this expression of helplessness and hurt occurs, the helper needs to assess and help decide what they are going to do in the future if they do not want to feel the same unpleasant feelings

("What will it take for you to change?" "What pleasant feelings would you like to experience?" "What will you need to do for these feelings to occur?"). Essentially, this is a crucial point because now the decision has to be made to abandon previous, repetitive, and dysfunctional patterns and the person must be able to decide on more appropriate functional patterns that will bring some pay-off ("gold stamps") to himself and to the system of which he is part.

In summary, it helps the helper to state his assumptions clearly from the beginning. It helps everybody if options are given to the parents and the family ("If you want to go on the way you have, you don't need me; if you want to change then perhaps I can help you." "If you want a clear-cut prescription and a miracle that will take care of all your problems, then you would be better off going to see someone else; I'll be glad to recommend someone." "If you want to deal with how you feel about yourselves and each other, then I'll be glad to help you."). This last statement does in no way mean that the helper is unwilling to give a prescription (unless he is unable). Prescriptions can and should be given, provided they do not become substitutes for feelings and are used for what they are, i.e. crutches that can give some immediate relief to the family.

THE USE OF HELPFUL PRESCRIPTIONS

It may be necessary at any time (but mostly the beginning) to give "miracles" and meet the system's expectations for a miraculous short-cut. This can be attempted if provisions are made for longer term goals.

The major issue in the use of prescriptions is *when to use them;* this is essentially an issue of choice between using behavioral versus psychodynamic interpersonal approaches. One cannot and probably should not be used (Lazarus, 1971) instead (or in spite) of another. Under certain conditions one method is more appropriate than the other. For example, if the problem is such that the child cannot be engaged in prolonged interpersonal confrontations, then it may be more appropriate to use behavioral management approaches. If the problem is specific and circumscribed, then specific methods should be used and behavioral prescriptions and contracts should be used. Sometimes a prescription is all that the parents or family may want. If the prescription works but other problems, less circumscribed and more general, still persist, eventually this basic dysfunctionality will come out and will be brought forth, *if:* (1) the helper has already demonstrated that he has no particular theoretical ax to grind, and (2) that he is flexible and competent enough to use whatever method seems appropriate. There is no question that many behavior management techniques are useful and the psychodynamic helper should be able to be knowledgeable about when and where they do work and when and where they do not. Woody (1971) has described in detail how insight-oriented and behavioral techniques can be integrated. This issue receives further consideration in Chapter 7.

Under which conditions are behavioral techniques practically useless? In the first place, *behavioral and psychodynamic approaches are not mutually exclusive.* Both can coexist successfully and help many couples and families in need. They complement and supplement each other and one does not need to subtract from the other.

In the second place, *behavioral techniques simply cannot be used when control over a member of the family cannot be achieved.* In other words, externally rebellious and adolescent children cannot benefit by behavioral techniques because the parents and the family have lost control over them. This statement does not imply that certain behavior applications to aggressive behavior cannot be made, as Patterson and Gullion (1968) have well demonstrated. It does mean, however, that certain adolescents resist and refuse any attempt, subtle, direct, or indirect at what they consider manipulation from a system they reject. This refusal is especially present when they see themselves as the family scapegoats. Under these conditions then, family approaches, whereby everybody in the family is used to help, *may* be more successful.

In the third place, *behavioral techniques should be used so systematically, as well as so sensitively, as to avoid the patterns of bribery or blackmail (or both) that have already been unsuccessfully exploited in the family.* If attempts of this kind are already part of the family history, there is the danger of equating behavioral approaches with previous, failed attempts at bribery and blackmail. Under these conditions, the similarity between behavioral management techniques and the frequent use of bribery and blackmail is such that at this point the use of different approaches should be explored. The options available to the family and what each form of help does and does not do should be freely described in order to let the system know that various options do exist, more options than they ever thought were available.

In the fourth place, *various techniques of rehabilitation can and should be used according to a successive sieves approach;* e.g. following the principle of starting with the least expensive and most specific approach, which is usually closer to the physical setting of the family, behavioral techniques should be used first. If this approach fails, other more time-consuming and generalized approaches, like the psychodynamic should be considered.

In the fifth place, *behavioral techniques tend to fail in systems where contracts are meaningless and where the degree of disturbance in the system is such that no contract is ever kept.* In these families there may be some hidden forces present that may work to keep the same system while giving "lip service" to desire for change. Usually when unresolved hostility is present, especially in the mother, she may tend to fail any attempt at behavioral management. Her degree of helplessness is such that, unless these underlying feelings are brought to the fore, she may tend to fail and frustrate the behaviorally oriented helper. Some of the people perhaps hurt so much that they cannot be helped no matter what approach is used. On the other hand, if people and systems want help and hurt enough to want to change, they may tend to seek and find what it takes to change.

Most Common Prescriptions

The following are some examples of common prescriptions that may be useful.

(1) One of the "easier" and more frequent prescriptions pertains to waking up of the imputed patient in the morning, especially if the responsibility for waking up is on someone else ("As soon as you get out of here I want you to buy the biggest, hand-

wound alarm clock you can find. No electric clocks, please. From now on Joe will need to learn to get up in the morning by himself."). Possible consequences resulting from delays or oversleeping should be discussed (miss breakfast, miss school bus, walking to school, etc.). Each one has the responsibility to wake himself up and no one should be responsible for another's getting up.

(2) Another prescription is to teach the family how to use time out for fighting, bickering, fussing, etc. ("What has fighting gotten this family?" "What rules is this family going to adopt from now on?" "Mrs. X, what are you going to do from now on whenever Jimmy and Helen bicker?"). Actions may be: have them state the rule "Fighting gets me nothing"; send them to separate rooms; put the kitchen timer on for five or ten minutes. ("Mr. X, what are you going to do when they fight in the back seat of the car?"). Actions may be: pull over on the side of the road; stop the car; and announce that you will resume riding five minutes after the fighting is stopped.

(3) In certain cases of learning disabilities, especially reading, the author has found that these children have not had any contact with (or there is a family taboo about) comic books. In that case, it is important to establish what is more relevant: (a) "What is more important to you that Jimmy read or what?" (b) "Let me first agree that comic books may be trash, but isn't the goal to have Jimmy read more?" (c) "Could we try to see how it works and if it doesn't, we can give it up?"

The instructions, then, would consist of having the family: (a) go to a drugstore to buy comic books (the first time in which comic books become a legitimate tax deductible expense!); (b) let Jimmy choose as many comic books (up to ten) of whatever kind he likes; (c) to start, give him one, just one comic book to read; (d) he can then get the others *one at a time* only after he has finished the first and has summarized it to one of the parents (completely without censure); and (e) in order to receive another comic book, repeat the procedure as fast as it is necessary.

(4) Written contracts can and should be encouraged, sometimes just for the expressed purpose of demonstrating and assessing whether the family is too dysfunctional to keep them. Contracts

have the function of clarifying in writing what each member of the family will do for the other members, as long as it is done on a reciprocal fashion. The helper can help in the writing of these contracts or ask that such contracts be reached through family conferences at home. The fact that sometimes these contracts are not kept is an indication that a strictly behavioral and contractual approach is not enough, especially if the family is unable to assert the importance of the individual family members.

(5) In cases of extreme underachievement and school failure where one of the parents, usually the mother, is actively engaged and involved in helping the child at home, the viewpoint to carry across is that apparently the child is choosing to fail even with parental help ("You have a choice: Jimmy apparently is failing with your help. Which do you want? Should he fail with your help or without it?"). The first step should be followed by a discussion of how Jimmy needs to separate himself from the mother and experience striking out and feeling, through trial-and-error, how to become responsible for his own behavior ("If he doesn't now, when and how is he going to learn to stand on his own feet?"). Clearly the prescription in this matter is to separate the seemingly helpful parent from the child, showing and demonstrating the destructive outcome of the parent's otherwise good intentions and actual love for the child ("If you want to continue like before, you do not need my help. If you want to try another way could you consider mine for awhile?").

The next step would be to help the child and the family develop order and study habits through definite structuring of the home, i.e. (a) homework as soon as the child comes home right after a slight snack and a change of clothes if necessary; (b) no T.V. for anybody in the family until all homework is done; (c) in extreme cases all other rewarding activities may need banning until definite study habits have been established and grades have improved ("How can Jimmy understand that studying is his primary responsibility if every weekend you take him fishing?"); and (d) home management is conducted through the use of parental manuals like Patterson and Guillion (1968) or Becker (1971).

Behavior management in no way needs to be antithetical to the psychodynamic family-oriented approach. The helper needs to be aware of the strengths of this approach, of its most optimal use, and of its limits, especially with parents who are too helpless, confused, and lacking in selfhood, to carry out such a program assertively. In fact, the present author would maintain that *no successful behavior modification program can occur unless a stronger realization of self-importance is achieved by the family and its individual members.*

In short, the radical behaviorist's denial of feelings is in keeping with the reality that in a large segment of the population asserting or attempting to reach expression of feelings may be an Herculean task. Some individuals may not have the ability or the linguistic skills necessary to achieve this goal or, perhaps, more importantly, *they hurt so much they are unable to talk.* Perhaps, it is this type of individual that may be helped by a system that denies importance of the existence and presence of feelings, since, according to radical behaviorists, feelings are unobservable, are hard to measure, and are private events. There is the possibility that this denial may bring behavior modification specialists to a reexamination of their own tenets (Lazarus, 1971).

The Need for a Cohelper

It is essential for the professional helper to know and to be aware of his limitations. This awareness should be translated into knowing if and when he can be helpful. To assume that one can be of help with any couple or family is not only presumptuous but hurtful. It would be helpful to the helper if he were aware of the conditions that most frustrate or defeat him ("Mr. and Mrs. White, your problems are of such intensity that I feel helpless to cope with them by myself. If you want me to help you I will need an extra pair of eyes and ears. What do you think?").

Personally, this author has found it helpful[7] to have a collaborator any time he could get one. In some cases, a member of the opposite sex may be essential to the welfare of a couple or a family, as well as of the helper. However, each individual will need to strug-

---

7. Harlan, Katherine, and L'Abate, L. The role of the cotherapist in family therapy (research in progress).

gle with his own need to be dependent or independent and to ask for help whenever it is appropriate for him. More extensive discussion of issues relating to the use of cohelpers has, of course, been presented in Chapter Two.

Closing Statement: I Examine Myself Everytime I Cannot Reach a Couple or a Family

The psychiatric externalization of name-calling that goes under the name of psychiatric nosology ("I cannot work with that individual because he is schizophrenic, psychopathic, etc.") has the direct function of avoiding looking at oneself or one's professional practices in terms of what is missing inside of one's self. It is easier and much more comfortable, personally and professionally, to reassure oneself of one's competence and self-esteem by declaring that people we failed to help belong to some kind of category which in turn "explains" or better excuses us from responsibility for not being able to work with them. At no time should the helper fall into this conceptual (and certainly most human) trap. Only if he asks himself, "How and why did I fail in reaching this family?" can there be hope for his improvement. A great many psychiatric and psychotherapeutic practices are stymied and rigidly perpetuated by the process, subtle to be sure, of externalization. Only by taking this responsibility upon himself can the helper hope to improve and change his techniques and to increase his batting average in helping.

Consequently, it is important for the helper to be in continuous touch with himself and his helpees, so as to make sure that he is neither ahead or behind them ("I want to make sure that you and I are square with each other. Are we?" "I feel good about how you and I seem to get along. However, I still don't feel comfortable with you about. . . ." "I am afraid that what I said did not go over well. Is there something here that needs clarifying?" "Wait a minute, Mr. Smith, you are way ahead of me. I need to get my bearings straight about you (this couple or family). Could you explain what it is that you want in another way?" "I concluded that this family puts facts before feelings or that facts are used at the expense of feelings. How does anyone feel about what I just said?").

The helper's self is, obviously, central to the success or failure of sexual, marital, and familial interventions. As Grosser and Paul (1964) suggested:

> As far as the issue of the therapist's feelings in the family therapy [and I would add in any helpful and hurtless interaction] setting is concerned, he is in a position analogous to that of the family members present. Just as they have to disclose publicly their previously hidden actions, feelings, and failures, he has to demonstrate his therapeutic skill with the family as his public (p. 877).

What is "therapeutic skill"? The ability to intellectualize and to know facts and literature by dropping names clearly gives no therapeutic surcease to anyone. Pointing the finger or finding faults with either past or present "fall" guys, like parents or teachers, is a form of externalization that takes away responsibility from the helpees ("I cannot change your past [parents] or your child's present [teachers], but perhaps I can help this family help itself to deal with each other better. If you help each other, you win. If you defeat each other, you all lose.").

HISTORICAL BACKGROUND OF PSYCHODYNAMIC INTERVENTIONS

Since William James, the importance of the self has been the subject of many theoretical viewpoints. Most of them have asserted the importance of the self, but like the weather, few have done anything about it in terms of empirical validation.

Self and Identity in Psychoanalytic Thinking

One's sense of identity is the awareness of being a person (self?) separate and distinct from all others. Overlap between these two concepts is great. When the self is conceptualized or made synonymous to identity, a variety of neopsychoanalytic writers need to be considered, e.g. Erikson (1959), Lynd (1958) and Wheelis (1958). Perhaps it may be helpful to the reader to visualize the ego as a circle, within a larger circle (the self), which in turn, is within a larger circle (the person).

Spiegel (1959) defined the self "as a frame of reference or zero point to which representations of specific mental and physical states are referred and against which they are perceived and judged" (p. 82). While most psychoanalytic writers differentiate between the ego and the self, others may tend to make the self synonymous with the whole individual personality:

> The development of a sense of self is strongly influenced by psychosexual and ego development, and by maturation from birth on. Partially as a result of perception, the infant soon develops a body ego in which he first begins to differentiate various aspects of his body image from objects in the external world. With the accumulation of identifications in the ego, as well as within the superego, multiple self-presentations are formed, the totality of which gradually form a stable concept of the self. . . . In those instances where a psychic conflict promotes ego and libidinal regression and culminates in a withdrawal of object cathexis, there is also a fluctuation in self-presentation, affecting one's sense of identity and sense of self (Eidelberg, 1968, p. 395).

A great many of the viewpoints expressed here are in essential agreement with those made independently of this formulation by Szasz (1959). He used concepts like "distress" and "pain" to describe states here called "helplessness" and "hurt." He states:

> . . . in all sorts of human relations one's partner's unhappiness or discomfort signifies *the badness of self* [italics by Szasz] . . . making one's self-esteem dependent . . . on the pleasure or pain (comfort or discomfort) of one's partner leads to all sorts of complications in human affairs . . . (Szasz, 1959, p. 164).

Szasz talked about "inhibited self-assertion" because any other expression may represent "excessive aggression." The pain in those we love or care for brings about the need to do something and to spring into action rather than bringing recognition that there is little anyone can do to decrease or prevent someone else's unhappiness.

Among psychoanalytic writers with a family approach, Bowen (1966) has been mostly concerned with the degree of differentiation of self within the family as a "combination of emotional and relationship system." He accords primary importance to this degree of self-differentiation, which includes concepts like "family ego mass" and "multigenerational interlocking of emotional field" and "parental transmission of varying degrees of maturity or immaturity over multiple generations." Bowen is unique among psycho-analytically-oriented therapists in his attempt at an operational definition of self according to a *Differentiation of Self Scale,* a measure which allows him to make (apparently) differentiations among family members along the continuum of differentiation-undifferentiation. Inside of this family ego mass, which apparently is the totality of individual selves of the family members, Bowen sees three major mechanisms that disrupt "the intensity of the ego fusion": (1) marital conflict; (2) dysfunction in one spouse, and (3) transmission of the problem to one or more children.

Although not directly influenced by Bowen in his practice (as he has been influenced by Satir), this writer sees himself as conceptually following, in part, Bowen's thinking, but without sharing the need for elaborate psychoanalytic jargon.

Guntrip (1971) has aptly summarized the contribution of various psychoanalytic writers to the theory and therapy of the self:

> . . . psychoanalytic theory today centers less and less on the control of instinct and more on the development of a stable care of selfhood. . . . The systematic study of the self, the subjective experience of human beings must now be recognized as an enlargement of the boundaries of science . . . in short, we have now arrived at the time when it is apparent that man's major problem is not how to understand and master his physical environment but to understand himself and find out how we can help one another to live truly self and other fulfilling lives (p. 148).

There are two general criticisms that can be leveled against Guntrip's review as a representative of most psychoanalytic thinking. The first criticism deals with the individual self being seen as separate from his loved ones ("The problem here is not relations to other people but whether one is or has a self"). How can a self exist without other selves? Furthermore, how can this self be helped to find itself without confrontation, negotiation, and compromise with other closely related selves? The length of psychoanalytic treatments with individuals raises serious questions about the assumption of a self without relations. This assumption needs comparative testing in the long time that it takes individuals to find their own selves in individual therapy in contrast to the time it takes to find themselves together with their loved ones in family therapy. The second criticism pertains to the disdain manifested by Guntrip, as well as other psychoanalysts (see Arieti, 1967, for example), against empirical validation of their concepts; or to put it in another way, it is impossible to test their views if their concepts are defined in ways which are not testable. Although the theory attests to the basic importance of the mother-child interaction in the formation of self, the ignorance of recent empirical literature and the holier-than-thou disdain against empirical validation makes psychoanalytic theory suspicious and questionable (besides the point that ultimately, from an economic practical viewpoint, its emphasis on treating the individual separately from his loved ones makes it so expensive that only a very small percentage of individuals can be helped by it).

Humanistic Viewpoints

The general humanistic viewpoint finds its roots in the self-consistency view of Prescott Lacky and more recently by Carl Rogers (Patterson, 1961), who views the self as a "basic factor in the formation of personality and in the determination of behavior" (p. 7). The self is expressed through one's self-concept and one's self-regard. Even though historically Rogers traces his thinking to sociologists like Cooley and Mead, his views have produced a specific school of psychological thought known for its therapeutic nondirectiveness, which is based on having sufficient regard for an individual so as to allow him to make his own decisions. An important aspect of this theory is the actual self-ideal, self-discrepancy that Rogers and his students attempted to measure through the Q-sort technique. Unfortunately, as Patterson (1961) noted:

> What is needed is a more formal theoretical statement which would lead to testable hypotheses for research, not only with clients in therapy, but in many other situations, with many other kinds of subjects (p. 11).

One of Rogers' students, Combs, developed a more detailed statement about the helping relationship and basic concepts for the helping professions that derives from Rogers' viewpoint (Arila, Combs and Purkey, 1971; Combs, Arila and Purkey, 1971). The helper's self-actualization, personal self, professional self and self-acceptance are viewed as keys to the process of help and change in others.

Of course, one of the current luminaries of humanism is Maslow (Goble, 1970). Maslow emphasizes the importance of self-actualization as a way of satisfying biological and psychological needs.

A more direct empirical derivation of self-concept theory is found in the work of Fitts (Fitts, Adams, Radford, Richard, Thomas, Thomas and Thompson, 1971; Fitts and Hamner, 1969). Fitts developed the *Tennessee Self-Concept Scale* (TSCS) and applied it to the study of delinquents, relating the self-concept to the phenomenological theory of Snygg and Combs and Rogers. His work, at this time, stands out as a landmark in the actual empirical validation of self-concept theory and its application to clinical populations. Unfortunately, the wording of this scale makes a certain degree of literacy necessary for administration. This methodological shortcoming can be bypassed through the use of audiotapes[8] or visual stimuli consisting of pictures, as described toward the end of this chapter.

Fitts relates the self-concept to a wheel model of interpersonal competence, self-actualization, psychopathology and the whole process of self-concept change. Fitts distinguishes between internal and external dimensions of the self-concept, discussing concepts like self-esteem and distortion of self perception. Another line of research on the self, especially dealing with children and using nonverbal stimuli that do not require a reading knowledge, can be found in the work of Ziller (Ziller and Grossman, 1967). Another contribution to self-theory from a developmental viewpoint can be found in Gale (1969). A collection of readings on the self from a humanistic viewpoint has been edited by Hamachek (1965), who recently reviewed most of the relevant aspects of the self-concept and its correlates (Hamachek, 1971).

This writer (L'Abate, 1971a) criticizes humanism on grounds of being: (1) too idealistically abstract (i.e. how many truck drivers or ditchdiggers can use such a concept as self-actualization?); (2)

---

8. The use of audio tape techniques in test administration of objective questionnaires (Woody, personal communication) would bypass any need for literacy.

paradoxically inhuman in its disregard, at least in the hands of some (but certainly not all) of its representatives, of empirical controls, denying quantification and other aspects of empirical inquiry; (3) impractical and having an antiempirical stance; and (4) low in concern for accountability (a quality that humanism shares with psychoanalytic thinking).

Social Interaction Theories

Self-theorists at the sociological level of analysis have been many, ranging from Cooley and Mead (as some of the original thinkers) to Goffman and Strauss (as followers of the same tradition). One of the best expressions of this school of thought is found in the work of McCall and Simmons (1966). The authors relate a role-identity model to the self as a determinant of action, considering the self as "situational as specific to its content and expectations." Thus, the self is seen as basic to the various role-identities that we assume in the course of our interactive careers from son to student, to husband, to father, to one's occupational self, etc. While psychoanalysts emphasize the intrapsychic self, these social interaction theorists emphasize the social self; i.e. what is apparent from one's interactions with others rather than one's doubts, anxieties, fears, etc.

As Cottrell (1969) suggests in his review of interpersonal interaction and the development of self: "Psychology has not yet accomplished the shift from a nomadic to a dyadic form of conceptualization of its problems" (p. 543). That is, the self cannot be viewed in and by itself as a structure, the way most psychologists see it and measure it, anymore than it can be viewed as a function.

There is little to criticize in such theorizing in so far that it is somewhat more testable and socially relevant and better validated than psychoanalytic theory. Unfortunately, the social interaction viewpoint suffers from its lack of connection to clinical applications. In other words, most sociologists or social psychologists are not concerned with validating their theories in the clinical arena. This lack of applications produces an unfortunate split to the point that most group and family therapists have a questionable academic background in group dynamics and sociological theory (because most of their training is usually in psychiatry or clinical psychology). Social workers may perhaps receive more relevant academic training than the other two mental health professionals, at least for interventions within the social interaction framework.

Nevertheless, the lack of clinical applications has deprived the social interaction theorists from developing more empirical ways of testing their concepts or of finding validation in clinical applications.

Cognitive Theory

Kelly (1955) differentiates sharply between his personal constructs theory and what he considers neophenomenological self-concept theory of Rogers and of his students (e.g. Raimy, Bugenthal, Snygg and Combs). Although he feels that some overlap may be inevitable, Kelly views the self as a construct or a concept:

> It refers to a group of events which are alike in certain ways and, in that same way, necessarily different from the other events. The way in which the events are alike is the self. That also makes the self an individual, differentiated from other individuals. The self, having been thus conceptualized, can now be used as a thing, a datum or an item in the context of a superordinate construct. The self can become one of the three or more things—or persons—at least two of which are alike and are different from at least one of the others (Kelly, 1955, p. 131).

Phenomenological self-concept theory, described previously under the rubric of humanism, emphasizes, according to Kelly, "the location of the self within an externally imposed system of dimensions." Basic to Kelly's definition of self is his *Role Repertory Test,* in which the self is defined in terms of similarities and dissimilarities to one's parents, spouse, siblings, friends, etc. The method basic to one's self-definition is called by Kelly "self-characterization" and is based on an autobiographical, thematic, and impromptu clinical interview in answer to questions like "Who are you?" "What kind of child were you?" "What kind of person do you expect to become?"

Behaviorism

There is no room in behavioristic approaches for the concept of self. Classical or instrumental learning is too molecular

(L'Abate, 1969) to include such a molar, complex, and interpersonal concept as "self." Perusal by the reader of representative views (Franks, 1967) should convince him that such a concept is either absent, foreign, or omitted (and perhaps even useless) to a level of conceptualization that makes only direct observable behavior its only subject matter and that rejects such an inferred entity as "self." Consequently, the contribution of behaviorism to a view of the self is either minimal, or nonexistent. Nonetheless, behavioristic approaches should not be dismissed because of their theoretical limitations. Many behavioristic procedures, including some of the behavioral prescriptions suggested earlier in this chapter, are positive avenues of helping parents and children to find more helpful avenues of self-assertion than they knew heretofore. When the helper prescribes, for instance, the use of an alarm clock. comic books, green stamps, pennies, or any other form of token rewards for the benefit of the child, he is essentially helping the child remain assured of his importance, without making him omnipotent, and helping the parents find novel avenues through which they can assert their love and care for the child. Could it not indeed be the case that most positive behavioristic approaches based mostly on output feedback (L'Abate, 1969b) into the self help to proclaim its competence and increasing self-confidence in the family system?

Developmentally, for instance, the child's self-concept is seen by behaviorists as the outcome of social labeling that the child learns to incorporate in his own vocabulary:

> The verbal responses the child learns to his own stimuli—internal, external, and behavior produced—are heavily involved in what has been called the self-concept. The self-concept will also ordinarily include the individual's labeling of other people's responses to him, such as "People like me," and so on. The individual's "self-concept" will also include verbal labels . . . learned . . . in many evaluative situations involving social, sensory-motor, and intellectual skills . . . (Staats, 1971, p. 141).

Consequently, since the concept of self shows a minimum of overlap between psychodynamic and behavioristic approaches, it may well represent the dividing line between the two. The degree of emphasis on the self may differentiate among various psychoanalytic, humanistic, and phenomenological approaches. Just as the presence or absence of emphasis on the self may well be the primary difference between psychodynamic and behavioristic approaches, so within psychodynamic approaches the main issue of interest and controversy is and will remain (because it is as yet unresolved) the difference between affect-oriented and cognition-oriented approaches. The integration of both, as found perhaps in Gestalt therapy, may be the next significant breakthrough in the helping process.

RESEARCH IN THE PROCESS AND RESULTS OF HELPING

How does the helper "know" he has done any good, above and beyond the personal feelings of satisfaction? Winter's (1971) recent review on the outcome of parental and familial therapies raises serious questions as to the adequacy of present-day techniques of evaluation, especially in regard to outcome:

> When some evaluation process is systematically employed, reality will not replace conjecture. . . . Clinicians have been traditionally weary and even antagonistic toward research. . . . There seem to be relatively few research studies of the efficacy of family therapy, and those which have been conducted are generally lacking in sophistication. . . . Perhaps family therapy simply does not work (p. 92).

With such a gloomy outlook he concludes with a statement to which this writer would subscribe:

> . . . we should move rapidly toward the development of techniques for measuring family improvement so we can eventually sort out reality from fantasy about what works in family therapy (p. 116).

With these criticisms in the foreground and a healthy amount of personal skepticism, this writer and his students have been attempting to fulfill Winter's final conclusion, i.e. to develop rapid methods of family assessment that would allow a quick evaluation of outcome (if any!).

Very briefly, present psychodiagnostic techniques have the following shortcomings:

1. *Too cumbersome.* If they are easy to administer, like projective techniques, they are hard to score. However, most of them were

built for individual rather than group or family administration.

2. *Too time-consuming.* Most techniques yet devised, whether objective questionnaire-type, structured interviews, or projective techniques take a great deal of time, going usually into hours.

3. *Too atheoretical.* Most empirically devised measures, tasks, or methods have been atheoretically devised. Very few instruments have been based on any theory of family functioning and dysfunctioning.

4. *Too costly of time in administration, scoring, and interpretation.*

Consequently, we started with Satir's views of family dysfunctions and reviewed the literature from this viewpoint. We found a great many similarities between her model and much of the empirical and psychological literature (see L'Abate and Golden, Note No. 5). As the review of the literature progressed and it was found increasingly consistent with Satir's original model (modified by us to fit an orthogonal structure), we developed techniques of assessment to test the model at what we call the phenotypical level (L'Abate, 1964). One technique consisted of adjective checklists derived as directly as could be done from the model.

A second technique consisted of many statements culled from published family therapy protocols that fit into the model. The respondent checks which statements are descriptive of himself or of selected others or of members of his past or present family. Whereas the first technique was based on a forced ranking of adjectives, the second test was originally built to allow free choice. Whether this format will be continued depends on the preliminary results from exploratory try-outs.

A third technique, which we hope will be especially relevant to adolescents, consists of hypothetical family stress situations to which the respondent can answer in terms of four choices representing the four major extremes of the orthogonal model: blaming, placating, computing, and distracting.

A fourth technique assesses the nonverbal level and consists of visual presentations, drawings that represent various situations among family members according to the four major dysfunctional extremes already mentioned *(Family Situations Picture Series).* Instead of using this family picture series projectively (that is, having family members tell stories, as is usually done), the plan is to use a sufficient number of them to reduce the projective process to objective scoring. Assuming a series of 264 pictures to encompass all the various combinations and permutations of relationships among family members (father to mother and vice versa, father to son and vice versa, mother to daughter and vice versa, son to son, daughter to daughter, and daughter to son) the respondent is asked to make a choice of whether each picture applies to his family. The response furnishes an objective (true-false) dichotomy from which to evaluate the consistency of perceptions among various family members. This method also reduces a rather cumbersome procedure, that is, scoring of thematic materials, to an easily quantifiable and quick scoring procedure.

In addition to the 264-item *Family Situations Pictures Series* (FSPS), a self-evaluation picture series is envisaged that will use the same methodology. The value of a visual-pictorial stimulus over a written word and statement is its range of applicability to a larger population, regardless of age or intellectual level (larger than written words or statements would allow). This *Self-Description Picture Series* (SDPS) would consist of the same, single family pictures used in the previous series presenting various moods (sad, mad, fearful, etc.). These pictures would be administered to various family members according to age and sex with the instructions to choose those pictures that show how they "show the family as each of you sees it." There would be a self-description as well as a family description of feelings.

The value of these pictorial techniques would not only be evaluative. It would be hoped that by focusing on dysfunctional situations in the family and the feelings of the various family members, the process of therapy would be already enhanced. These techniques could then be used on a before-after basis with the use of brief programmed role-playing sessions, and training in the use of angry verbalizations before the start of family therapy *per se.* Thus, structured, truly laboratory techniques could be used in a way which would enhance consistency between assessment and therapy. Some information is already given by viewing dysfunctional situations and by having to consider personal and familial feelings. Such family enrichment programs[9] consist of programmed instructions about:

1st Stage: Pretraining assessment, nonverbal techniques and sculpting, exercises, nonverbal role playing;

2nd Stage: Role-playing of dysfunctional patterns: blaming, irrelevancy, placating, computing;

3rd Stage: Use of constructive feelings, use of feelings, feeling states, and constructive communication. Post-training assessment;

4th Stage: Follow-up interview with consideration of plans for the future.

An unfinished and as yet incomplete area of research is assessment and evaluation of the genotype; that is, the assessment of the explanatory level below the phenotypical (L'Abate, 1964) that helps to explain (in addition to and in conjunction with the historical level) the *raison d'etre* and major *leit-motif* of the family and of the individual. At the individual level, it is relatively easy (or it should be) to assess the genotype through the use of measures of *self-esteem* if one were to agree with Satir that this is the individual genotype: how one feels about one's self. On the other hand, we have been increasingly impressed, both clinically and theoretically, with the possibility that *helplessness* or *powerlessness* as originally thought by Adler (1964, 1969), may fit the definition of genotype. Consequently, we are presently reviewing the literature on both counts and considering the possibility of a posture that may well include both aspects, if both are independent from each other. Another genotypical aspect that is almost impossible to assess empirically (but which needs increasing theoretical, empirical, and clinical recognition) is included in concepts like *pain* and *hurt*. Is this the feeling that overcomes us when we feel and experience *helplessness?*

The ultimate goal, of course, will be to integrate assessment and therapy and to relate one to another within a more consistent framework than has been possible before. If clear patterns of family dysfunctioning can be identified, how can they be related

---

9. L'Abate, L. *Family Enrichment Programs: Experimental Manual.* Atlanta, Georgia: Institute for Psychological Services, 1971.

to genotypical, familial as well as individual sources? By the same token, how can these genotypical patterns be related to historical child-rearing antecedents?

SUMMARY

This chapter presents a therapeutic approach based on interpersonal, psychodynamically oriented intervention. This approach makes three assertions concerning the origins and directions of dysfunctionalities in couples and families. It presents an approach toward helping couples and families that should derive as much as possible from the three original assertions. This approach makes the therapist responsible for asserting himself in a helpful and hurtless fashion. At the core of conjugal and familial dysfunctions one finds the concept of "self," a concept that is basic to many seemingly different theoretical viewpoints. The historical relationship of various psychodynamic approaches (psychoanalytic, humanistic, social, and cognitive) to the concept of self is reviewed briefly in terms of how this concept separates these approaches from perhaps more molecular, learning- or reinforcement-based approaches. A brief review of research presently taking place in the author's laboratory concludes the chapter.

REFERENCES

Adler, A.: *Superiority and social interest.* London, Routledge and Kegan, 1964.

Adler, A.: *The science of living.* Garden City, Doubleday, 1969.

Arieti, S.: *The intrapsychic self: feeling, cognition, and creativity in health and mental illness.* New York, Basic Books, 1967.

Arila, D. L., Combs, A. W. and Purkey, W. W.: *The helping relationship sourcebook.* Boston, Allyn and Bacon, 1971.

Becker, W. C.: *Parents as teachers: a child management program.* Champaign, Research Press, 1971.

Bowen, M.: The use of family theory in clinical practice. *Comprehensive Psychiatry, 7*:345-374, 1966.

Combs, A. W., Arila, D. L. and Purkey, W. W.: *Helping relationships: basic concepts for the helping professions.* Boston, Allyn and Bacon, 1971.

Cottrell, L. S. Jr.: Interpersonal interaction and the development of the self. In D. A. Goslin (Ed.), *Handbook of socialization theory and research.* Chicago, Rand McNally, 543-570, 1969.

Eidelberg, L. (Ed.): *Encyclopedia of psychoanalysis.* New York, Free Press, 1968.

Ellis, A.: *The essence of rational psychotherapy: a comprehensive approach to treatment.* New York, Institute for Rational Living (undated).

Erikson, E.: *Identity and the life cycle.* New York, International Universities Press, 1959.

Fitts, W. H. and Hamner, W. T.: *The self-concept and delinquency.* Nashville Mental Health Center's Research Monograph, No. 1. Nashville, Nashville Mental Health Center, 1969.

Fitts, W. H. *et al.: The self-concept and self-actualization.* Dede Wallace Center's Monograph No. 3. Nashville, Dede Wallace Center, 1971.

Franks, C. M. (Ed.): *Behavior therapy: appraisal and status.* New York, McGraw-Hill, 1969.

Gale, R. F.: *Developmental behavior: a humanistic approach.* New York, Macmillan, 1969.

Ginott, H.: *Between parent and child.* New York, Macmillan, 1965.

Goble, F.: *The third force: the psychology of Abraham Maslow.* New York, Grossman, 1970.

Grosser, G. H. and Paul, N. L.: Ethical issues in family group therapy. *American Journal of Orthopsychiatry, 34*:875-885, 1964.

Guntrip, H. J.: *Psychoanalytic theory, therapy, and the self.* New York, Basic Books, 1971.

Hamachek, D. E. (Ed.): *The self in growth, teaching, and learning: selected readings.* Englewood Cliffs, Prentice-Hall, 1965.

Hamachek, D. E. (Ed.): *Encounters with the self.* New York, Holt, Rinehart and Winston, 1971.

L'Abate, L.: *Principles of clinical psychology.* New York, Grune and Stratton, 1964.

L'Abate, L.: A communication-information model. In L. L'Abate (Ed.), *Models of clinical psychology.* Atlanta, Georgia State University, 65-73, 1969.

L'Abate, L.: An empiricist's rebuttal to humanistic ideology. Unpublished mimeographed paper. Atlanta, February 17, 1971(a).

L'Abate, L.: The laboratory method in clinical child psychology: two applications. Paper read at the XVII International Congress of Applied Psychology, Liege, Belgium, July 30, 1971(b).

Lazarus, A. A.: Where do behavior therapists take their troubles? *Psychological Reports, 28*:349-350, 1971.

Lynd, H. M.: *On shame and the search for identity.* New York, Harcourt, Brace, 1958.

McCall, G. J. and Simmons, J. L.: *Identities and interactions.* New York, Free Press, 1966.

Mullan, H. and Sangiuliano, Iris: *The therapist's contribution to the treatment process: his person transactions and treatment process.* Springfield, Thomas, 1964.

Patterson, C. H.: The self in recent Rogerian theory. *Journal of Individual Psychology, 17*:5-11, 1961.

Patterson, G. R. and Gullion, M. Elizabeth: *Living with children: new methods for parents and teachers.* Champaign, Research Press, 1968.

Satir, Virginia: The family as a treatment unit. *Confinia Psychiatrica,* 8:37-42, 1965.

Spiegel, L.: The self, the sense of self, and perception. *Psychoanalytic Study of the Child, 14*:81-109, 1959.

Staats, A. W.: *Child learning, intelligence, and personality: principles of a behavioral interaction approach.* New York, Harper and Row, 1971.

Szasz, T. S.: The communication of distress between child and parent. *British Journal of Medical Psychology, 32*:161-170, 1959.

Wheelis, A.: *The quest for identity.* New York, Norton, 1958.

Winter, W. D.: Family therapy: research and theory. In C. D. Spielberger (Ed.), *Current topics in clinical and community psychology.* New York, Academic Press, 85-121, 1971.

Woody, R. H.: *Psychobehavioral counseling and therapy: integrating insight and behavioral techniques.* New York, Appleton-Century-Crofts, 1971.

Ziller, R. C. and Grossman, S. A.: A developmental study of the self-social constructs of normals and the neurotic personality. *Journal of Clinical Psychology, 23*:15-21, 1967.

CHAPTER	BEHAVIORAL INTERVENTIONS
FIVE	

DESPITE ITS ROOTS in time-honored learning theory, behavior therapy or behavioral modification was bypassed for years by marriage and family counselors and therapists. During the sixties, however, behaviorism emerged as a powerful treatment orientation, and progressively it has been applied for sexual, marital, and familial problems.

Behavioral procedures have their theoretical rationale in learning theory. According to the insight-oriented therapies (from psychoanalysis to client-centered therapy) emotional and behavioral problems are caused by unresolved psychological conflicts; however behavior therapy discounts the presence of emotional conflicts and looks instead to faulty learning. In other words, a behavior therapist would not be concerned with underlying emotional problems that would have to be unraveled and resolved through increased self-understanding, but would instead view problem behaviors as simply maladaptive habits that had been learned. Treatment would be directed at unlearning or relearning: i.e. any behavior that is learned can be unlearned or extinguished by eliminating its reinforcing properties, and any conditioned response can be counterconditioned and a more appropriate response or behavior can be cultivated via conditioning.

Reinforcement constitutes the most basic ingredient of behavior therapy. Reinforcement may be explained as follows: *when an act or behavior occurs, the consequence will contribute to whether the act is prone to be repeated;* that is, if an action leads to a pleasant or rewarding consequence, the person will be apt to repeat the action, whereas if it produces a negative or non-rewarding reaction, he will be apt to turn to another form of responding. For example, in the marriage relationship, if a wife dresses in a certain manner and her husband compliments her or reacts favorably to her appearance, she will be more prone to dress in that manner again than to dress in a different style, such as in a way to which her husband had previously not responded or to which he had been negative. To take a further theoretical look at reinforcement, let us consider the following statement:

> Reinforcement means simply that a performance is followed by a stimulus. The stimulus serves as a reinforcer, but whether such a bonding procedure has a noticeable influence on subsequent perform-ance, that is, whether it increases the frequency of the same type of performance later, depends upon the collateral conditions. In be-havioral counseling and therapy, a reinforcement contingency be-comes the basis for the intervention; this means that the relationship between the reinforcer and the exact properties of the performance are used to define what is to be cultivated by the counselor-therapist. In practical terms, if the desired performance is a certain class of verbal responses from a client, e.g. information-seeking responses in vocational counseling, the properties include such ele-ments as references in the counseling session to the seeking of such information. The reinforcer is defined as a verbal or nonverbal re-sponse from the counselor-therapist, and the reinforcement con-tingency is the counselor-therapist's responding to information-seeking responses from his client in counseling as a means of reinforcing the occurrence of this type of verbal responses. Reinforcement is usually presented according to a schedule. This is an established way of providing the reinforcing stimulus, and typically includes one of the following formats of responding: on a fixed-ratio, at a fixed-interval, at a variable-interval, or on a variable-ratio (Woody, 1971, p. 32).

The nature of this discussion does not accommodate an extensive review of learning theory or conditioning, but a thorough academ-ic exposition may be found in Ferster and Perrott (1968).

In the foregoing definition, a critical term was introduced: *re-inforcement contingency*. The reinforcement contingency is the vehicle by which the therapist implements his intervention. The following statement should clarify the concept:

> A reinforcement contingency is either positive or negative. A positive contingency denotes that a rewarding stimulus follows the performance. These rewards may be objects or tokens that have a prescribed value or can be redeemed for prizes (e.g. money, candy, privileges), or social recognition (i.e. acceptance from a significant other, peer, or authority figure), or verbal praise (e.g. a counselor-therapist saying "good," or "that's a fine idea," or "I would certainly

agree with that plan"). All of these positive stimuli have been used in behavioral modification, but in behavioral counseling the most frequently used reinforcer is verbal praise, that is, positive responses, from the counselor-therapist. Negative reinforcement refers to the procedure of eliminating an unpleasant situation by acting. That is, an unpleasant condition is created when an unacceptable behavior occurs, and when the behavior is altered to be acceptable the unpleasant condition (e.g. mild electric shock) is removed. Negative reinforcement is said to have occurred when the performance (i.e. behavior) that eliminates an aversive (i.e. unpleasant) stimulus increases in frequency. Incidentally, punishment should not be confused with negative reinforcement. Punishment follows a performance, whereas in negative reinforcement the aversive stimulus precedes the performance (Woody, 1971, pp. 33-34).

It might be added that the loss or withdrawal of a positive reward is interpreted as a punishment.

Subsequent sections of this chapter will clarify how reinforcement contingencies are indeed intrinsic to marital and family relations, and techniques will be described for identifying and altering these contingencies. At this point, however, it seems important to underscore how suitable behavioral modification procedures appear to be for marital and family problems. Liberman (1970) states:

> Couple and family therapy can be particularly potent means of behavior modification because the interpersonal milieu that undergoes change is that of the day-to-day, face-to-face encounter an individual experiences with the most important people in his life—his spouse or members of his immediate family. When these therapies are successful, it is because the therapist is able to guide the members of the couple or family into changing their modes of dealing with each other. In behavioral or learning terms, we can translate "ways of dealing with each other" into consequences of behavior or *contingencies of reinforcement.* Instead of rewarding maladaptive behavior with attention and concern, the family members learn to give each other recognition and approval for desired behavior (pp. 106-107).

Liberman (1970) indicates that therapy progresses best when each member of the interlocking, reciprocal behavioral system within the family learns how to change his responsiveness to the other members. In explaining how family difficulties arise and are maintained, he states:

> Typically, families that come for treatment have coped with the maladaptive or deviant behavior of one member by responding to it over the years with anger, nagging, babying, conciliation, irritation, or sympathy. These responses, however punishing they might seem on the surface, have the effect of reinforcing the deviance, that is, increasing the frequency or intensity of the deviant behavior in the future. Reinforcement occurs because the attention offered is viewed and felt by the deviant member as positive concern and interest. In many families with a deviant member, there is little social interaction and the individuals tend to lead lives relatively isolated from each other. Because of this overall lack of interaction, when interaction does occur in response to a member's "abnormal" behavior, such behavior is powerfully reinforced (p. 107).

A familiar example of the latter point is found with the young child who feels neglected by his mother; he will often misbehave in order to get her attention, and the fact that she reacts with anger or hostility will usually lead him to repeat the same unacceptable behavior: *getting some emotional reaction, even if it has to be negative, is better than getting no emotional reaction whatsoever.* The solution, which will be repeatedly exemplified in subsequent discussions of techniques, is to train the parent to withhold negative emotional responses to the unacceptable behavior and instead to offer positive emotional responses when the child behaves acceptably. Obviously the parent, who has a history of not responding positively enough to make the child feel that he is getting adequate emotional attention, will have to be helped to learn to respond positively as well as to learn to control negative responses. This same principle can easily be applied to a multitude of situations between spouses; for example, there are countless incidents in probably every marriage (at some point in time) in which negative reactions to a non-preferred behavior on the part of a spouse leads to the continuation of that behavior, yet the non-preferred behavior could be more effectively counteracted by not responding emotionally but responding positively to an opposing behavior that is more desirable.

Before turning to specific behavioral modification techniques for sexual, marital, and familial relations, it seems appropriate to summarize what distinguishes the behavioral approach from its insight-oriented counterparts. In brief, the distinctions are:

1. The behavioral definition of etiology is couched in learning theory terms. Therefore, problem behaviors are viewed as faulty learning or maladaptive habits. Emotional conflicts as etiological components do not exist, at least not in the sense that insight-oriented approaches would maintain; thus threatment need not give attention to resolving underlying conflicts, only to altering overt behavioral patterns.

2. As might be inferred from the foregoing etiological set, the behaviorist does not believe in symptom substitution. The insight-oriented therapist believes that emotional conflicts must be resolved (otherwise the overt behavioral problem, which is considered to be only the "tip of the iceberg" and not causative, will be replaced by another symptom or problem that is provoked by the emotional conflict). The behavior therapist believes that eliminating the observable, conscious behavior and reinforcing a more appropriate response will totally eliminate (or at least significantly alleviate) the problem permanently. Much to the surprise of some therapists, as behavioral research accumulates, the long-feared symptom substitution concept appears to be only a myth.

3. In accord with the two preceding points, behavioral treatment does not necessitate increased self-understanding nor conflict resolution. Rather, behavioral treatment is designed to help the person with the problem unlearn or extinguish the unacceptable or undesirable behavior, to identify and eliminate the contingency that led to the behavior problem being reinforced and maintained.

4. The behavior therapist does not attribute any importance to the qualities of the relationship between him and his client and thus negates the importance of the "facilitating conditions" (such as accurate empathy, nonpossessive warmth, and genuineness) that insight-oriented therapists endow with change power in psychotherapy (e.g. Carkhuff and Berenson, 1967). In behavior therapy, therefore, the conditioning techniques are assigned critical value, and the behavioral treatment could, at least theoretically, be provided by any number of therapists, any of whom would get comparable results from application of the technique, regardless of his relationship (be it positive or negative) with the client.

5. The behavior therapist assumes clear-cut responsibility for the outcome of the therapy. Whereas the insight-oriented therapist believes that the responsibility for introspection and eventual behavioral change rests on the shoulders of the client, the behavior therapist accepts that he is the expert being called upon to solve a dilemma with his expertise, and that he must prescribe an appropriate means for achieving behavorial change.

6. The success or failure of the treatment intervention differs between the insight approaches and the behavioral approach. The insight-oriented approaches, in general, accept that the real objective for treatment is increased client-insight; therefore, if the client terminates treatment with increased insight, the therapy may be deemed successful, even if he still possesses the problems that led him to seek treatment (the assumption being that as long as he understands why he has the problems and accepts that the problem is a concomitant of a self-concept or personality structure that he prefers to live with because it is satisfying and fulfilling, then the problem is irrelevant). The behavior therapist, on the other hand, accepts specific behavioral objectives at the onset of treatment, and his intervention cannot be deemed successful until he has helped the client eliminate the target unacceptable behaviors, and hopefully aided the client in attaining new, more rewarding behaviors.

It must be acknowledged that these six points are, to some degree, an all-too-simple synthesis of complex issues; each of these issues has received elaboration elsewhere (Woody, 1969, 1971). Further, it should be pointed out that while this chapter is focused exclusively on behavioral techniques and remains within the domain of pure behaviorism, there are a number of extenuating circumstances that suggest that the most efficacious form of therapeutic intervention involves the integration of behavioral and insight techniques. This integration process, termed the *Psychobehavioral Frame of Reference* will receive consideration in the last chapter.

REINFORCEMENT CONTINGENCIES

As mentioned previously, the most rudimentary element of the behavioral approach is to make use of positive reinforcement. This necessitates, of course, the identification of reinforcement contingencies within the marital or familial relationships. From these contingencies, reinforcement properties are controlled and altered to improve behaviors and relations.

Therapeutic Relationship

In approaching the task of helping a couple or a family deal with reinforcement contingencies, it is necessary to establish a therapist-client (or helper-helpee) relationship that will accommodate a free-flow of information. Although the behaviorist might attribute no change power to the so-called "facilitating conditions," it seems paramount to the outcome of the behavioral intervention to have effective interpersonal communication, and this typically means that the helper must demonstrate his ability to be empathic, nonjudgmental, warm, genuine, in other words, exhibit all human relations constructs that the insight-oriented approaches consider to be crucial. In the process, this stage of relationship building serves both to develop a high degree of communication between the helper and the couple or family members and to create a pull for all primary members involved to be committed to achieving change–at least this is the first step toward actually promoting change.

Data Collection

Given an adequate communicative bond, the helper must next carry out the basic task of collecting data that can be transformed into the contingency framework, which will lead to the structure for treatment or intervention techniques. Interviewing for behavioral procedures can be strikingly similar to that used for psychodynamic procedures; namely, an effort is made to understand the developmental, current, and expected influences on the life of the helpee. Special attention is commonly given to factors that provoke anxiety and situations that are perceived as pleasant or unpleasant. There are a few instruments, such as questionnaires, that are designed especially for behavioral interventions (see Wolpe and Lazarus, 1966; Wolpe, 1969; Lazarus, 1971); and it is possible to extrapolate from rather traditional psychological tests (Greenspoon and Gersten, 1967). For the most part, however, such specialized instruments only supplement what is the real crux of the matter: *astute diagnostic interviewing and clinical judgments must be used for developing a behavioral treatment plan.*

Behavior Analysis

Kanfer and Saslow (1969) have offered one of the most meaningful set of guidelines for a behavioral analysis available to date:

1. A detailed description of the particular behavioral excesses or deficits which represent the patient's complaints, and of the

behavioral assets which may be available for utilization in a treatment program.

2. A clarification of the problem situation in which the variables are sought that maintain the patient's current problem behaviors. Attention is also given to the consequences of psychiatric intervention on the current adjustment balance of the patient in his social environment.

3. A motivational analysis which attempts to survey the various incentives and aversive conditions representing the dominant motivational factors in the patient.

4. A developmental analysis suggests consideration of biological, sociological, and behavioral changes in the patient's history which may have relevance for his present complaint and for a treatment program.

5. An analysis of self-control, which provides assessment of the patient's capacity for participation in a treatment program and of the conditions which may be necessary to control behaviors with untoward social consequences.

6. An analysis of social relationships which provides the basis for assessing social resources in the patient's environment which have affected his current behavior and may play a role in the therapeutic program.

7. An analysis of the social-cultural-physical environment to assess the degree of congruence between the patient's present milieu, his behavioral repertoire, and the type of therapeutic goals which the therapist can establish (pp. 443-444).

From these data, whether gained through interviewing (structured or unstructured) and/or psychological tests, the helper is left with the subjective task of ordering and weighting the data, and deducing the most suitable treatment approach: *there is no substitute for behavioral knowledge and clinical expertise.*

Since clinical judgment pervades the task of ordering and weighting data and deducing the treatment approach, it seems illogical to attempt to posit a simple equation. Obviously, such a task is extremely complex, and the behavioral approach is just as vulnerable to bias as any other treatment approach when it comes time for the helper's expertise to enter. In terms of handling the data, however, Kanfer and Saslow (1969) recommend:

The compilation of data under as many of the headings as are relevant should yield a good basis for decisions about the areas in which intervention is needed, the particular targets of the interventions, the treatment methods to be used, and the series of goals at which treatment should aim (p. 430).

As for what "headings" should be used, this depends to a large extent on the idiosyncratic frame of reference used by the helper; in other words, each helper should try to construct the categories or headings for the data that are most cogent to his set for clinical judgments, as would relate specifically to the behavioral approach. Greenspoon and Gersten (1967) suggest that the data simply be grouped into four classes of contingencies or contingent stimuli: positive verbal, negative verbal, positive nonverbal, and negative nonverbal. This may prove to be a bit too simplistic, for while the data might well be grouped into these four categories, it would seem that most clinical cases would necessitate the development of numerous subcategories. This means tailoring each set of headings to the helper and helpees involved.

Technique Selection

The next challenge is to select a behavioral technique. Woody (1971) states:

Behavior therapists presume to operate on algorithms; i.e. they employ rules of procedure that lead to the solving of a problem. In the rationale for behavior therapy, it is implicit that the proper application of conditioning will produce a predictable change in behavior. This would lead one to assume that, given a specified behavior, the conditioning procedure could almost be mechanically determined, but thus far, human nature being what it is, such cut-and-dried technical prescriptions are not tenable (p. 123).

The helper making use of behavioral techniques cannot rely on a prescribed formula; he must depend upon his clinical skills. Moreover, and in support of the integrative "Psychobehavioral" framework to be described in the last chapter, Klein, Dittmann, Parloff, and Gill (1969) state:

Many people suppose that the therapist begins by clearly and systematically defining the patient's problems in terms of manageable hierarchies and then selects appropriate responses to be strengthened or weakened. We found little support for this conception of behavior therapy diagnosis in our observations. Indeed the selection of problems to be worked on often seemed quite arbitrary and inferential. We were frankly surprised to find the presenting symptomatic complaint was often sidestepped for what the therapist intuitively considered to be more basic issues. Most surprising to us, the basis for this selection seemed often to be what others would call dynamic considerations (p. 261).

Parenthetically, their observations were of the behavior therapy activities at Temple University, one of the foremost behavior therapy centers under the auspices (at that time) of Drs. Joseph Wolpe and Arnold A. Lazarus.

Review of major behavior therapy texts reveals that some sources attempt to match behavior problems with specific techniques, e.g. Eysenck and Rachman (1965) and Yates (1970); Woody (1971) provides a synopsis of these systems. In the end, the helper is left with the requirement that he make value judgments about what technique would best deal with the reinforcement contingency being treated. This necessitates a thorough knowledge of behavior theory and its related techniques, extensive understanding of the psychological-sociological-cultural-physical influences and conditions within the helpee's life, and an on-going evaluation of the effects of the behavioral intervention (with the format geared to accommodate technical alterations if needed). It should be noted that selection of the appropriate technique is a central issue to the outcome of treatment, because the technique is vested with the key to whether treatment is or is not effective.

HELPEE-IDENTIFICATION OF REINFORCEMENT CONTINGENCIES

The preceding section purposefully emphasized the decision-making responsibility that the helper holds in behavior therapy. But much of his responsibility can optimally be discharged by helping the couple or family members accomplish their own identification of reinforcement contingencies. This would mean that the initial stage of a behavioral intervention for sexual, marital, or familial difficulties would involve the bringing-out of information, with the couple or family members doing much of the ordering and weighing of the influences. The helper would serve as a behavioral consultant, asking them probing questions and leading them into reasonably accurate introspection, while at the same time formulating his own expert opinions about the critical reinforcement contingencies. Philosophically, this type of involvement for the helpees has the advantages of (1) allowing them a self-determining stance, (2) placing some degree of responsibility for outcome on their interactions, and (3) making the decision partly theirs so that there will be maximum motivation to accomplish the conditioning tasks.

Helpees often cannot assume this responsibility because of a background of poor communication with the spouse or family members. Thus one of the first tasks must be to defuse the exchanges relevant to analysis of the problems; that is, frequently family members are defensive after a chronic history of difficulties to the point that they cannot talk about the problem, much less deal rationally and objectively with the intrinsic elements. To circumvent this barrier, the helper should enter into somewhat of a psychodynamically-oriented counseling role, such as by interpreting what the family members are doing to each other in their inability or refusal to deal with the problems. The helper can progressively move toward a behavioral role by asking them to look at these "games" or defensive behaviors in learning theory terms. It is common to find a first clearcut example of reinforcement, both positive and negative (but particularly the latter), in the interactions within the therapy session.

A second major barrier is an inability to identify the emotional components of the relationship. This is common because disturbed family relations and marital problems often stem from faulty transmission of feeling and from a gross inability to communicate and to respond to emotional or affective needs. It is somewhat surprising how many persons actually lack the words to describe emotional needs or feelings; so one basic technique is to provide them with a list of adjectives and have them try to label statements or actions occurring within the therapy session. From this, they can be encouraged to analyze and label the feelings or affective cues that occur outside the session. Without this ability to identify and label, the couple or family members will be unable to gain eventual

control of the responses in order to promote behavioral modification within their relations. Since the relationship between spouses
or family members is often too poor to accommodate any outside-
the-session analysis, it is occasionally necessary to direct their an-
alytic and labeling attempts to persons outside the family, persons
for whom they do not have a "loaded" apperceptive mass. With
this technique, for example, a husband and wife can make their
independent analyses of the actions or comments of a third-party,
e.g. a house guest or friend that they have not seen for a long time,
and their labels can be compared in the therapy session. If the
helper detects that there are certain sets of circumstances, such as
particular kinds of persons or types of interaction, that cause
greater perceptual distortions than others, he can actually prescribe
the situations and/or persons on whom the helpees can practice
their analysis and labeling. Specifically, the helper might want to
have them encounter special kinds of feelings at a given stage in
their treatment. A rule of thumb is: *It is best to start with nonthreatening, clear-cut affective situations and progress to situations
that are more complex and capable of provoking greater degrees
of anxiety.* A fuller understanding of this guideline should
emerge in a subsequent discussion of systematic desensitization to
anxiety-provoking stimuli or situations.

A special technique to facilitate an improved perceptual awareness of affect is to make use of video tapes or films. In other words,
the helper can present materials that are designed to convey a very
specific kind of emotional message. Similarly, audio tapes, such as
of the couple's or the family's therapy session, can be played back
for analysis or narrative excerpts from books or short-stories can be
discussed (and in these instances, the selection should allow for
both a better perceptual awareness of affect and for a therapeutic
message, such as a short-story that has elements that are comparable
to the helpee's personal situation). The previous chapter by Schauble was, of course, aligned with this methodology (see Chapter
Three).

A third barrier to a helpee's assumption of responsibility in reinforcement contingency identification is that spouses or family
members often do not really have any clear-cut idea what they

want, need, or expect from the others–therefore, it is not surprising that their relations have been historically poor and less than satisfying. One technique for identifying needs or expectations is as follows:

1. The helper should select an affective statement and abruptly stop the communication exchange;
2. He should write the statement down, and have each helpee write out what (A) he *expects* the other person to say in response and (B) what he would *prefer* that the other person say in response;
3. These written statements should be exchanged; a discussion of why there are differences between spouses' or family members' perceptions, as well as why there were differences between what was expected and what was preferred, often leads to increased understanding about how affect is communicated.

Incidentally, the more provocative the topic statement, the more revealing seem to be the responses–if blind defensiveness can be avoided. This technique makes the person giving the statement pay attention to what he would really like to accomplish from his messages and thus to alter his messages according to the biases of the receiver, such as a spouse; it also allows the receiver to gain better understanding of the affective intent of the sender's communication style.

A related technique, one that especially gets at what spouses and family members would prefer from their relationships, is to create "mental marriages" or fantasy relationships. Thus a husband could be asked to create a mental marriage to another person, or a child could be asked to fantasize another mother. The helper then probingly explores whether each person believes he could be a fulfilling partner to the other or to another person, and if so (or if not), why (or why not); and what the other person would have to have as qualities; what persons they know who have these qualities; why their immediate relationship, either between the family members or with these other persons (if they are actual known persons), is not better. The underlying premise is, of course, that family members frequently do not know what they want and do not recognize what they have available. Specifically, upon introspection about the qualities of others, it frequently becomes clear that many of these qualities are already available, at least potentially, within their existing familial relations. The objective is for them to develop more realistic attitudes, more clearly communicated expectations, and more accurate perception.

Each of the foregoing techniques, while promoting a definite degree of insight, is designed to set the stage for a better awareness of the reinforcement contingencies in the marital or family relations. When an ability to communicate about affect and label accurately the emotional messages has developed, actual interactions can be analyzed for reinforcing properties. Because of the stormy nature of the present or immediate past, it is sometimes advisable to take a developmental approach, that is, to review the evolution of the relationship. This technique serves several purposes: (1) the spouses or family members have an opportunity to cathart or ventilate, which can have at least a quasi-therapeutic value by "clearing the air" once and for all, (2) the helper can gain a systematic review of conscious material, giving special recognition to what is emphasized by each spouse or family member and what is omitted (as the omissions emerge), and (3) the helper can begin to process the grist for the reinforcement contingency mill.

The hypothesizing of cause-and-effect relationships (i.e. the reinforcement contingencies) is always open to debate, and there comes a point at which the helper will have to ask the couple or family members to set aside their differences of view regarding etiology or causation and to "assume that X might be what caused it," with the understanding that this assumption will allow for an exploration of whether those presumed reinforcers are (or were) present. It is at this point that there must also be some agreement as to what the behavioral change objectives should be—and again, there may be enough disagreement to warrant an injunction in the name of exploration of alternatives or hypotheses.

Since many spouses and family members have difficulty in delineating what they would like to have within their relationships, one technique is to make use of fantasy for purposes of conjuring up the "ideal relationship," e.g. have spouses focus on the "ideal mate" for themselves, purposefully avoiding anyone who is already known (to avoid unnecessary defensiveness). When using this technique, spouses and family members frequently realize that they have virtually no idea about what they want from each other, that they often contradict themselves, and that they are not very effective in communicating their expectations. It is not unusual for spouses or family members to benefit from merely exploring and delineating their expectations, with their reaction being one of "I never knew that's what was expected—of course, I can handle that!"

In those relationships where there has been poor communication of expectations and inadequate handling of affective material, it is sometimes helpful to encourage the persons to share fantasies and dreams. Many persons seeking marriage and family therapy claim that they do not dream (which would be a good research question: Does a disturbed marriage or family relationship lead to repression of dreams?). However, if the helper gives the suggestion: "You can remember your dreams, now that you have a reason to do so," it is common to find an instantaneous increase in dream production. A certain degree of caution should be exercised to assure that spouses or family members do not start sharing dream or fantasy materials for destructive or sadistic purposes. If used properly, this technique can lead to a wealth of information for the therapist, improved mutual understanding of affective needs, and (occasionally) related behavioral changes.

Role playing and psychodrama can also be used to clarify exactly what goes on (or went on in the past) within the relationships and what would be the preferred changes in their relationship. Since it is often difficult for helpees to appreciate which of several alternatives might be the most rewarding because they have never experienced them with their spouse or family members, role playing can lead all persons involved to appreciate via feelings what a given role might hold in store for each. Likewise, psychodrama yields similar appreciation of feelings and often increases insight into why problems developed. Both of these techniques provide the helper with a means of making first-hand observations of (1) what occurs in the relationships, and (2) what might be created if certain behaviors (those being role played for example) were reinforced. Role playing is particularly useful for reinforcing assertive behaviors in specific areas for a spouse or family member

(Lazarus, 1971). Psychodrama, while requiring special therapeutic skills, has the potential of promoting behavioral changes in a variety of areas.

After delineating expectations and perhaps after exploratory role playing, an effective technique for both improved diagnostic understanding and behavioral change involves having the spouse or target family member simulate behaviors. As mentioned, role playing or simulation affords an opportunity for all persons involved to feel what the new behavior would be like, but more importantly perhaps, simulation offers an often much-needed excuse for making behavioral changes. In other words, some persons feel they cannot afford to change their behavior even if they could and want to, because it would be admitting defeat and would be giving in to a spouse or family member with whom they have been competing for control of the relationship. The use of the simulation of the ideal relationship may provide the reason or justification for them to acknowledge that the behavioral alteration is both possible and desirable.

A behavioral contract constitutes a technique that can serve to define the objectives for the marital or family therapy, and it can also lead to behavioral change simply because the expectations are spelled out. Again, the fact that many persons have never stopped to delineate expectancies or preferences often leads to maladaptive behaviors, and a behavioral contract offers them an opportunity to call a moratorium on their conflicts and to make rather sudden and drastic changes in their responses to each other. The behavioral contract is merely a spelling out of the conditions under which each person will be positive toward the other. For example, if a husband and wife have had a long standing series of disagreements over each other's behavior, the contract would state what each would be expected to do and not do in relationship to each other. Following is an actual behavioral contract drawn up by a husband and wife. This couple had been married for about six years; neither had ever liked the way he was treated by his mate. They had finally separated, but a separation was not wanted. They had three therapy sessions in which their relationship was explored in a behavioral manner and a commitment to change was reinforced.

Then they were told that, since finances (for treatment) were a real problem and since the rate of progress depended on their personal commitment to change, if they could specify what they wanted from each other and operate for the next three months as though under a binding contract, the helper would meet with them to help them "ratify the agreement." The couple represented a blue-collar family and neither had extensive education, but they wrote up the following agreement:

1. Whenever either of us starts to get nervous, instead of taking it out on the children or other partner we will dismiss ourselves into another room or outdoors until we cool off. Then we will come back in and discuss the problem sensibly. No blowing up; instead we will do a "self-analysis." We will be cooperative until the issue is resolved.
2. We will give no threats of leaving of any kind; nor will we tell the other mate to "take off," "get out," etc.
3. We will not argue or gripe about who does the most work around the house.
4. The housework can be let go a little once in a while. John (the husband) will decide when things are clean enough.
5. If the other partner offers help, we will not refuse it.
6. We will quit assuming the other partner wouldn't want to do something for us.
7. There will be no swearing in front of the children, and no screaming at them.
8. If June (the wife) has to work, she will not go to work if either child is visibly ill, if the child is running a high fever, or seems to be really sick. If John has any fears concerning the children's health and June is at work, he will call her and she will come home immediately. June is responsible for the health of the children.
9. When we meet an acquaintance, friend or neighbor, we will not discuss family problems, such as, "who does the most work," etc.
10. We will not make any decisions during an argument, if one occurs.
11. Neither partner will make any big decisions without first consulting the other partner.
12. We will not be quick to jump to conclusions if the other partner isn't on time or something comes up suddenly. We will not make assumptions without checking with the other partner as to whether they are valid.
13. We will try to cultivate mutual trust.

14. If June isn't working, John should be home by 6:00 p.m.; if June is working, John can have 2 beers 5 nights a week before coming home.
15. If John goes out for a "night on the town," unless these are special circumstances, June will go with him; "special circumstances" should be discussed with June before going.
16. We will make a list of what are the husband's duties, the wife's duties, and their shared duties.

The couple found that the concreteness and specificity of their behavioral contract provided them with a reason not to follow previous behaviors, and in the process they were able to start positively reinforcing each other. The list of items clearly indicates how the contract does not have to be all-inclusive and can be couched in everyday language (and should be, if it is to be optimally meaningful to those involved).

Following the identification of reinforcement contingencies and the delineation of desired changes or preferred new behaviors, the task is to train the couple or family consistently to practice reinforcement techniques. In other words, the helper strives to get them to become reasonably objective about accomplishing behavioral change, to understand reinforcement principles academically, to be able instantly to recognize when both preferred and maladaptive contingencies occur, and to be able to control their responses. Gaining control of responses is difficult for everyone, as any experienced helper can attest from his own training in how to respond in a counseling-therapy situation, and the seemingly most effective way to cultivate this ability within the couple or family is much like a professional training program; i.e. they should be educated in what is the way to respond, they should practice responding in that manner, and they should analyze their responses so they can increase their sensitivity to the cues that lead them to respond properly and improperly (as defined by the designated contingencies).

The helper can also play another role: he can use his own response style and his overt behavior as a framework for modeling. In other words, he can demonstrate how he reinforces their healthy or appropriate behavior and refuses to respond to (i.e. reinforce) their "nutty" behavior. Indeed, it is extremely important that the helper not only demonstrate his competencies as a model for teaching purposes but takes care to be sure he does not get manipulated into reinforcing the avoidance and maladaptive "games" that so often pervade marital and family relations. Liberman (1970) has noted: "The behavioral approach, with its more systematic and specific guidelines, makes it less likely that a therapist will adventitiously reinforce or model contradictory behavior patterns" (p. 117), as compared to insight-oriented approaches.

The material in the foregoing section is designed to capture the essence of behavioral interventions for sexual, marital, and familial relations. Specifically, the important ingredient is for spouses and/or family members to learn how to avoid reinforcing inappropriate behaviors or responses and how to reward or reinforce those behaviors or responses that will lead to more satisfying marital and family relations. There are instances, of course, when there is a particularly troublesome area, and the helper will have to intervene with an intensive technique. In the following sections, consideration will be given to the following problem areas, each of which seems to be especially prominent in marriage and family therapy: anxiety-provoking situations; obsessive-compulsive behaviors; heightened affect (positive and negative); and sexual preferences and variations.

ANXIETY-PROVOKING SITUATIONS

When a stimulus, such as a certain kind of situation between persons, strikes a vulnerable spot in the ego-structure of an individual, the functioning of the organism is disrupted by anxiety. Anxiety takes on a variety of forms, from mild stress that is easily dealt with, to fears that lead the person to avoid particular kinds of experiences (such as with phobias, in which the person fears a specific stimulus), to the transformation of anxiety into psychosomatic disorders, to a flooding of anxiety that leads to being oblivious to reality in panic or hysteric-like behavior. Many professionals assert that the one common dimension across all emotional conflicts and behavior problems is anxiety—this shows how critical the factor of anxiety is in human behavior.

Within the interpersonal relationships of marriage and the family, anxiety plays a critical role, and because of the camouflaged nature of anxiety, it is frequently unrecognized and other factors are seen as causing or maintaining the problems. An appropriate treatment objective, regardless of the problem and the primary goal, would be for the helper to aid the helpee recognize when his responses and/or behaviors are influenced–perhaps exaggerated– by anxiety, and then help him alleviate significantly or eliminate entirely the provocation power of the anxiety-evoking stimuli.

Systematic desensitization, one of the foremost behavioral modification procedures, is designed to counteract anxiety. Systematic desensitization is based on the reciprocal inhibition principle. Wolpe (1964) defines the reciprocal inhibition principle as follows:

> *if a response inhibitory of anxiety can be made to occur in the presence of anxiety-evoking stimuli it will weaken the bond between these stimuli and the anxiety* (p. 10).

In other words, if a person experiences anxiety or fear and can immediately induce a relaxed, comfortable feeling, the next time he encounters the stimulus that evoked the initial anxiety, it will be less powerful; and eventually repetition of this sequence causes this stimulus to lose its power to evoke a significant degree of anxiety.

To apply systematic desensitization to sexual, marital, and familial problems, the following is a step-by-step approach:

1. An examination should be made to determine what situations or stimuli lead a sexual partner, a spouse, or a family member to have anxiety. If the helpee experiences anxiety in several different kinds of situations, there should be a categorization, with all of the ingredients for each situation being identified.
2. The ingredients for each situation should be ranked by the helpee as to provocation power and a hierarchy developed; that is, a situation that provokes a small, but discomforting, degree of anxiety should be at the bottom of the hierarchy, a situation that provokes slightly more anxiety should be listed next, and so on progressively until the situation that produces the maximum amount of anxiety (which might even be panic) should be at the top of the list.
3. The helpee should be taught how to relax and induce a pleasant feeling upon need (to use to counteract the anxiety when it is evoked in the treatment).

4. The helpee should be led to experience (such as through imagination, verbal descriptions, pictures, or in actuality) the first step on the hierarchy, i.e., that step that produces a low-degree of anxiety, and as soon as he experiences anxiety, he should be told to relax and focus on a pleasant situation; after conjuring up relief from the anxiety, i.e. a pleasant feeling, he should be asked to refocus on the situation that previously provoked anxiety, and if he experiences anxiety on this trial, he again is told to relax. This process is repeated until the situation no longer evokes a significant amount of anxiety, and then the helpee can move up the hierarchy to the next level of fear-evoking stimuli; this level is treated as described until it no longer evokes anxiety, then the next step on the hierarchy is dealt with; this process is repeated until the entire hierarchy has been covered.

There are several points within the preceding method that should be made. First, *the hierarchy is not a fixed, static entity;* at any point, the helpee may want to reorder the stimuli, or add new ones, or eliminate some of the steps (often a step suddenly loses its anxiety-provoking status, apparently because desensitization to a lower-level stimulus has generalized to other stimuli as well). Second, *care must be taken to move progressively;* to have stimuli be greatly different in anxiety-provoking power could lead to an unnecessary and untherapeutic experiencing of anxiety, so caution should be exercised to assure a gradated sequence of anxiety. Third, although the reciprocal inhibition principle calls only for a pleasant situation to be conjured up to counteract the anxiety-evoking stimulus, research (which will be discussed in the last chapter) indicates that *the procedure can be complemented and made more efficacious by the helper's supplementing the relaxation procedure with purposeful clinical suggestions that the stimulus will be of less anxiety-evoking power the next time it is experienced.* Fourth, there is some question as to how much relaxation actually contributes to the process of systematic desensitization (as compared, for example, to the persuasion and clinical suggestions offered by the helper), but apparently *relaxation is an important part of the method and may even contribute to therapeutic change by itself via conditioning for musculature relaxation.* Fifth, *it may be necessary to have several hierarchies, and these too should be treated in a gradated manner;* that is, the hierarchy that seems less threatening should be dealt with first, and so on until the most threatening hierarchy is dealt with last, after all of the others have been successfully treated, thereby capitalizing on the confidence gained from having experienced success in overcoming other feared situations and on the possible generalization effects. Sixth, as mentioned, *there can be several ways of experiencing the anxiety-provoking stimuli,* such as verbal descriptions, mental images, pictures, and the actual situations or objects. As with the use of several hierarchies, it may be advisable, depending upon the helpee, to use a gradated approach to the different avenues of stimulus presentation; for example, it could be that for a given hierarchy the helpee would find talking about the anxiety-evoking stimuli less threatening than creating visual images, and both of these avenues might be less threatening than asking him actually to progressively experience the situations. This has been but a brief account of systematic desensitization; more extensive coverage of the theoretical and technical aspects may be found elsewhere (Lazarus, 1971; Wolpe, 1969; Wolpe and Lazarus, 1966; Woody, 1971).

Systematic desensitization can be applied to a host of sexual, marital, and familial problems. Two of the major types of problems are: social anxiety and sexual anxiety.

Social anxiety may be defined as an uncomfortable, fearful state that occurs in human interaction. Specifically, some persons feel uncomfortable when entering a group of unknown others or when talking to a person they perceive to be of a higher status than themselves. Sometimes this gets transformed into a phobia; for example, agorphobia, a fear of leaving one's home, is surprisingly present among housewives: while they may be able to leave the home with their husband or family and they may be able to go to selected (usually necessary) places, such as the grocery store, for the most part they remain at home indoors, believing that they could leave anytime they want to do so, but somehow never quite getting around to going out. Similarly, both males and females frequently end up altering their vocational and educational aspirations and their social interactions because of anxiety or fear associated with the relevant situations. It is easy to see how relations between a husband and wife could be disrupted if one of them hesitates, i.e. fears, doing something that the other wants or feels a need to do, e.g. socialization. Likewise, differences in values and secondary needs among family members can lead to certain members' feeling more pressure, i.e. more anxiety, than other members; and the consequence can be a lessening of their interpersonal relationships. Treatment, therefore, should root out sources of social anxiety, as might relate to marital and family relations. It can readily be said from an insight-oriented point of view that these kinds of anxiety reflect such ego factors as low self-esteem or a poor self-concept, and indeed this might be the case; but even this could be explained from a behavioral stance, namely, that the poor self-concept was due to ineffective social reinforcement previously. Thus insight-oriented counseling may provide a means for identifying much-needed sources of social reinforcement. Systematic desensitization can then be applied to the specific existing sources of anxiety (those sources that restrict successful interpersonal functioning), and other reinforcement techniques (such as positive reinforcement from a spouse) can be used to shape new, more rewarding social behaviors.

Sexual anxiety plays a prominent part in many marital problems. Of particular importance are: impotence in men and frigidity in females. These problem behaviors, although often unrecognized, are frequently the source of less than satisfactory sexual relations. In other words, full-blown clinical impotence and frigidity may be easily recognized because of the helpees' inability to be sexually responsive, but milder versions, in the form of sexual anxiety (perhaps rooted in discomfort from or fear of an intense emotional relationship, to be discussed later in this chapter), are typically more difficult to recognize and more difficult for the helpees involved to acknowledge.

Systematic desensitization has been exceptionally successful in cases of both impotence and frigidity. The approach, in brief, is to identify the series of sexual activities that the couple engages in, place them in a hierarchy (as described previously), have the couple begin to act out the situations at home, with the understanding that the moment the anxiety reaches a significant degree, they will cease the action and retreat to a nonthreatening, probably nonsexual, situation. A possible abbreviated hierarchy might be:

1. Sexual intercourse with light on;
2. Sexual intercourse in the dark;
3. Oral-genital activity with light on;
4. Oral-genital activity in the dark;
5. Being nude on the bed and petting;
6. Being nude on the bed and preparing to pet;
7. Undressing in bedroom, knowing that sexual activities will follow;
8. Walking up the stairway to the bedroom with the intention of having sexual relations;
9. Petting and kissing downstairs, knowing that this usually precedes sexual relations;
10. Exchanged signals, verbal or nonverbal, that sexual activities are desired.

This is a hypothetical list, but it parallels what is commonly created. In actuality, the list might be either more extensive or even briefer; and in all likelihood, it would be much more specific in terms of what the sexual actions would be, tailored, of course, to the persons involved. Treatment would start with the couple's identifying how they could induce a relaxed, anxiety-free state, and then with acting out the lowest level on the hierarchy; when they had become desensitized to this level, they would progress on to the next level, and so on. Obviously this approach requires a considerable amount of personal commitment from both parties, and it is not uncommon to find one of the partners having difficulty cooperating; usually this occurs when the partner who presumably is free from the problem becomes sexually excited and resents having to cease the sexual activities and regress to a nonanxious situation. While one can appreciate the sexual frustration that the presumably problem-free partner might experience, the mutual cooperation is tantamount to success, and the helper must emphatically convey this importance. In these instances, counseling about why the frustration cannot be tolerated should be provided. Incidentally, the refusal to cooperate, as might be expected, is frequently due to alienation from or hostility toward the partner, and this might necessitate therapeutic attention before the systematic desensitization can be applied. Alternatives to having a cooperative partner or spouse are: (1) the helper can attempt to treat the individual with the problem via imagery (combined with clinical suggestions that he can overcome the problem) instead of actually acting out the steps on the hierarchy; and (2) some helpers believe that it is appropriate to arrange for a surrogate partner, that is, have the helpee practice the sexual acts in the systematic desensitization format with someone other than a spouse, e.g. a prostitute (the ethical factors in this practice are obviously not clear-cut, and must be reconciled by each helper). This systematic desensitization approach is quite compatible with the currently "in vogue" services provided by Masters and Johnson (1970). Their treatment approach capitalizes on systematic desensitization, as well as on development of sensory awareness (but the latter is restricted to sensing and not acting out initially, thereby allowing for a desensitization to the potentially fear-evoking elements to occur before the couple enters into higher-order sexual activities).

Systematic desensitization in general and behavioral rehearsal in specific (the latter following a gradated hierarchy of roles to be rehearsed) have proven to be highly effective with a wide range of forms of social and sexual anxiety. Incidentally, it might also be noted that: (1) these techniques can be applied to individuals or in groups; (2) while the hierarchy should typically be tailor-made for the helpee involved, a helper experienced in systematic desensitization can create a standardized hierarchy for a given problem that will be applicable to almost everyone experiencing that problem; and (3) the hierarchy of scenes can be video taped for effective, controlled presentation (Woody and Schauble, 1969a, 1969b).

OBSESSIVE-COMPULSIVE BEHAVIORS

Many marriages and families seem to be disturbed by obsessive-compulsive behaviors. Commonly one member of the family has a behavior that the others find aggravating, such as smoking constantly and dropping the ashes on the floor, excessive alcohol consumption, over-eating and becoming obese, requiring everything to be in order around the house and cleaning even when it does not merit it, and on and on. While family members may be prone to explain the problem as "that's just one of his eccentric qualities," the behavior continues and negates the best possible degree of interpersonal relations. Moreover, the person with the obsessive-compulsive behavior often does not like it either, such as the person who recognizes drinking alcohol leads to emotional distance from his spouse and family but still cannot keep from indulging, or recognizes that over-eating leads to obesity and that an unattractive physical appearance "turns off" his spouse but the eating cannot be controlled. What may be labeled "eccentric" or "aggravating" by the layman can be termed "maladaptive approach responses" by the behaviorally-oriented professional. In other words, the helpee is drawn to a stimulus (such as an object or an act) that does not produce any benefit and indeed may produce destructive effects, but he cannot control the impulse and goes along with the compelling tendency.

From the onset it must be recognized that obsessive-compulsive behaviors represent probably the most difficult to treat set of problems encountered by a professional helper. Without doubt, an alcoholic, a drug user (even the drugs which are not physically addictive), a chain-smoker, an over-eater, and representatives of comparable obsessive-compulsive acts, do not readily respond to treatment by permanently ceasing the maladaptive behavior. Behavioral modification techniques, however, have been quite successful, at least as would be relative to other available techniques (such as those within the insight-oriented approaches to therapy).

Obsessive thoughts are often disturbing to an individual. When this is present within marital therapy, the helpees seem to reveal a tendency toward recurring thoughts that provoke guilt and feelings of inadequacy. While an elaborate set of psychodynamic hypotheses for this would be possible, the important point for this discussion is that behavioral interventions can eliminate them. Wolpe and Lazarus (1966) describe a "thought-stopping" technique, where the patient is instructed to shout-out (or at least think emphatically) "STOP!" whenever the plaguing thought comes to mind. They acknowledge that this is a clinical technique and that its applicability to everyone with recurring thoughts has not been validated.

Clinical hypnosis has been successfully used for the elimination of obsessive-compulsive behaviors, whether they be thoughts or acts. Here too there is some question as to whether the technique is suited for everyone, and moreover there is even question as to whether the so-called "hypnotic trance" actually exists or whether it is merely a state of self-induced readiness to accept suggestions from oneself or a therapist (Barber, 1969). In any case, clinical hypnosis may be defined as follows:

> Hypnosis refers to the state in which the client has achieved a degree of relaxation and confidence to allow him to relegate a limited command-of-ego functioning to the counselor-therapist, who alters his habituated behaviors, whether attitudinal or acting-out, by offering suggestions designed to benefit the client and derived from the counselor-therapist's clinical appraisal of the client's functioning and needs (Woody, 1971, p. 85).

It is important to note that there is a relationship between suggestions and hypnosis, but there are also differences:

> Clinical suggestion is a specific technique that is separate from, but related to, hypnosis. It is not hypnosis in and of itself; in other words, when a counselor-therapist makes a suggestion based on clinical evidence to his client, he is not practicing "hypnosis." Therefore, a counselor-therapist could make subtle, planned, clinically-derived suggestions, following the conditioning principles, as a means of modifying his client's behavior without fearing that he is practicing "black magic" or without opening himself to the misconceptions about highly-trained professionals who use hypnosis clinically. There is reason to believe that if these suggestions are offered to the client when he is relaxed, the effects might be enhanced. Thus, induced relaxation and clinical suggestions can be combined, and, if they are carried to a certain point on the continuum (which is different to each client), the procedure evolves into hypnosis (Woody, 1971, pp. 85-86).

The point in making this distinction is that some helpees will probably respond to straightforward suggestions from the helper and will alter their obsessive-compulsive behavior—and this technique should probably be tried initially with all problems—but for those helpees who are resistant to or cannot change from clinical suggestions, the helper should be prepared to offer a truly hypnotic approach, one that purposefully induces relaxation and presumably a heightened state of suggestibility, and to posit suggestions. Hartland (1967) offers guidelines for formulating clinical suggestions, and he sets forth a technique called "Ego Strengthening," which purportedly treats many problems, including obsessive-compulsive ones, via giving hypnotic suggestions that the helpee can overcome certain inadequacies; he explains the success of the ego-strengthening technique in terms of the person's ego gaining needed buttressing from the suggestions that have special power because of the hypnotic state (Hartland, 1965). It should be noted that such hypnotic techniques as these have not consistently proved to be efficacious; apparently, this is due in part to differences in psychological characteristics between helpees and due in part to differences in appreciation of and skill with hypnotic procedures between helpers.

Closely related to clinical hypnosis is the technique called "covert sensitization." Cautela (1967) has been a primary proponent of covert sensitization, which he explains as follows:

> It is called "covert" because neither the undesirable stimulus nor the aversive stimulus is actually presented. These stimuli are presented in imagination only. The word "sensitization" is used because the purpose of the procedure is to build up an avoidance response to the undesirable stimulus (p. 459).

This technique has purportedly proved to be successful in treating such maladaptive approach responses as homosexuality, alcoholism, stealing, and various forms of obsessions and compulsions. In brief, the technique of covert sensitization progresses as follows:

1. The helper induces a state of relaxation and heightened suggestibility in the helpee;
2. The helpee conjures up an image of himself progressing through a sequence of behaviors that lead up to performing the maladaptive approach response (the helper facilitates this imagery by verbally describing the scenes in as vivid and realistic manner as possible); and
3. When the act is performed in imagery, the helper describes noxious consequences, such as social condemnation, and then describes a pleasant feeling of relief as the helpee imagines distancing himself from the unacceptable stimulus.

For example, the helper might describe the alcoholic entering a bar, and as the helpee visualizes this scene, the helper would progressively describe in detail the actions leading up to the first drink of alcohol. When this happened he would visualize himself vomiting all over himself, the bartender, and persons near him in the bar, and experience their ridicule of him, with relief coming only after he has left the bar and breathed in fresh air with a conviction that he will not drink again. And with the homosexual, behavior leading up to overt homosexual acting out would be described and as the homosexual activity started, a feeling of revulsion would be created (such as vomiting on the partner's genitals). This technique obviously has certain properties strikingly similar to clinical hypnosis, as there is a distinct attempt to capitalize on the suggestibility of the helpee, but it is a conditioning procedure in that efforts are directed at reinforcing an expectation of negative consequences from the maladaptive approach response. As with numerous other clinical techniques, both behavioral and insight, covert sensitization has not proved to be useful with all helpees, but it does seem to be effective with at least some persons, with the success depending upon the motivation for therapy held by the helpee and the clinical expertise of the helper.

Negative practice is another technique used for obsessive-compulsive behaviors, but it should be noted immediately that the technique has proven to be totally unpredictable as to whether it will eliminate the problem or whether it will actually cause the unacceptable behavior to occur more often. At one point or another in its history, negative practice has supposedly cured almost every imaginable problem, but in each problem area there seem to be more failures than successes—but this is an opinion (there is little research to provide documentation). The idea of the technique is that the helpee is required to repeat the unacceptable behavioral act over and over until he is bored, fatigued, and no longer getting any satisfaction from the act; the extreme repetition of the act, resulting in its taking on strong negative properties, theoretically extinguishes the act from the helpee's repertoire of preferred behaviors, and the behavior becomes associated with unpleasant outcomes. In practice, the helper would assign or require the helpee to repeat the undesirable behavior over and over, not just until it became boring but until it became definitely unpleasant. The classic example is the situation in which a teacher makes a child caught throwing paper-wads make hundreds more and painstakingly toss them, one by one, into a wastebasket (hopefully after school hours and alone in order that there would be no social recognition reward from peers). Thus the overly fastidious housewife would polish the same table for hours, the profane husband would relentlessly say a list of profane words, etc. Because of its sporadic and unpredictable efficacy, it seems illogical to recommend this technique for any specific problem. On the other hand, the rationale is seemingly sound in terms of theory and there have been just enough clinical successes to support that negative practice should be at least considered when evolving a behavioral modification treatment plan.

Aversion therapy is a most promising, yet somewhat distasteful, procedure. It is promising in that it apparently treats successfully numerous problems that are not amenable by other techniques, and it is somewhat distasteful in that it involves the inflicting of pain or discomfort on the helpee. The following is a brief description:

> Aversive therapy employs unpleasant stimuli as both negative reinforcement and punishment. When the client performs the undesirable act, the aversive stimulus is administered and continues until the client stops doing the undesirable act. Thus, the reward comes when the aversive stimulus is stopped, i.e. when the problem behavior (the undesirable act) has stopped, and has been replaced by other, acceptable acts. The client is also conditioned to expect punishment when an unacceptable situation arises. The aversive stimulus is usually a mild electric shock, an unpleasant noise, or an emetic. (Note that the electric shock is very mild, and is not electroconvulsive therapy.) (Woody, 1971, pp. 96-97).

This is a capsule description, but more extensive coverage is available elsewhere (Rachman and Teasdale, 1969; Marks, 1968). To take a few examples: each time the alcoholic takes a drink of liquor, he is given an emetic to make him vomit or is given a mild electric shock—until such time as he felt no attraction to alcohol; the chain-smoker would be free to smoke, but an electric shock would be administered each time he inhaled–until he reached the point at which he might light a cigarette and never quite get around to smoking it and eventually until he would not even light one.

It should be noted that one of the alternatives for this technique, and one that allows for the helper to dismiss any philosophical qualms he has about administering pain or discomfort, i.e. the aversive stimulus, to a helpee, is to allow the helpee to become his own aversion therapist; that is, there are small portable shock-boxes (which operate off of a pen-light battery) which the helpee carries with him, and as he finds himself performing the undesirable act, he administers mild (but strong enough to be unpleasant) electric shocks to himself. The one limitation with this alternative is keeping the helpee motivated, because it is fairly common for a person to back out of his plan, if he is left totally autonomous, as the self-administered treatment becomes unpleasant. The helper's role in this case is to consult with the helpee about keeping an appropriate reinforcement schedule and to reinforce the helpee's wish to rid himself of the problem.

Aversion therapy has, as mentioned, been successful in treating problems that other techniques fail to change, and it has been particularly effective with chronic sexual deviations (or variations), alcoholism, smoking, drug addiction, and social withdrawal. Because of its applicability to sexual problems, aversion therapy will receive additional coverage in the subsequent section on sexual preferences and variations. Suffice it to say, aversion techniques can be applied to a variety of behaviors that occur in sexual, marital, and familial relations. For example, the helpee could pinpoint behaviors that he does, perhaps of an obsessive-compulsive nature, that disrupt his marital or familial relations, and set about to eliminate their occurrence, either by having the helper present him with provocative stimuli and administer the aversive condition or by a self-administered aversion program. A popular magazine recently cited a British press release that described how one husband sought aversion therapy from a British therapist for purposes of developing an aversion to his mistress (who was presumably leading him to be dissatisfied with his marriage) and developing a positive reaction, via conditioning, to his wife. This may seem like a simplistic, even facile, approach to dealing with a marital problem, but some helpees may choose to pursue this kind of treatment format, albeit the "easy way out" for some cases.

To summarize, obsessive-compulsive behaviors are frequently found within poor marriage and family relations. While it is simple to pass over these behaviors in the name of eccentricity, the fact that they do "grate on the nerves" of the spouse or family members and are often distasteful even to the person doing them, more than justifies special consideration in sexual-marital-familial therapy. Behavioral modification, as illustrated in the foregoing techniques, encompasses the resources to deal effectively with these kinds of problems. Finally, in working with obsessive-compulsive behaviors, the helper should remember that such behaviors, even though not preferred by others, are often consciously or unconsciously reinforced; thus, care should be exercised to eliminate the undesired reinforcement contingencies.

HEIGHTENED AFFECT

Until they have become totally disillusioned with their efforts to form rewarding interpersonal relationships, probably all human beings would profess to want love and other positive feelings from others. Unfortunately, the reality of the situation is that there are many persons who are unable to accept heightened affect, even if it is positive. Whether this inability is explained by psychodynamic theories or by behaviorism, the fact remains that this inability to handle heightened affect leads some persons into all sorts of disturbed, frequently illogical, behaviors that produce poor interpersonal relations. Further, what is "heightened" affect is a relative matter; what may seem like mild emotion to one person might seem like an intolerably threatening emotion to another. There is, therefore, no way to establish a general baseline for assessing the degree or intensity of affect with marital and familial relations; it must be deduced from the idiosyncratic perceptual set of each person involved.

Intimacy

Intimacy provides probably the most basic affective dimension in marriage and family relations. The essence of familial relations and the relationship between a husband and wife is that the persons involved will interact in an intimate fashion, unmatched in degrees of openness and caring by any other relationship ever experienced. An analysis of unhappy marriages and families often reveals that one (or more) of the persons involved demonstrates gross uneasiness, to say the least, about intimacy in the relationship.

It is interesting to note that many of the exercises used in encounter and/or sensitivity groups, done in the name of humanistic treatment, are directed toward getting the participants to try out and experience new kinds of intimacy. For example, they might be asked to write out and share with each other what they would have accomplished if they "controlled the other fully for one day." A behaviorist might look at these so-called humanistic exercises and point to the conditioning elements: typically the participants are asked to try exercises in sharing and experiencing that are of a low-order intimate or affective nature and to progress to more intense ones. From the behavioral point of view, this is the process of teaching the persons, in learning theory terms, how to experience intimacy, sharing, or other affective ventures; in a true hierarchical procedure they are becoming systematically desensitized and are building up an ability to handle higher-order intimate or affective situations as the stimuli lose their anxiety-provocation power and as the participants are reinforced, particularly through social recognition, for behaving in the designated intimate-affective manner. Parenthetically, the assertion that conditioning elements are present in encounter group exercises is further supported in a recent system of structured exercises offered by Russell (1971), in which the humanistic exercises are prescribed according to the chronological sequence of the life of the group.

Dependence/Independence

Closely paralleling intimacy as a critical basic dimension in family relationships is the concept of dependence/independence. Within marriages and families, members are expected to be both dependent on each other and to accept the dependence demonstrated toward them. But conversely, human nature leads each person to want a certain amount of independence, in the name of maintaining personal self-identity, and this means that there will be a tendency to push away from each other and consequently away from dependency from others. Combine these dependency/independency needs with a unique developmental history where the spouses or family members have learned to trust or distrust, as a result of their childhood relations and subsequent experiences, and it is not at all surprising that many marriages and families with problems reveal an ever-present difficulty in handling dependence/independence.

Treatment

What the foregoing two concepts suggest is that marriage and family therapy should examine the helpees' ability to handle or fulfill the requirements of intimacy and dependency/independency within their marital or familial network. Exploration and elaboration of these concepts can lead to increased insight and a recognition of what behaviors need to be reinforced in order for relations to improve, i.e. be more rewarding. Therefore, while the initial consideration of intimacy and dependency/independency takes on definite insight-oriented properties, the objective is to define in behavioral terms what needs to be altered; and the techniques used, even if they are sensitivity-type exercises, can be distinctively behavioral.

The first step in heightening appropriate affect is to cultivate an acceptance, hopefully by both spouses or all involved family members, that the affects identified as needing special attention deserve a commitment from them. This means a preparation for change in these affective areas and a dedication, albeit to varying degrees among the spouses or family members, to altering the affective states.

From the commitment stage, the couple or family members should be taught how to apply the basic principles of reinforcement. Of particular importance, as described earlier in this chapter, each person should strive to be able to recognize the reinforcement contingencies that are operating within the marital or familial relations, and to develop a set that will accommodate: (1) identifying the class of response emitted by another person; (2) immediately and accurately deciding whether that response should be reinforced, such as by a positive reaction; and (3) consistently responding positively to those affective response classes that are to be increased or heightened and withholding any response to those affective response classes that should be eliminated or decreased in frequency of occurrence.

As stated previously, encounter or sensitivity exercises are designed to stimulate, particularly in a sensual fashion. The helper can prescribe various techniques from this rubric, with the plan being to select techniques that will be directed at specified target affective factors and that will progressively lead to a better handling and use of affective responses. There is also the alternative of having the couple or family members participate in an encounter/sensitivity group experience. This alternative, however, introduces several questions, such as: Would it be preferable, because of the existing psychodynamics and behavioral patterns, for the couple or family to make use of encounter/sensitivity techniques within their own constellation or would it be preferable to have them involved in such experiences with outsiders? And if the latter is preferred, the question must be asked: Should the couple (or family) participate together in an encounter/sensitivity group or should they participate individually in separate groups (the implication being the participation together with outsiders would potentially provoke different feelings than participation on an individual basis, such as feeling more threatened by having to share their spouse with another person in an affective encounter)? The third possibility is to allow the couple or family to explore the effects of encounter/sensitivity techniques in essentially an unsupervised, undirected manner. For example, there are numerous audio taped experiential programs on the market that allow a couple to listen to a cassette tape recording for guidance through a series of encounter/sensitivity exercises designed to increase mutual awareness and appreciation; and there is a variety of "do-it-yourself" books or manuals on the market that, like the audio taped programs, describe how to make use of encounter/sensitivity exercises. Within each of these encounter/sensitivity alternatives, the helper is faced with the ethical responsibility of assessing potential benefits or detriments of such experiences. It is only logical that he would not prescribe any exercise–whether he implements it or it is a do-it-yourself procedure or it is an experience succinctly out-side his services–which he cannot justify according to psycholog-ical/sociological/behavioral information gleaned from his clini-cal vantage point. Therefore, at this point in time, the popularity of sensitivity exercises and their seeming potential benefits (for at least some persons) require that professional helpers have a thor-ough orientation to encounter/sensitivity techniques, thorough enough to allow them to make a learned judgment about their ap-plicability (regardless of who applies the techniques) to the per-sons whom they serve. Likewise, the helper should be familiar with the other professionals who might be involved with his helpees on a temporary basis, such as encounter group leaders from whom his helpees might seek a one-time encounter group experience. Part of his professional responsibility would be to offer an opinion on the qualifications of a particular group leader and the clinical advis-ability of participating in such an experience. Parenthetically, some encounter/sensitivity group leaders assume the position that their experiences are "non-therapeutic," and that since they are "self-development" or "educational" in nature, there is no reason why any person, regardless of personality or characteristics, should not participate in them and no reason why they should communi-cate their involvement with the participants to any other profes-sional helper working with the persons on an ongoing basis. This kind of posture is, of course, what leads some professionals to avoid and/or denounce encounter/sensitivity activities, because it seems evident, from the professional's point of view, that such powerful intervening experiences like encounter/sensitivity groups cannot be blindly applied, must be offered to persons who have been carefully screened to ascertain that the experience will prob-ably be beneficial, and must be provided by a leader who has ade-quate preparation for the handling of human behavior–even if the activity is not labeled "therapeutic" as such. The next chapter will give extensive consideration to the use of encounter/sensitivi-ty experiences (see Chapter Six).

Assertive practice and behavioral rehearsal, both techniques in which the persons act out prescribed roles and progressively work toward greater degrees of affective interaction, are suitable for improving a person's tolerance for and ability to appropriately use heightened affect. Through these techniques, the person vicariously experiences the affect and in the process learns alternative ways to react and feel and, moreover, becomes desensitized to elements that might have previously provoked excessive anxiety or undue reactions, such as defensiveness. Thus, a helpee might use assertive practice and/or behavioral rehearsal to become better able to cope with his spouse or family members.

Similarly, clinical suggestions can lead to more effective functioning in affective situations. The hypnosis format is especially appropriate, because the helpee is consciously indicating that he wishes to change, that he will focus on the target affect, that he will explore alternative behavioral responses, that he believes the so-called "trance state" will increase the probability that his responses will be altered, and that he attributes change-power to the helper to whom he is, at least nominally, relinquishing a significant degree of ego control.

In making use of assertive practice, behavioral rehearsal, clinical suggestions, and hypnosis, the approach is one of: (1) identifying the behaviors relevant to the critical affective areas; (2) experiencing vicariously, either through acting out or highly focused visual imagery, the affects (to become desensitized to stimuli that previously evoked inappropriate anxiety and to enlarge their repertoire of ways to behave in affective situations); and (3) having the helper capitalize upon his professional status and power of persuasion for the offering of suggestions relevant to convincing the helpee that he can–in fact–feel and respond differently, such as by enjoying rather than fearing certain affective interactions with a spouse or family members. These techniques can be confined to therapy sessions, but the ultimate goal is to have adaptations made in daily interactions and it seems advisable to attempt to move these techniques to outside-the-session activities as soon as is feasible. Specifically, couples or families should be encouraged to explore new affective styles at home, but to do so in a carefully planned, progressive fashion.

Audio and video tape recordings constitute an important method for developing more desirable affective experiences. In Chapter

Three, Schauble elaborated on numerous relevant issues, but a be-havioral reiteration and extension seems appropriate. The basic premise is that a tape recording of a segment of interaction, such as a portion of the therapy session or a discussion at home or an as-signed problem-solving discussion, can be played back and this will provoke a reliving of the experience which, in turn, can be used to increase understanding of the psychodynamics and reinforcing properties and to facilitate efforts to find new ways for responding. There are three general approaches to the use of audio and video tape recordings: interpersonal process recall, affect simulation, and recorded vicarious desensitization.

Interpersonal process recall (IPR) involves the tape recording of a counseling or therapy session. Following the session, an "in-terrogator," who might be the same helper, e.g. counselor-therapist, or a second helper, plays the recording of the session back to the helpee and leads him into exploring what went on in the session. The interrogation procedure prepares the helpee by acknowledging that when people interact, such as the helpee with the helper or a spouse with a spouse, there is the observable response but underly-ing it may be a covert response, such as a feeling or thought that was not voiced, and that by placing himself back in the scene via the recording, the helpee can not only reexperience the session but can also explore the interaction to a more refined or sophisticated degree. Thus the recording is played back, and the tape is stopped at any point the interrogator or the helpee suspects that something significant occurred, be it voiced or not. The helper and the helpee explore the possible meaning, covert and overt, of verbal com-ments, facial expressions, body movements, and gestures. A more thorough theoretical and technical description may be found else-where (Kagan, Schauble, Resnikoff, Danish and Krathwohl, 1969; Woody, 1971); of special relevance to this discussion are the de-scriptions of a comparable method used in the context of marital and family therapy (Alger and Hogan, 1967, 1969).

Affect simulation evolved from the interpersonal process recall method. Affect simulation involves the use of confrontive vignet-tes. An audio or video tape of professional or lay actors is created that presents scenes designed to stimulate intense degrees of feelings, e.g. hostility, affection, fear of hostility, and fear of affection. For a given affect, several degrees of intensity are recorded; for example, if feelings related to seduction were the target, the first scene would have an actor talking seductively but in a low-keyed or mild manner, while in the next scene he would be a bit stronger in his seductive comments and behavior, and in the next scene he would be even more seductive and so on. Therefore, a helper: (1) would diagnose the critical types of affect for his help-ee; (2) would develop or obtain commercially developed stimulus materials, i.e. audio or video recordings of a hierarchy of scenes relevant to the critical affect; (3) would present a simulated affective scene to the helpee; and (4) would explore with him his feelings and response repertoire. The objective is, of course, to desensitize the helpee to unnecessary or disturbing feelings, to gain insight into why he feels or responds the way he does in related situations, and to attain more effective ways to deal with interactions or situations that involve this type of affect. Any helpee might need to have stimulus materials directed at several types of affect, but in some cases, a generalization effect is possible; i.e. a person becomes able to handle effectively heightened affect of one type, and through the conditioning process also becomes able to better handle another type of affect as well. The affect simulation method is described in greater detail elsewhere (Kagan and Schauble, 1969; Woody, 1971).

Recorded vicarious desensitization involves the audio or video taping of scenes devoted to a target affect and presenting these recorded stimuli in the hierarchical fashion used in the systematic desensitization format. There are several distinguishing features for this method. It allows the helper to make use of standardized stimuli, thereby controlling the intensity of the stimuli for all helpees. It is adaptable to individual or group treatment. And, like the affect simulation method, it allows for an element of social modeling; that is, the helpee can typically identify with the persons in the recording who are effectively handling their affect. This method is described in detail elsewhere (Woody and Schauble, 1969b). It should be noted that research on the video taped vicarious desensitization method revealed that the desensitization process can be optimally effective if the respite from anxiety-evoking stimuli, i.e. the relaxation period, is augmented with purposeful, systematically given clinical suggestions that the person can overcome his maladaptive reaction to the stimulus and that he can find reward from a more appropriate reaction (Woody and Schauble, 1969a).

Social modeling is a concept intrinsic to interpersonal process recall, affect simulation, and recorded vicarious desensitization. Indeed, it could probably be labeled a technique in and of itself, but clinical efficacy seems best accommodated when it is made a component of a broader treatment procedure, such as these three audio or video tape recording techniques. In brief, social modeling involves the helpee identifying with the actions of another and modifying his personal response style because of the consequences witnessed for the other person's actions. For example, a couple watching a filmed segment of another couple interacting in a certain manner would be apt to adopt some of the filmed behavior if the other couple's interaction led to a positive, rewarding outcome, whereas if the other couple's interaction led to a negative consequence, they would be less apt to adopt that behavioral pattern. When using social modeling as a relatively discrete treatment modality, the helpee is exposed to behaviors of people who are fairly similar to him but who have a higher status (which serves as a motivator to model after them) and a more rewarding or more appropriate behavioral response style. Thus, the helpee is influenced progressively to alter his behaviors to be similar to the more effective behaviors of the social models. The models may be presented via audio or video tape recordings or via films (which could be specially prepared or could be carefully selected commercial films), or they could be encountered through assigned real-life experiences. Again, the brevity imposed by the purposes of this text restricts a thorough discussion; more extensive information on social modeling may be found elsewhere (Bandura, 1965, 1969).

To summarize, audio and video tape recordings can provide a highly effective vehicle for gaining insight into the psychodynamic and behavioral aspects of responses, for becoming desensitized to affective stimuli that have previously provoked unnecessary, inappropriate, or detrimental anxiety-ladened reactions, and for developing an enlarged repertoire of behavioral responses or coping behaviors. While either audio or video tape recordings may be used, video tape recordings, because of the greater vividness, seem to be more powerful than audio tape recordings.

SEXUAL PREFERENCES AND VARIATIONS

Sexuality constitutes one of the most frequent contributory sources to marital and familial discord. A person who has sexual frustrations or conflicts, such as guilt, can easily find himself lacking responsiveness to a spouse, family members, or outsiders. Moreover, because of the sensitive nature of sexuality, it often becomes the scapegoat for other problems (when a presumed sexual problem is explored in therapy, it is not uncommon to find that sexual relations are the effect, not the cause). Such situations are further complicated since sexuality is too often treated with "kid-gloves" instead of being dealt with directly.

A person's expressed views relevant to sexuality often do not reflect his true feelings or beliefs. That is, everyone is brought up in a society that literally prescribes that certain sexual acts are unacceptable and others, while not talked about, are at least given tacit approval. This is clearly evidenced in laws related to homosexuality, where society makes it illegal for two consenting adults to engage in homosexual acts (and society goes so far as to assign policemen to roles where they pretend to be homosexuals, such as in parks and public toilets, for purposes of luring someone with a homosexual preference into acting out so that they can be arrested). Likewise, some religious doctrines essentially relegate all sexual acts, even between spouses, to a state of being tolerated but not endorsed. Many persons carry over into adulthood a child's views of sexuality as "right" or "wrong" as gleaned from parental opinions and reactions; added to these perceptions are also certain misperceptions due to childhood distortion. If childhood perceptions and misperceptions never get assessed and integrated into the value system of a unique adult, one may mechanically attempt to live according to a set of beliefs that are not applicable or appropriate to his adult situation.

As might be assumed, approaching the issue of sexual preferences in marital and/or family counseling-therapy necessitates that consideration be given to exactly what are the beliefs, the morals, and the values of the persons involved. As mentioned, all too often what is professed to be beliefs actually are the illogically conceived or inaccurately perceived sets of beliefs, morals, and values of other persons, typically society in general or their parents in particular. Thus the basic therapeutic task is the identification of an idiosyncratic set of attitudes toward sexuality and then the adaptation of the individual's manifest behaviors to this set.

The term "variation" is used in the heading for this section purposefully to avoid the term "deviation" and to connote that a certain sexual act may be but a variation of a more basic sexual preference. In other words, the concept of "deviation" implies a view or act that is not in accord with the majority; it is, therefore, relative to a much larger entity than the person. In developing effective, rewarding relationships, particularly in a marriage, the objective should be two-fold. First, there obviously has to be some consideration given to the concept of deviation, because to manifest certain sexual behaviors that violate laws or the rights of other individuals cannot be considered appropriate from either the point of view of society or the long-range satisfaction of the individual. And second, the major objective for treatment should be the development of an individualized sexual set that, while not conflicting with societal norms to the point of illegality or infringement on others outside the marriage, allows for optimal sexual fulfillment for the sexual partners involved. For example, a couple should strive to find what sexual acts will best express what sexual relations are designed to convey; this will usually be several "messages," because sexual relations between a husband and wife may satisfy a primary sexual drive, but they may also communicate certain types of affect, such as attraction, appreciation, love, and commitment.

The initial step in the provision of therapy for sexually-related matters is, in a sense, exploration. The basic objective is to simply get the involved persons, e.g. the husband and wife, to talk about sexual issues as a way of: (1) creating a sharing of the emotional concomitants associated with sexuality; (2) identifying the sexual preferences and how they came into being; and (3) fostering a motivation to achieve agreement about sex within the relationship. The attainment of this objective is highly reliant upon the professional helper's communicating to the helpees a healthy, open, supportive attitudinal tone.

One of the most amazing things is how often seemingly sexually sophisticated persons, often with a fairly wide range of sexual experiences, know very little about sexuality *per se* and are greatly restricted, perhaps even constricted, in their sexual beliefs and related behaviors. Therefore, the rudimentary level of counseling-therapy for sexual problems should focus on the dissemination of information. This level is quite behavioral in the sense that learning theory is being relied upon to expand the person's knowledge of and appreciation for the sexual ramifications of a relationship.

Implicit in this informational stage is the emphasis on the relationship; that is, if the sexuality is to be maximally beneficial, sexual acts between persons, such as a husband and wife, must be expressive of true feelings, the feelings that are the structure for the relationship. Without doubt there are elements within most, if not all, marriage relations that would result in sexual acts being destructive if allowed to be the communication mode. In other words, there are instances where a couple will use their sexual behavior to reflect their negative feelings toward each other, such as a spouse who will not be responsive. This destructive use of sexuality may be conscious, but often it is unconscious; for example, the spouse who cannot achieve an orgasm during sexual intercourse may be doing so because of intense anxiety about sex (perhaps because of illogically conceived sexual attitudes) or because of unacknowledged negative feelings about the sexual partner. Obviously these negative feelings must be uncovered and recognized, and other means of manifesting them must be decided upon, with sexual relations being kept as an expression of positive feelings.

To summarize the informational level, this can be accomplished via exploratory discussion, with the helper providing information about sexuality in almost a didactic fashion, or via assigned readings or experiences (e.g. attending sexually-oriented movies and discussing them subsequently with the helper).

If the informational stage can lead to a mutual awareness of the partners' sexual attitudes, it should be possible to move to the stage of reciprocal agreement about what sexual acts should be used for and what alternatives in behaviors can accomplish these needs. Specifically, it is not uncommon to find that sexual acts are confined to a few variations in behaviors, and that an expanded range of sexual acts would greatly enhance communication and the relationship. Again, merely providing information about sexual variations may improve the sexual relations. Moreover, discussion of sexual variations provides a means for alleviating unnecessary guilt associated with a certain sexual act; for example, the quest to enrich sexual relations might feasibly mean, for a given couple, including extensive petting, sexualized verbal expressions, masturbation, sexual intercourse, oral-genital sexual activity, and possibly even variations that involve objects or materials, such as a vibrator for genital stimulation, pornographic pictures, provocative garments, and items with a fetish-like appeal. While everyone need not feel that this entire range of sexual variations is necessary, it does seem logical to believe that everyone could benefit from giving open-minded consideration to what each variation could potentially contribute to their sexual relations. Too often, sexual preferences are repressed or suppressed and sexual variations that could lead to personal and interpersonal gratification are avoided or denied in the name of propriety or morality.

In the previous discussion of increasing sensuality and heightened affect, it was noted that there were encounter/sensitivity techniques that had implications for sexual problems; for example, Masters and Johnson (1970) make use of these techniques in a desensitization framework when treating couples with problems in sexual responsiveness. These techniques may be of value in initiating change in sexual actions.

After sexual preferences and potentially rewarding variations have been delineated, it is appropriate to encourage the persons to try out certain variations (those that seem to have the potential of contributing gratification). The helper's role should be one of advisement on behavioral contexts and actions, and guidance in planning a systematic, gradated approach, one that will not frighten or abuse either of the sexual partners.

At this point, it is important to reemphasize that the concept of deviation, with its connotation of unacceptability, is relative. It is particularly dependent upon a societal frame of reference and is cogent to public acts but of little relevance to private acts. Therefore, it might be asserted that *any form of private sexual activity between consenting adults should not be labeled deviant and should be viewed as an idiosyncratic expression or variation.*

Also before proceeding further, it should be reemphasized that many sexual limitations within relationships are rooted in lack of information, ill-formed or illogical attitudes, and conditioned responses. As mentioned earlier, the simple action of providing information about the physiological, psychological, and sociological aspects of sexuality, combined with an opportunity for partners to ventilate sexual feelings with each other, will provide many couples with the means to improve their sexual relations. Elaboration and clarification of how their attitudes and expressive modes were settled upon will provide further opportunity to enhance their sexual relations.

Identification of habituated sexual behaviors and the deriving of rewarding alternatives can also circumvent an out-and-out therapeutic intervention. In regard to the latter, it is not uncommon to hear how couples respond differently in special situations, as compared to their sexual responses in their everyday environment; for example, couples, because of the closeness of their living quarters and the interruptions caused by the children, have been known to rent a motel room on an occasional weekend night only a few miles from their home and have sexual relations there that far exceed their performances at home. Therefore, in accord with this same principle (and without the cost of a motel room!), the helper should encourage couples to find alternative conditions for their sexual acts within their normal life space. For example, some couples limit their sexual relations to the nighttime, and switching to the daytime provides sexual excitation; some remain partially clothed, whereas nudity might increase the excitation; some find that sexual relations outdoors, if conditions are private enough, adds a special degree of excitation; and the number of augmenting circumstances is unlimited. The point is that people all too often get into an established routine or "rut," and a quick and easy means to bringing more rewarding relations into a marriage is for the helper to aid the couple in structuring for themselves a more flexible, free-wheeling, id-expressive approach to the situational context for sexual activities, rather than remaining in the non-gratifying, boring (but seemingly safe) routinized activities: *flexibility, expressiveness, and creativity should be guidelines.*

The principle of desensitization is extremely important to the efforts to develop more rewarding sexual relations. Most prominent is the task of expanding the range of sexual activities for purposes of allowing optimally appropriate behavioral expression of the affective elements of the relationship. Since *human behavior is so often governed to a significant extent by personal values and behavioral habits that have been propagandized into existence and perpetuated by misperceptions of sources of ego support,* it is to be expected that many marital and familial relations will be more reflective of past influences from others, often in the abstract (such as society and the church), than of the true personal needs and commitments presumably intrinsic to the relationship between spouses and family members. Thus the adoption of new sexual behaviors may bring on anxiety, which might be manifested as a clearcut anxiety response or, and probably more likely, as an unconscious element within an overt behavior that appears to be due to another issue entirely. Therefore, changing sexual behaviors necessitates therapeutic efforts to lower any type of anxiety that might be associated with new forms of sexual expression.

As described in the previous section on heightened affect, several forms of affect may be related to sexual expression, and the technique used to alter affect, particularly to increase positive affective exchanges, can be used for sexual relations. For example, behavioral rehearsal, assertive practice, clinical suggestion, and hypnosis can be applied to the task of developing a broader, more rewarding range of sexual experiences, and the use of the audio and video taped stimulated recall techniques, such as the interpersonal process recall and the affect simulation methods, can open up the spouses to discussions of new ideas and revisions in their attitudes that can lead to alterations in sexual activities.

If, however, there is a degree of anxiety associated with sexuality that merits special attention, other behavioral techniques can be employed. As described earlier, the systematic desensitization method has proved to be very effective for the elimination of anxiety found in some maladaptive sexual responses, such as impotence and frigidity; and systematic desensitization provides a means to teach or train the person or couple to be more responsive in their sexual relations. Likewise, within systematic desensitization is the issue of muscular relaxation, and while it has not been conclusively demonstrated exactly how much therapeutic influence muscular relaxation has in and of itself, it has been found that sexual anxiety can be eliminated or alleviated by training the person experiencing the anxiety to induce a relaxed state; and if that is insufficient, it can progress on to a more thorough systematic desensitization scheme.

Satiation provides another avenue toward tension reduction. The idea here is that if a particular kind of sexual act, or even sexual activity in general, produces a reaction that does not allow for a true, healthy sexual response, the person can be exposed to related stimuli to a degree that they lose their negative properties. For example, if a person became unduly anxious over nudity and it is evident that this is impairing the sexual expression within the marriage, the person could be assigned to look at pictures of nude persons (such as from nudist magazines or in movies) and/or could be assigned to spend more time at home nude, particularly in nonsexual situations (such as when watching television alone or while reading or while sleeping).

This kind of satiation is designed to enhance sexuality, not detract from it. A contrasting technique is negative practice. As previously described, negative practice attempts to satiate by having the act or stimulus repeated in such a format that it becomes painful, distasteful, or negative. When using satiation to lower anxiety, the obvious objective is to get the person to be comfortable with the stimulus by recognizing that a negative consequence does not occur simply by encountering the stimulus; that is, the sexual stimulus, such as nudity, need not be feared. In view of the potential for over-exposure to the point of the stimulus becoming noxious, the helper should make sure that negative circumstances and a negative format are not associated with the stimulus. Moreover, as the person is becoming comfortable with the stimulus, it is important for the helper to provide supportive actions, such as clinical suggestions and insight-oriented explorations as to positive rewards from overcoming the anxiety associated with the stimulus.

Although there is a limited amount of documentation supporting that negative practice, exceeding the perimeter and format of the satiation described above, can extinguish certain maladaptive approach sexual responses, the clinical evidence is far from clear-cut. Indeed, it is known that some sexual responses have ended up being reinforced to occur. For example, one hospital attempted to use negative practice with transvestites, homosexuals, and persons with sexual fetishes, and without exception the sexual act that the patient professed a wish to eliminate occurred more frequently after he entered into negative practice. Incidentally, these patients were, however, successfully treated afterward via the application of aversion therapy, a technique that will be described subsequently. On the other hand, there is undoubtedly a cotery of professionals who would maintain that negative practice can be used successfully to treat maladaptive approach sexual responses. Note, however, that undue anxiety is typically labeled as a maladaptive avoidance response, and thus the type of response–maladaptive approach versus maladaptive avoidance–may provide the guideline for distinguishing the clinical usefulness of satiation and negative practice.

A related technique is verbal satiation therapy. DiCaprio (1970) uses language symbols, e.g. words, that would presumably trigger unpleasant feelings or unacceptable behavior as the material for verbal repetition, visual fixation, and auditory exposure. Purportedly, satiation via verbal stimuli (whether seeing it, saying it, or hearing it) can lead to a reduction of unwanted negative responses. In other words, the assumption is that if the person can read, say, or hear sexual words associated with sexual acts that evoke anxiety, they will become able eventually to actually enter into those sexual activities if the language symbols have been presented to the point of satiation. Leventhal (1968) presents a relevant case study where suggestion, relaxation, and desensitization (with the latter having certain satiation effects) were directed at acts that were previously "taboo" (e.g. sexual words were used to overcome sexual anxiety).

Implosive therapy is another method designed to take a fear or anxiety state that functions as a motivator of behavior and cause it to occur enough without negative consequences to the person so that it eventually loses its power to provoke fear. Stampfl and Levis (1967) describe the method as follows:

> At each stage of the process an attempt is made by the therapist to attain a maximal level of anxiety evocation from the patient. When a high level of anxiety is achieved, the patient is held on this level until some sign of spontaneous reduction in the anxiety-inducing value of the cues appears (extinction). The process is repeated, and again, at the first sign of spontaneous reduction of fear, new variations are introduced to elicit an intense anxiety response. This procedure is continued until a significant diminution of anxiety has resulted. After a few repetitions of a particular scene, the patient is given an opportunity to act out the scene by himself. He is encouraged to verbalize his own role-playing behavior. Between sessions the patient is instructed to re-enact in his imagination the scenes which were presented during the treatment sessions. This homework provides additional extinction trials. As therapy progresses he is given more instructions on how to handle fearful situations through use of the implosive process (p. 500).

Implosive therapy incorporates formulations from psychodynamic systems into a learning theory or behavioral approach to treatment. Some professionals question the suitability of implosive therapy because it creates unpleasant anxiety and could potentially lead the person into a severely disturbed state (perhaps even emotional disintegration or psychotic-like functioning). However, the increasing array of supportive research seems to indicate significant value, but the nature of the technique requires that the helper be fully prepared to "stay on top" of the anxiety, thereby being responsible for keeping the anxiety within tolerable limits and goal-directed at the extinction of the anxiety.

Aversion (or aversive) therapy has proved to be highly success-

ful in the treatment of numerous sexual variations, such as homosexuality, transvestism, excessive masturbation (meaning that the
person masturbates as a way of avoiding potentially more rewarding interpersonal sexual activity), and sexual fetishes. In each of
these instances, while the variation might be satisfying to some individuals, those seeking treatment have found their variation to be
interfering with their life in some manner.

In aversion therapy, the person performs the maladaptive approach sexual response, an aversive stimulus (such as mild electric
shock, unpleasant noise, or an emetic drug) is applied, and it continues until the person stops the unacceptable sexual act. Woody
(1971) provides an illustration:

> To illustrate the technique, let us assume a young man is being
> treated for homosexuality. He is told what the procedure will be,
> and is then placed in a therapy room with a slide projector con-
> taining sexually stimulating pictures of nude or seminude men and
> women. Electrodes are attached to his wrist, and a picture is pro-
> jected on the screen. If it is female, nothing happens, but if it is male,
> a mild electric shock would begin and would continue until he
> pressed button to change the picture to that of a female. The electric
> shock would then be stopped, restoring calm and giving relief from
> the aversive stimulus. This example illustrates the differences between
> negative reinforcement and punishment. If a shock occurred each
> time a picture of a sexually seductive male was flashed on, regardless
> of how the client reacted, it would be punishing. If, on the other
> hand, the electric shock could only be eliminated by the client's taking
> action in the desired direction (substituting a picture of sexually se-
> ductive female for the sexual male), negative reinforcement would
> be occurring. Note that punishment would condition the client to
> have a negative reaction whenever a picture of a seductive male was
> shown, while negative reinforcement would condition a redirection
> of his sexual response from men to women. Further, apparatus is
> available to measure psychophysically whether a picture is sexually
> stimulating; therefore, another approach could be to give the electric
> shock only when sexual arousal was measured for the target pictures
> (i.e. seductive males) (p. 97).

More thorough coverage of the aspects of clinical application of
aversion therapy may be found elsewhere (Marks, 1968; Rachman
and Teasdale, 1969; Woody, 1971).

The unfortunate thing about aversion therapy is that it requires the creation of unpleasant circumstances for the helpee, and many helpers find this requirement distasteful enough to lead them to refuse to use the technique (and conversely, some helpers question why certain other helpers prefer to use aversion therapy, intimating that they suspect there might occasionally be an element of sadistic gratification). On the other hand, the fortunate thing about aversion therapy is that it seems highly efficacious in the treatment of maladaptive approach responses, and particularly so for problems that are resistant to other forms of psychotherapeutic treatment, such as sexual "deviations" (or variations), drug addiction, and alcoholism. Therefore, one seemingly appropriate rule-of-thumb might be: *In the case of maladaptive approach responses, it might be preferable to take steps to ascertain if a positive reinforcement procedure and/or insight-oriented techniques can accomplish the therapeutic objective effectively, but if not, aversion therapy should be used.* One prominent psychiatrist who uses aversion therapy stated: "I do research on aversion therapy in hopes that I can find out why it is so effective in order that I might eventually be able to locate a more pleasant treatment plan that will be equally as effective." To summarize, the use of aversion therapy might be viewed with ambivalence: it is unpleasant, but it does seem to be successful in treating maladaptive approach responses, and it should be used only with persons who seek treatment to change maladaptive behavior.

The use of systematic desensitization and clinical hypnosis (and the related techniques of assertive practice, behavioral rehearsal, clinical suggestions and muscular relaxation), satiation, negative practice, implosive therapy and aversion therapy frequently raise a question in the minds of patients: Is it possible that if I become immune to the attraction of my currently preferred sexual stimulus that I might also become immune to any and all sexual stimuli? For example, one woman in implosive therapy for impulses that she identified as being lesbian in nature feared that becoming desensitized to female anatomy might lead her to become repulsed by her own anatomy and that of her husband (and other men) as well; and male homosexuals often express this same fear, namely if they quit being homosexuals, they fear they may end up not having any sexual preference. This is certainly an understandable concern, but one that need not be feared: *The behavioral treatment plan should encompass both the elimination of the undesired maladaptive response and the creation of a desirable alternative response.* Moreover, returning to the basic question, there is no reason to believe that any of the previously mentioned behavioral modification procedures would lead to total loss of sexual motivation; but it is important to insure that the helpee does not move into such a form of denial (which, if it happened, would be for neurotic purposes and should be psychotherapeutically counteracted). In other words, the treatment plan should encompass the development of a suitable, rewarding mode of sexual expression, and this goal should be attained before treatment is considered completed and termination occurs.

It should also be pointed out that the nature of these techniques, particularly those involving negative conditions (e.g. implosive therapy and aversion therapy), necessitate that the helpee be oriented about what to expect in the treatment: *Knowledge of the treatment plan should enhance rather than detract from the treatment outcome.* In aversion therapy, for example, it is sometimes found that a helpee realizes that in-depth psychotherapy (i.e. insight-oriented) will be a long-term process and that the best behavioral treatment (perhaps the only effective one) would involve negative or painful circumstances; in some cases the person will decide after therapeutic consultation that he really does not care to "pay the price" of treatment, be it in terms of time, money, or discomfort, and will choose instead to keep the questionable sexual variation. In these instances, of course, insight-oriented counseling-therapy might be provided to foster adjustment to the particular sexual variation, i.e. to be free from worry or guilt about it.

Each of the foregoing behavioral techniques has focused on sexual variations, but it should be obvious, without exceptions, that these techniques are applicable to other areas of behavior or other types of problems as well. Although there are numerous guidelines that should be applied in the selection of a behavioral technique (see Chapter 3 in Woody, 1971), perhaps the most basic dimension is determining whether the target behavior or problem is a maladaptive approach or a maladaptive avoidance response.

REFERENCES

Alger, I. and Hogan, P.: The use of videotape recordings in conjoint marital therapy. *American Journal of Psychiatry, 123*:1425-1430, 1967.

Alger, I, and Hogan, P.: Enduring effects of videotape playback experience on family and marital relationships. *American Journal of Orthopsychiatry, 39*:86-93, 1969.

Bandura, A.: Behavioral modification through modeling procedures. In L. Krasner and L. P. Ullmann (Eds.), *Research in behavior modification.* New York, Holt, Rinehart and Winston, 310-340, 1965.

Bandura, A.: *Principles of behavior modification,* New York, Holt, Rinehart and Winston, 1969.

Barber, T. X.: *Hypnosis: a scientific approach.* New York, Van Nostrand Reinhold, 1969.

Carkhuff, R. R. and Berenson, B. G.: *Beyond counseling and therapy.* New York, Holt, Rinehart and Winston, 1967.

Cautela, J. R.: Covert sensitization. *Psychological Reports, 20*:459-468, 1967.

DiCaprio, N. S.: Essentials of verbal satiation therapy: a learning-theory-based behavior therapy. *Journal of Counseling Psychology, 17*:419-424, 1970.

Eysenck, H. J. and Rachman, S.: *The causes and cures of neurosis.* San Diego, R. R. Knapp, 1965.

Ferster, C. B. and Perrott, Mary Carol: *Behavior principles.* New York, Appleton-Century-Crofts, 1968.

Greenspoon, J. and Gersten, C. D.: A new look at psychological testing: Psychological testing from the standpoint of a behaviorist. *American Psychology, 22*:848-853, 1967.

Hartland, J.: The value of "ego-strengthening" procedures prior to direct symptom-removal under hypnosis. *American Journal of Clinical Hypnosis, 9*:211-219, 1967.

Kagan, N. and Schauble, P. G.: Affect simulation in interpersonal process recall. *Journal of Counseling Psychology, 16*:309-313, 1969.

Kagan, N., Schauble, P., Resnikoff, A., Danish, S. J. and Krathwohl, D. R.: Interpersonal process recall. *Journal of Nervous and Mental Disease, 148*:365-374, 1969.

Kanfer, F. H. and Saslow, G.: Behavioral diagnosis. In C. M. Franks (Ed.), *Behavior therapy: appraisal and status.* New York, McGraw-Hill, 417-444, 1969.

Klein, Marjorie H., Dittmann, A. T., Parloff, M. B. and Gill, M. M.:

Behavior therapy: observations and reflections. *Journal of Consulting and Clinical Psychology, 33*:259-266, 1969.

Lazarus, A. A.: *Behavior therapy and beyond.* New York, McGraw-Hill, 1971.

Leventhal, A. M.: Use of a behavioral approach within a traditional psycho-therapeutic context: a case study. *Journal of Abnormal Psychology, 73*: 178-182, 1968.

Liberman, R.: Behavioral approaches to family and couple therapy. *American Journal of Orthopsychiatry, 40*:106-118, 1970.

Marks, I. M.: Aversion therapy. *British Journal of Medical Psychology, 41*: 47-52, 1968.

Masters, W. H. and Johnson, Virginia E.: *Human sexual inadequacy.* Boston, Little, Brown, 1970.

Rachman, S. and Teasdale, J.: *Aversion therapy and behaviour disorders: an analysis.* Coral Gables, Fla., University of Miami Press, 1969.

Russell, J.: Personal growth through structured group exercises. *Voices: the Art and Science of Psychotherapy, 7* (2):28-36, 1971.

Stampfl, T. G. and Levis, D. J.: Essentials of implosive therapy: a learning-theory based psychodynamic behavioral therapy. *Journal of Abnormal Psychology, 72*:496-503, 1967.

Wolpe, J.: The comparative clinical status of conditioning therapies and psychoanalysis. In J. Wolpe, A. Salter, and L. J. Reyna (Eds.), *The conditioning therapies.* New York, Holt, Rinehart and Winston, 5-20, 1964.

Wolpe, J.: *The practice of behavior therapy.* New York, Pergamon, 1969.

Wolpe, J. and Lazarus, A. A.: *Behavior therapy techniques.* New York, Pergamon, 1966.

Woody, R. H.: *Behavioral problem children in the schools: recognition, diagnosis, and behavioral modification.* New York, Appleton-Century-Crofts, 1969.

Woody, R. H.: *Psychobehavioral counseling and therapy: integrating behavioral and insight techniques.* New York, Appleton-Century-Crofts, 1971.

Woody, R. H. and Schauble, P. G.: Desensitization of fear by video tapes. *Journal of Clinical Psychology, 25*:102-103 (a), 1969.

Woody, R. H. and Schauble, P. G.: Videotaped vicarious desensitization. *Journal of Nervous and Mental Disease, 148*:281-286 (b), 1969.

Yates, A. J.: *Behavior therapy.* New York, John Wiley, 1970.

ENCOUNTER INTERVENTIONS: HUMAN POTENTIAL GROWTH GROUPS

THE USE OF HUMAN POTENTIAL growth groups has become one of the most recent "shining lights" in mental health and other human helping. Although for many the movement represents a "shining light," others, both professional and lay persons, view it as a hypnotic light that can lead the follower to unknown, possibly dangerous, lands. In other words, advocates of the human potential growth groups have tended to promote a religionist appeal, which has produced a "movement," characterized by various faddish trappings and by many "true believers." In the opposing camp, professional and lay segments of the population have outrightly denounced such groups: many professionals strongly caution: (1) against the intense head-on encounter methods on grounds that they might exceed the ego's control-power and lead to emotional disturbance; and (2) against involvement in a group that is led by non-professionals (in many instances) and by a person (professional or layman alike) who adopts a "true believer" approach to behavioral change.

The human potential growth movement is plagued by widely divergent approaches to purportedly the same objectives and via basically the same method, i.e. encounter. These many variations end up, however, being quite disparate in structure, techniques, processes, parameters, and outcomes. *Awareness* constitutes one of the major thrusts; this term encompasses approaches to body and sensory stimulation, with the purpose being to cultivate new receptors for the interactional messages in order that greater psychological insight and appreciation for self can occur and lead to improved internal and external functioning. It is from this thrust that the term "sensitivity" evolves; and it is, of course, one of the most frequently used synonyms for the entire human potential growth movement, i.e. sensitivity groups. *Body correction* is another major

235

thrust; here the effort is toward bringing maximum mental and physical potential into being, such as through the use of bioenergetics (bodily actions designed to release emotions and eventually produce a body that truly reflects the mind). *Role playing and fantasy* provide another major thrust, and both these techniques are also used in insight-oriented psychotherapy and conditioning-oriented behavior therapy. In encounter approaches, however, role playing and fantasy are used again to promote inner-determined growth. In addition, there are a variety of interactional groups, such as confrontation groups (where ex-drug addicts intensely confront current drug addicts in a therapeutic milieu), theme groups (where the participants restrict their explorations and confrontations to a very specific topic or problem), leadership groups (which attempt to prepare the participants to become leaders of others), nude groups (which make use of the removal of clothing and bodily exposure in the presence of others as a vehicle for the person to "strip away" other defenses and enter into interaction in an open and uncamouflaged manner), and training groups or T-groups (which strive to help the participants understand the group process rather than promote individual growth). And there are other related forms.

All of the foregoing human potential growth groups are basically "encounter" in approach, and there is usually some emphasis on "sensitivity" or "sensory awareness." Likewise, the popularity of training groups or T-groups has contributed to the generic definition. Thus, when one hears about encounter groups, sensitivity groups, T-groups, and so on, there is no way of being sure exactly what the group is designed to accomplish, how it will proceed to try to fulfill its goals, or what the leader's qualifications are. These are all synonyms for a potpourri of approaches, activities, and purposes which are presumably aligned to some degree with the human potential growth group movement.

One of the most common formats for human potential growth groups is the marathon. The marathon format calls for the group to run for a seemingly inordinate continuous length of time; for example, the group might meet for 12 to 18 hours for several days in a row, or for long hours on one weekend, or for as long as participants can tolerate the circumstances (usually participants are only allowed to sleep if the other group members will agree to it). The assumption is that continuous and prolonged encounter will lead to forced intimacy and confrontation, the elimination of defenses because of both mental and physical fatigue, and accelerated intrapersonal and interpersonal growth. It is precisely the forced intimacy and confrontation, the elimination of defenses, and the accelerated growth factors that lead many professionals to caution against the marathon experience on the basis that it might induce a reckless plummeting that could result in destructive outcomes. In summary, the marathon group capitalizes on group pressure as much or more than the interventions of the group leader, and group pressure is maximal in an extended session. Bach (1966), one of the foremost proponents of marathon groups, describes his approach to marathon and offers his "ten marathon commandments" (note the religious connotation, something that is quite common to many human potential groups).

In the following discussion the terms "encounter" and "growth" will be used generically for the human potential growth movement. The two major divisions, and the seemingly most well formulated divisions, of the human potential growth movement are: training groups or T-groups, and gestalt groups, each of which will be discussed in detail.

ENCOUNTER

An initial step for this discussion must be the defining of the key term: *Encounter.* In achieving a definition of encounter, there will also be direct reference to the techniques that go into the growth approach.

The theoretical rationale for growth groups is decidedly humanistic or existential. However, the preceding chapter on behavioral intervention notes how encounter techniques could be presented in a behavioristic fashion; and later in this chapter, it will be pointed out how exemplars of the growth movement, such as gestalt therapy, can actually be defined theoretically in behavioristic terminology. But in considering the humanistic philosophy and theory of human growth that underlie encounter activities, the following statement presents an accurate and concise rationale:

Within each of us there is the power to grow, to *be more,* to be whole, to function at a higher level both personally and inter-personally, and to find greater satisfaction in everything we do. Man's potential for growth is an unknown quantity; the limits are yet to be attained. Organisms grow or they die—there are no other alternatives, and it is important for each of us to get a glimpse of what man can become, of what I can be. The mobilization of one's potential re-quires an investment of self and a dedication to an exciting and challenging life-long adventure of self-discovery. The goal is *self*-actualization (rather than self-*image*-actualization), the actualization of those aspects of our potentialities which we have overlooked, avoided, or ignored and not the adoption of phony social roles which tend to further split and disintegrate us (Foulds, 1971, p. 10).

This framework clearly creates a humanistic charge for partici-pants in encounter experiences.

In turning to a definition of the encounter or growth group, Foulds (1971) states:

Growth groups are relatively unstructured group experiences that provide opportunities for personal development and experiential learning for growth-seeking individuals. The focus of these groups is on the here-and-now, moment-to-moment experiencing of individual participants and the interactions among them. Psychological *arche-ology* is discouraged, and participants are encouraged to live as fully as possible in the present and to relate authentically in the *now.* The facilitator or leader attempts to create a psychological climate of safety and trust in which each person may feel increasingly free to risk being transparently real, to trust his feelings, to communicate his needs and preferences openly and honestly, and to be more aware of his personal freedom and the responsibility associated with this. Participants are urged to *talk straight* at all times (with directness, clarity, and congruence), to become aware of their social masks and manipulative behaviors, and to discover ways in which their intended *helpfulness* sometimes inhibits growth and change in an-other person. The group provides an opportunity for persons to experience themselves more fully and to engage in authentic en-counter and confrontation with self and each other as a method for self-discovery and release of human potentials through expanded awareness. A variety of time structures are utilized for growth groups (pp. 2-3).

Again, apparent in this statement is the responsibility of the indi-vidual. This goal contributes to the position that the group leader should avoid any title or role definition that would cast him into "leadership" distinctly separated from "participation"; consequently, group leaders, even the professionals, avoid being viewed as "therapist" or "counselor" by studiously striving to be seen and sensed as a facilitator or, at the most, a helper. As might be expected, the growth group is designed not to be a "therapy" group, even if the participants are clinical cases and/or have involvement with psychotherapy; the group is viewed as providing an experience in self-development or "education" (or possibly "*re*education," but not to the extent that counseling and psychotherapy endorse "*re*education"). As a result of these factors, some encounter leaders attempt to exempt themselves from professional ethics, a practice which causes many professionals to denounce the actions of encounter group leaders. As will be evident in a subsequent section of this chapter, the denunciations from many professionals are also rooted, to a large extent, in the rather limited documentation for change power that has to date been accumulated for the human potential growth activities.

Further clarity of the process of encountering, particularly in the marathon context, is presented by Ruitenbeck (1970):

> The encountering experience in the marathon actually is a four-phase process. Individual expressions are (a) reacted to, and (b) these reactions are shared in a "feedback"; (c) the feedback in turn generates counterreactions (d) from the original expressors as well as from the rest of the group. All members of the group are expected to participate. No one should wait to be "brought out." Everyone is expected to put himself voluntarily into the focus of the group's attention, to seek out the group and to turn attention to himself, preferably a number of times. This applies to everyone in the marathon—there are no *observers,* only *active* participants (p. 91).

And as mentioned earlier, even the group leader attempts to involve himself as a "participant." It might be noted that this practice is another source for negative criticism, because theory of group process would suggest that by virtue of convening the group (not to mention his exceptionality because of presumably group leadership skills and possibly professional identity) the encounter leader cannot actually participate in an equalitarian fashion; he can only participate as a simulated-peer participant. Thus critics feel the leader is misrepresenting his involvement and that his input is self-serving at the expense of the integrity of the other participants.

By this point, it is logical to begin to question why the human potential growth groups have attained such contemporary prominence. One reason is that apparently traditional psychotherapy was inadequate for the needs of the public; this inadequacy led to group psychotherapy; and again, group psychotherapy, while seemingly contributing more than traditional psychotherapeutic interventions, has failed to serve the breadth of motivations reflected by persons seeking help. The use of a group format seems to better serve the *normal* kinds of human problems, e.g. feelings of isolation and alienation of one's self from the world. These kinds of feelings, according to Ruitenbeck (1970), feed into certain characteristics of our citizenry:

> Americans, perhaps more than other people, are more *inclined* to reveal themselves. . . . This display of emotion and the encouragement to act them out, which is so much a part of the new group experiences, is very much part of the American personality *per se* (p. 59).

There seems reason to question the hypothesis that Americans are more inclined to reveal themselves than are other nationalities; what may, however, be the case is that complex American society does, in fact, deprive many persons of appropriate outlets for sharing self revelations and interpersonal exchanges (such as might be found in a Catholic-dominated society where church-prescribed family behaviors and personal values combine with the required confessional to satisfy these sorts of intrinsic needs—if they do exist).

In accord with the possibility that complex societal factors are influencing the upsurge of the human potential growth movement, Ruitenbeck (1970) states:

> The attraction of encounter groups, marathons, play therapy, psychodrama and other forms of group therapy where the patient actually is allowed to participate and even act out some of his desires and aggressions, that attraction it should be said is the greatest and most widespread in the urban centers of contemporary America. I feel that

this has a great deal to do with the decline in community life in those centers, if it ever existed in the first place, and with the steady rise in alienation and estrangement of big-city people. The loss of a sense of community and the absence of meaningful social activities probably has contributed to the desire to participate in the groups mentioned above. Often one hears the remark, even in traditional groups which I have conducted for a number of years, that the group activity provides the patient not only with a platform to air his problems but also with the opportunity to establish genuine relationships and encounters. True again this might not have been the primary goal of traditional group therapy but it certainly has become an important by-product of the process (pp. 50-51).

Further, along these same lines, Ruitenbeck (1970) states:

The sense of temporariness pervades many facets of American society and colors its character. . . . Thus, in effect, the sense of *encounter* is short and only temporary. The nature of encounter implies a sense of impermanency. This fits well with the general pattern of American social life, where social and interpersonal relationships are often of a temporary nature. Also in the new groups perhaps less emphasis is being placed on the therapeutic aims and what counts is more and more the here-and-now experience. In a society where one senses the lack of permanency, it seems rather obvious that *any* approach in group therapy that emphasizes the immediate experience rather than the long run or permanent results would have the appeal of experimentation for that society (p. 66).

Ruitenbeck's analysis is also aligned with the inferred relationship between the *permissiveness* endorsed by society and maintained within the human potential growth groups and with the *now*-emphasis of our era, both of which are found in our society and in the growth groups.

The foregoing hypotheses about a cultural stimulus to the human potential growth group movement remains purely conjecture. However, these same societal factors (such as complexity of living, temporariness, permissiveness, depersonalization, alienation, etc.) are viewed by many professionals as contributing to the widespread problems affecting sexual, marital, and familial relations (see Chapter 1 for elaboration of this point).

Another *raison d' être* for the upsurge in the human potential growth groups may well be the sensual appeal. In other words, many people derive gratification from participating in a group experience that clearly violates many of the tenets of social propriety and allows for the evolution of a unique, ego-gratifying system. Since it is an encapsulated experience, one that the participants will leave to return to their more conventional and more restrictive (yet necessarily predictable) life styles, some professionals claim that there is a tendency for the growth groups to cater to id-gratification. While this may not be as overt as sexual acting out, many participants in growth groups clearly describe the experience as an "ego trip" and report an after-effect termed "encounter high," in which there are feelings of elation and exemption from the demands of reality. These feelings reportedly subside with the person's returning to essentially his pre-encounter existence; or, while still "high" he may promote encounters in the real world (such as with a spouse or employer) which cannot be undone and which he must live with after his mania-like responses have been dissolved. Thus, there is reason to believe that much of the appeal and continued expansion of the human potential growth movement has to do with the simple principle of *hedonism*. It feels good to do it (i.e. to have an encounter, with all of its related ingredients); it is a matter of *encounter for encounter's sake*. The philosophical question that must be answered by each individual is whether he wishes to pursue an experience offering both the potential benefits *and* liabilities that accompany a hedonistic endeavor.

It should be evident that the human potential growth groups are quite distinct from the traditional therapy groups. But as a final clarification of encounter, a contrast between growth groups, and therapy groups should be made:

> In the traditional group the orientation is primarily historical in that questions as "why" and "where from" are fundamental to the functioning and the concept of what therapy is about of the group. Thus the traditional group basically does not depart from the essential premises of classical psychotherapy. Some of the traditional groups might have been more open and flexible in seeking the answers to "why" and "where from" but they remain firmly within the context of traditional psychoanalysis. Such is not the case with the marathon groups. In the marathon group subjective truths are shared, irrational and ineffectual behavior appears incongruent, to be dropped in favor of new, more intimate, and more

competent behavioral patterns. The latter emerge and are practiced in the course of the marathon. Such orientation thus primarily is *ahistorical* and emphasizes the "what" and "how now" rather than the "why" and "where from" (Ruitenbeck, 1970, p. 78).

And as was mentioned earlier, the growth group leader presumably works diligently: (1) to avoid being viewed as a "leader" or "therapist" or "professional helper" in favor of being viewed as a "facilitator of growth"; and (2) to promote a sense of "self-development" or "education" as opposed to "therapy" or "reeducation."

TRAINING GROUPS

Previously it was mentioned that there are two human potential growth group approaches that seem to be substantially better formulated than their counterparts. These two approaches are: training groups (also known as laboratory groups and T-groups), and gestalt groups. This section and the next will focus respectively on these two approaches.

A training group or T-group is viewed basically as a learning process. The group leader functions as a resource person to the participants for aiding them in better understanding their behavior in the group and the group's processes:

> Trainers in these sessions usually encourage participants to explore in some depth their own feelings and motivations, as well as those of other group members. The objective is to stimulate an exchange that is inhibited by a minimum of reserve and defensiveness in order to achieve a maximum of openness and honesty (Ruitenbeck, 1970, p. 143).

While there are definite encounter elements, such as confrontation, it should be underscored that the emphasis is on the participant's involvement in the group, the group processes, and group decision-making; there is less emphasis on outside-the-group individual growth, though logically there would hopefully be a generalization of the beneficial learnings.

In describing the learning process within training groups, Seashore (1970) indicates that there are five underlying assumptions:

1. LEARNING RESPONSIBILITY. Each participant is responsible for his own learning. What a person learns depends upon his own style,

readiness, and the relationships he develops with other members of the group (p. 15).

2. STAFF ROLE. The staff person's role is to facilitate the examination and understanding of the experiences in the group. He helps participants to focus on the way the group is working, the style of an individual's participation, or the issues that are facing the group (p. 15).

3. EXPERIENCE AND CONCEPTUALIZATION. Most learning is a combination of experience and conceptualization. A major T-Group aim is to provide a setting in which individuals are encouraged to examine their experiences together in enough detail so that valid generalizations can be drawn (p. 15).

4. AUTHENTIC RELATIONSHIPS AND LEARNING. A person is most free to learn when he establishes authentic relationships with other people and thereby increases his sense of self-esteem and decreases his defensiveness. In authentic relationships persons can be open, honest, and direct with one another so that they are communicating what they are actually feeling rather than masking their feelings (pp. 15-16).

5. SKILL ACQUISITION AND VALUES. The development of new skills in working with people is maximized as a person examines the basic values underlying his behavior, as he acquires appropriate concepts and theory, and as he is able to practice new behavior and obtain feedback on the degree to which his behavior produces the intended impact (p. 16).

In the foregoing statements it is extremely important to grasp the assumptions because they functionally define the respective responsibilities and appropriate actions for both the group leader and the participants.

Training groups have received broad application in managerial training and development. From an analysis of this managerial context, Campbell and Dunnette (1968) offer the following "ultimate aims of all T-group training," with the connotation being clearly that they are applicable to other than managerial training and development; the aims are:

(a) a spirit of inquiry or a willingness to hypothesize and experiment with one's role in the world; (b) an "expanded interpersonal consciousness" or an increased awareness of more things about more people; (c) an increased authenticity in interpersonal relations or simply feeling freer to be oneself and not feeling compelled to play a role; (d) an ability to act in a collaborative and interdependent manner with peers, superiors, and subordinates rather than in authoritative or hierarchical terms; and (e) an ability to resolve conflict situations through problem solving rather than through horse trading, coercion, or power manipulation (p. 74).

In summarizing from various sources, Campbell and Dunnette state that there are six direct or proximate outcomes desired:

1. Increased self-insight or self-awareness concerning one's own behavior and its meaning in a social context (p. 75).
2. Increased sensitivity to the behavior of others (p. 75).
3. Increased awareness and understanding of the types of processes that facilitate or inhibit group functioning and the interactions between different groups—specifically, why do some members participate actively while others retire to the background? (p. 75).
4. Heightened diagnostic skill in social, interpersonal, and intergroup situations (p. 75).
5. Increased action skill . . . refers to a person's ability to intervene successfully in inter- or intragroup situations so as to increase member satisfactions, effectiveness, or output (p. 75).
6. Learning how to learn . . . his ability to analyze continually his own interpersonal behavior for the purposes of helping himself and others achieve more effective and satisfying interpersonal relationships (p. 75).

It is interesting to note that each of these six desired outcomes are well within the objectives of essentially all forms of counseling and psychotherapy (with behavior therapy providing some exception because of its lack of concern with self-insight and interpersonal relations, except as would relate to the target behavioral problems being treated). Granted, however, that counseling and psychotherapy hold other objectives as well, but it seems fair to assert that there are commonalities between acknowledged therapeutic interventions and training group experiences.

Of special importance to this treatise, training groups have been used for sexual, marital, and familial issues, with marriage being a primary area of interest. When applying the training group or laboratory training method to marriages, Golembiewski (1970) states that there are four change-objectives:

First, learning designs seek to enable couples to "experience more depth, breadth, and complexity in their marriage" (p. 346).
Second, laboratory learning designs seek to help couples "establish

a new norm about how open they are with each other" (p. 347).
Third, laboratory designs for married couples seek to sensitize
participants to their needs for separateness as well as for to-
getherness (p. 347).

Fourth, the laboratory approach to learning by married couples
highlights the kind of debilitating games that husband and wife
commonly play with one another (p. 347).

Many techniques can be used in training groups, according to
Golembiewski (1970), but there are several important approaches
worth noting. One is dual sensitization, designed "to help individuals to become more effective simultaneous participants/observers
in interaction with their mates" (p. 348). Another approach is
sharing of secrets (between mates within the group) while being
observed by the other group members for purposes of breaking
down barriers in communications; the intention is:

> . . . to turn the massive energies necessary to preserve deception
> into forces that bind the married couple together. The observing
> couples provide support and feedback, as well as help the central
> couple avoid the argumentation or fighting or down-putting that are
> such common games for couples (Golembiewski, 1970, p. 348).

Golembiewski also endorses training groups for dealing with distancing and avoidance of intimacy.

The training group approach (or laboratory method) seems to
have a sound academic rationale, solidly based on extensive group
dynamics research. As compared to many of the other versions of
human potential growth groups, the training group approach is relatively well defined; moreover, there is clarity in the delineation of
objectives for the method and for the responsibilities and types of
responses for the group leader. As mentioned earlier, much or most
of the research on training groups is aligned with managerial/
leadership training and development; there has, to date, been only
limited research analysis of the application of the training/lab-
oratory method to other problems, such as sexual, marital, and
familial relations. Even within the realm of managerial/leader-
ship training groups, there is disagreement among professionals as
to the efficacy of the method. In an exhaustive review of relevant
research on the use of training group experiences in managerial
training and development, Campbell and Dunnette (1968): (1)

acknowledge that there are many limitations evident in existing research on training groups and, consequently, evaluations of efficacy
must be tenuously posited; and (2) assert that, contrary to the findings of others, they believe that training groups do lead to behavioral changes in the "back home" setting.

At this point in time, the prudent and scientific position would
seem to be that the professional helper should gain academic
knowledge and experientially-based appreciation of the training/
laboratory group method and should consider the applicative value
for helpees on an individual basis (i.e. it would seem ill-advised to
make a generalization for all helpees). Although the research for
efficacy is lacking, there seems to be promise in the method, but its
application would best be made within the framework of tailor-
ing-to-individual-needs.

GESTALT GROUPS

The second seemingly best developed encounter approach is the
gestalt group. Indeed, Ruitenbeck (1970) deems gestalt therapy to
be "the most astute and perhaps successful" (p. 114) of marathons
and encounter groups; in distinguishing it from other forms of
therapy, he states:

> Gestalt therapy is closely related to the approach of existential anal-
> ysis. Both forms of therapy stress the here-and-now situation and
> both encourage the element of *confrontation* in the analytic situ-
> ation. If there is anything different between the forms of therapy
> then it is perhaps that the Gestalt therapists stress more the element
> of *feeling* in the analytic process and also the *contemporary* aspects
> of the process of psychotherapy. The Gestalt therapists deemphasize
> or debunk the past and pay little attention to the future (p. 115).

He indicates that the effort of the gestalt approach is to establish
a continuum of awareness. To accomplish this objective, great reliance is placed on nonverbal techniques, particularly as a means
for achieving sensory awareness. One of the major techniques is to
urge the helpee to "stay with a feeling," meaning that the helper
invokes a preference for the helpee not to dispel a feeling or
mood or state of mind that is unpleasant or one from which he
would be habitually inclined to move away (note that this helper-
injected preference seems more closely aligned with behavioral in-

terventions than with insight-oriented interventions, an issue that will be discussed subsequently). In other words, the "stay with it" technique counters the aspect of human behavior that reflects an almost phobic avoidance within neurotic behavior:

> . . . the neurotic has habitually avoided vigorous contact with a variety of unpleasant and dysphoric experiences. As a result, avoidance has become routinized, and major dimensions of experience have never been adequately mastered (Ruitenbeck, 1970, p. 139).

Bioenergetics, the integration of body and mind, also plays a major technical role in the gestalt approach.

There appear to be five kinds of tasks for the gestalt therapist to fulfill: patterning, control, potency, humanness, and commitment (Fagan, 1970). In *patterning,* the role of the therapist is manifested as being a perceiver and constructor of patterns:

> As the therapist begins his contact with the patient requesting help, he has available a body of theory which is largely cognitive in nature, a background of past experience, and a number of awarenesses and personal responses derived from the ongoing interaction that have large emotional and intuitive components. From these, which may be given varying degrees of importance by a specific therapist, he begins to form an understanding of the interaction of events and systems that result in a given life style that supports a given symptom pattern. *Events* refers to the things that have happened or do happen to the patient; *systems* includes all those interlocking events that interact on a specific level of existence, such as biological systems, self-perceptions systems, family systems, etc. The patient is visualized as a focal point of many systems, including the cellular, historical, economic, etc. The more the therapist can specify the entire interaction, or be sensitive to the possible effects of systems he is not directly concerned with (such as the neurological), or intuit the connecting points between systems where the most strain exists, the more effective he can be in producing change. He can act on a level and at a point that promises the most positive change in symptoms or conflicts at the least cost of effort, and where the least disruptive change will occur to other systems (p. 89).

And in considering the techniques to be used in this patterning, Fagan indicates that regardless of procedure there should be three criteria: "how rapidly the symptom has been removed, what positive behavior has replaced it, and how little disturbance has been created in the interlocking systems" (p. 90). Parenthetically, it is interesting to note how compatible these criteria are with those maintained by behavior therapists (for example, behaviorally-oriented therapists place much greater emphasis on how rapidly the symptom has been removed than do insight-oriented therapists). In *control,* the gestalt therapist strives to be able to persuade or coerce the helpee into adhering to the decided upon procedures (another behavioristic element):

> Control is not used here with cynicism or a Svengali attitude, nor is there any implication of ignoring the value of genuine concern and liking for the patient; it simply reflects the reality that unless patients do some of the things that therapists suggest, little will happen, and that which does happen will be mostly by accident (Fagan, 1970, p. 92).

Motivation and rapport are two major aspects of implicit control. In *potency,* the gestalt therapist must demonstrate his ability to be of assistance to the helpee in moving in the direction that he chooses and to "accelerate and provoke change in a positive direction" (Fagan, 1970, p. 96). In *humanness,* the gestalt therapist makes his contribution to the treatment through "being," his personal characteristics:

> Humanness, as it is used here, includes a variety of involvements: the therapist's concern for and caring about his patient on a personal and emotional level; his willingness to share himself and bring to the patient his own direct emotional responses and/or pertinent accounts of his own experiences; his ability to recognize in the patient groupings toward deepened authenticity, which need support and recognition; and his continued openness to his own growth, which serves as a model for the patient (Fagan, 1970, pp. 100-101).

In *commitment,* the gestalt therapist reveals both major and minor commitments through continuing involvement and acceptance of assumed responsibilities within the therapeutic relationship. Since this commitment requires high levels of interest and energy, Fagan (1970) states:

> Gestalt therapy places most emphasis on the therapist's commitment to himself in terms of enhancing his involvement and excitement in the day-to-day tasks. It also provides or suggests ways for the

therapist to assist himself in exploring his own boredom and doubts when they occur. In these respects it enhances both therapist and patient interest and offers ways of getting both "unstuck" when faced with the inevitable impasses (p. 104).

Within these five tasks, it should be readily evident that there are two major thrusts: a humanistic sharing of oneself and behavioristic intervention (the latter being termed behavioristic phenomenology within the gestalt framework).

A humanistic sharing of oneself must be manifested by both the helper and the helpee. Such a revelation or sharing by the helper obviously runs counter to the dictates of many theories of counseling and psychotherapy, such as those that are psychoanalytically-oriented.

Because of the humanistic sharing requisite within gestalt interventions, there is a distinct emphasis on experiential conditions. Kempler (1970) describes his conceptualizations of gestalt therapy for family problems from an experiential/gestalt vantage point:

> There is no obscuring of the therapist behind a title. He brings his personality and life experiences to the family encounter. It is his uniqueness in this family (he is not likely to be caught up in its painful, interlocking behavior patterns—at least not initially) and his willingness to engage fully with others that are his most valuable therapeutic "techniques." In other words, in experiential psychotherapy within families, there are no "techniques," only people. At every turn, the therapist is obliged to struggle for his right to be seen as he perceives himself, and not to permit distortions such as, for instance, an implication that he is all-knowing or all-powerful. By such example, the family members are likewise encouraged to struggle for what they perceive as their identities. It is during the vigorous clarification of who we are to each other that therapy occurs (p. 160).

While Kempler's statement seems to capture aptly the essence of the humanistic sharing that the helper must communicate during a gestalt intervention, it should be pointed out that many gestalt-oriented helpers (particularly those who recognize or make use of the behavioristic elements) would dispute his dismissing of techniques other than the experiential or humanistic sharing.

Several references have been made to behavioristic elements within the gestalt approach. Despite the dogmatic adherence to a single theoretical position that is so all too often maintained by some professional helpers, there is reason to believe that no one approach has a monopoly on therapeutic efficacy, that probably all approaches can contribute beneficially to at least some persons, and that the most scientifically advanced way for selecting a therapeutic intervention would be on the basis of clinical judgment, hopefully evolved from scientific postulates that have been validated through extensive and rigorous investigations, for each helpee. Moreover, there is reason to believe that: (1) many theoretical approaches have more in common with each other than they have differences (yet the differences typically get emphasized when proponents try to substantiate their espoused theoretical positions); and (2) specific techniques from seemingly quite diverse theoretical approaches can be integrated, many times creating the most efficacious way for dealing with the target behavioral or emotional difficulties. In Chapter 4, L'Abate dealt with related issues, and the next chapter will give consideration to the integration issue, particularly as relates to behavioral and insight techniques; this integrated approach is termed the *Psychobehavioral* frame of reference.

Because there are so many seemingly behavioristic elements with the gestalt approach (an approach, ironically, that is usually identified as being humanistic), gestalt therapists seem to be giving an increasing amount of recognition to how they can make use of reinforcement procedures. Kepner and Brien (1970) describe how gestalt therapy may be viewed from a behavioristic vantage point:

Symbolic behavior refers to "mental events" such as thinking, imagining, daydreaming, etc. Such behavior is not directly observable by the therapist, but the client's attention may be directed toward his own phenomenology, that is, toward what he is *feeling,* chiefly by way of fantasy or actual visualization. Gestalt therapists are especially interested in the client's symbolic representations as these are the coverants that determine his overt behavior. Visualization may involve imagining a dialogue with another person or with a whole cast of characters. In working with visualization, the client is instructed to stay with the imagined situation and to let it change as it will. The therapist then deals with the client's feelings, movements, etc., in relation to the visualization as it is emerging. For example, one client, in visualizing an encounter with his father-in-law, has a fantasy about being pursued by Indians. As the fantasy develops, he is able to turn around and shoot back, thereby saving himself. The visualization was a symbolic representation of a problem; it showed his initial avoidance of it by running away, and his possible solution, namely, confronting the pursuer and asserting himself. By making these coverants overt, the client was able to discover an alternative response to avoidance (p. 44).

While the gestalt therapist might rely more heavily on symbolic representations in fantasies than the behavior therapist (the latter probably giving primary attention to fantasies about real life or possible real life situations and only secondary attention to symbolic representations), it should be evident that the gestalt use of fantasy is strikingly similar in process and technique to the behavioral use of fantasy, e.g. behavioral rehearsal; and both are quite similar to the insight-oriented psychodrama. It should also be pointed out that gestalt therapy demonstrates what astute behavioral therapists have long maintained: it is possible to reinforce such nebulous entities as emotions (neblous because they are idiosyncratically defined and difficult to quantify in behavioral objective form) and even humanistically-oriented concepts like self-actualization.

To further emphasize the compatibilities between gestaltism and behaviorism, Kepner and Brien (1970) state:

Thus we may view human problem behavior, that is, "pathology," as learned behavior and psychotherapy as essentially a reeducational process. All psychological learning theories attempt to specify the variables that determine behavior. The behaviorist is primarily concerned with and attempts to account for external events, that is, for stimuli and responses. The phenomenologist, on the other hand, assumes certain "givens" about the nature of man and is concerned with what goes on inside the person, that is, with the rich, variegated, and elusive internal world of the individual. The behavioristic phenomenologist deals with this world of personal experiencing in such a way as to make it external, overt, specifiable, and communicable (p. 45).

Clearly this type of interpretation of gestalt therapy aligns it with behavioral interventions. It is only fair to admit, however, that this integrative position, while seemingly justifiable on philosophical and theoretical grounds, would not be accepted by some gestaltists, namely those who give total allegiance to the experiencing, being, and sharing tenets. The latter would seem to represent the portion of espousers found in probably every theoretical camp, those who, for their own ego-needs or lack of academic understanding, choose to refute a significant segment of the theory and blindly hold to a portion of the whole theory.

SCIENTIFIC STATUS OF ENCOUNTER GROUPS

Though there has been widespread acceptance of human potential growth groups, there is still reason to question whether the movement is within the purview of science, art, or religion. As the following discussion will indicate, there certainly seems to be reason to question that the practice of group encounters can be classified as "scientific": there is just too little experimental documentation. With the exception of certain practitioners of the training/ laboratory method and the gestalt approach, it seems doubtful that most encounter group leaders could be termed "artists": there is no set of clearly delineated principles, no succinct set of skills to be cultivated through learning, self-expression, and practice, and no theory of aesthetics. Because of the lack of research, the ambiguous functional definitions, and the "true-believer" atmosphere within the human potential growth movement, at this point in time the most appropriate status would probably be that of "religion."

Even advocates acknowledge the gross limitations within the practice of encounter groups. Burton (1969) indicates that the principal deficiency in encounter is that it lacks a theory, and that it "has not yet gotten around to specifying its dangers, and it ignores those who have been hurt by it and even the suicides" (p. 23). Further, he points out that ". . . encounter is perhaps still too young to have an ethic" (p. 24), and that there are a number of encounter leaders who are not trained psychotherapists and who are of questionable repute:

> A kind of anarchy takes over in which the leader with the greatest charisma, and perhaps the most diversified "awakening" techniques, is most desired and has the greatest following. Each leader builds a personal following by collecting testimonials and quickly forgets

his obligation to science. While industry has set some standards for its human relations counsultants, the broader exponents of encounter have not and do not promise to do so (p. 24).

The lack of qualifications proven to be prerequisites for effective group leadership and thus the consequent attitude that "anybody who has been in an encounter group can lead one" common in encounter circles has unquestionably thrown a potentially valuable approach into disrespect and aroused open contempt in the eyes of many professional helpers.

In a detailed review and analysis of contemporary group practices, with special reference to those that may be classed under the rubric of encounter, Parloff (1970) indicates that the three recognizable major aims are enhancing organizational efficiency, enhancing interpersonal skills, and enhancing the sense of well being. He notes that there is a paucity of research and that which is available varies greatly according to the sources of the judgments, i.e. the participant's or trainee's "opinion of the effectiveness of his behavioral change tends to be far more optimistic than that of observers" (p. 276). In addition, he states:

> In summary, participants in encounter groups report favorable reactions and are frequently described by others as showing improved interpersonal skills. That evidence is meager that such participants undergo significant attitude change or personality change, and evidence that group training improves organization efficiency is not compelling. What is clearest is that these groups provide an intensive affective experience for many participants. In this sense, the groups may be described as potent. As is the case with all potent agents, they may be helpful when properly administered, inert in "subclinical" dosages, and noxious when excessive or inappropriate (p. 279).

The potential production of such indiscriminate results scarcely provides the sort of research-based evaluation that would seem to be necessary for *professional* helpers.

When perusing the research that encounter advocates point toward for substantiating their claim to beneficial effects, one cannot help but be struck by the fervent claims of research validation for their activities (e.g. Rogers, 1970). But close inspection quickly reveals that the so-called research is clearly faulty from a research design point of view. For example, heavy reliance is placed on self-reports (particularly during the "psychic high" period immediately following the encounter group experience) and on rating scales that might prove to be reliable (because of the consistency within or between raters) but have little claim to validity. Parenthetically, behavioral science has demonstrated that it is impossible to have validity without reliability, but it is possible to have reliability without validity–the latter may be the case within encounter group research. Moreover, long-term follow-ups are essentially missing. At this point in time, the most logical position seems to be that encounter groups may feel good and may produce some immediate beneficial effects, but these effects are possibly dependent to a significant degree on the idiosyncratic qualities of the encounter group leader or facilitator (particularly the charismatic appeal and skill at persuasion), and that a claim of permanent change cannot be posited.

Implicit in many status reports, such as those cited by Burton (1969) and Parloff (1970), is the possibility of dangers from an encounter group experience. Overall, it seems that the position taken by reputable professionals is two-fold: first, the encounter method *per se* is not dangerous, but it can be powerful and this (as Parloff noted) could lead to beneficial or deleterious effects; and second, the power of the encounter method makes it mandatory that the encounter group leader be able to evaluate the probable impact on each would-be participant (this means an academically-based diagnostic judgment) and be prepared to handle therapeutically unpredicted situations that might arise during the course of the encounter group experience. Because of this possibility, the encounter group leader, regardless of rationalizations (such as the group being "educational" rather than "therapeutic") should be professionally trained or have ready access to a professional consultant (who should no doubt function, in part, as a supervisor).

To be more specific about possible dangers, Parloff (1970) states that if encounter groups are improperly conducted, there are the dangers of:

(1) psychosis and other serious emotional reactions; (2) mild or moderate emotional disturbances; and (3) "re-entry" problems (p. 280).

Parloff sees professional group therapists as being "guided by the ethical standards developed and enforced by their own professions and professional societies" (p. 297) and recommends that clinical practice rely on the following three principles:

1. INFORMED CONSENT. Prior to entrance into the encounter group the patient/client should be provided with as full information as possible to permit him to make a decision as to whether the purposes, leaderships, techniques, duration, costs, etc., are acceptable to him (p. 298).

2. FREEDOM OF CHOICE. Since the prerequisite conditions of informed consent are difficult to achieve, it is necessary that scrupulous attention be paid to preserving the client's right of free choice. This includes the client's right to withdraw from any given activity or from the group itself without being exposed to pressures from the group members or leadership. . . . Ethical standards require that proper respect be shown for the convictions, sensibilities, and values of the clients. It is unethical to attempt to impose any morality on the subject that is contrary to his own (p. 299).

3. ESTABLISHMENT OF SAFEGUARDS. It is the leader's responsibility to provide adequate facilities and resources to protect the subject against the possibility of psychological and physical injury. The most relevant safeguards are, of course, the leader's sensitivity to the psychological states of the participants and his skillful regulation of stress levels in order not to exceed the coping abilities of the individuals involved (p. 300).

It is important to note that these comments are directed at the *professional;* and the lack of professional ethical standards and related signs to verify proper service, as found with some encounter group leaders who believe that professional skills are irrelevant, should be a warning to lay and professional persons alike to avoid contact with the nonprofessional group leader.

There are some professionals who are far less accepting of the encounter group movement's potential for beneficial effects. For example, Ruitenbeck (1970) considers sensory awareness to be honorable but believes that encounter groups promote sensory awareness in such a way that it ". . . tends to occur precisely within a context that reinforces an already well-rooted reaction against mind and thought" (p. 234); and he sees the emphasis upon "antiintellectualism" as a potentially great danger:

Moreover in a society which already has deemphasized the achievements of knowledge and education and which tends to compromise ad infinitum with the nonintellectual forces in our midst, we will arrive at a culture where the blandness and dullness of its inhabitants will signify the total disintegration of personal and individual values (p. 234).

Ruitenbeck goes on to assert that people do not recognize these effects because they "are still caught up in the glamour of the movement . . ." (p. 234). Likewise, he points out that: ". . . they promise so much and still have produced little in terms of long-term individual growth and happiness" (p. 236). He believes encounter groups fail to let people know that: ". . . this world is not all made of honey and roses and that human misery is as much a part of our experience as anything else" (p. 238). Including these conservative, negative views does not connote endorsement; they were included to illustrate a segment of professional opinion about encounter groups, and there is ample reason to question this stance as much as there is to question the true-believer stance on the opposite end of the continuum.

In terms of sexual, marital, and familial relations in specific, the rationale for the human potential growth group movement is certainly compatible. The concepts of openness, honesty, owning of feeling, affective communication, caring, self-actualization, sensory awareness, intimacy, and sharing are definitely much needed in probably everyone's sexual, marital, and familial relations, given the premise that an optimal hygiologic framework is the desired outcome. However, the question remains, because of the lack of research documentation and the variety of nebulous or ill-defined properties in application, whether the human potential growth group approach is well-understood enough to allow for generalization. It would seem that *encounter may be of value to many people, but the prescription of such an experience and the provision of the encounter intervention can only be made through professional clinical judgments for each helpee.* With this framework, the professional helper would diagnose the needs of the helpee and select a human potential growth experience accordingly; stated simply, it would be *encounter by professional prescription.*

REFERENCES

Bach, G. R.: The marathon group: intensive practice of intimate interactions. *Psychological Reports, 18*:995-1002, 1966.

Burton, A.: Encounter, existence, and psychotherapy. In A. Burton (Ed.), *Encounter: the theory and practice of encounter groups.* San Francisco, Jossey-Bass, 7-26, 1969.

Campbell, J. P. and Dunnette, M. D.: Effectiveness of T-group experiences in managerial training and development. *Psychological Bulletin, 70*:73-104, 1968.

Fagan, Joen: The tasks of the therapist. In Joen Fagan and Irma Lee Shephard (Eds.), *Gestalt therapy now: theory, techniques, applications.* Palo Alto, Science and Behavior Books, 88-106, 1970.

Foulds, M. L.: The growth center model: proactive programs of a university counseling service. Paper presented at the American Psychological Association's Annual Convention, Washington, September, 1971.

Golembiewski, R. T.: Enriching marriages through the laboratory approach: tentative steps toward the "open couple." In R. T. Golembiewski and A. Blumberg (Eds.), *Sensitivity training and the laboratory approach.* Itasca, Calif., F. E. Peacock, 345-349, 1970.

Kempler, W.: Experiential psychotherapy with families. In Joen Fagan and Irma Lee Shepherd (Eds.), *Gestalt therapy now: theory, techniques, applications.* Palo Alto, Science and Behavior Books, 150-161, 1970.

Kepner, Elaine and Brien, Lois: Gestalt therapy: a behavioristic phenomenology. In Joen Fagan and Irma Lee Shepherd (Eds.), *Gestalt therapy now: theory, techniques, applications.* Palo Alto, Science and Behavior Books, 39-46, 1970.

Parloff, M. B.: Group therapy and the small group field: an encounter. *International Journal of Group Psychotherapy, 20*:267-304, 1970.

Rogers, C. R.: *Carl Rogers on encounter groups.* New York, Harper and Row, 1970.

Ruitenbeck, H.: *The new group therapies.* New York, Avon Books, 1970.

Seashore, C.: What is sensitivity training? In R. T. Golembiewski and A. Blumberg (Eds.), *Sensitivity training and the laboratory approach.* Itasca, F. E. Peacock, 14-18, 1970.

THE PSYCHOBEHAVIORAL
FRAMEWORK: INTEGRATING
THERAPEUTIC APPROACHES

T HAT NO ONE THEORETICAL approach is adequate for all helpees has been constantly stated throughout this book. This repetition is purposeful and is intended to convey one of the major thrusts: the integration of therapeutic approaches.

Stated briefly, the assumption is made that the best helping approach (defined as theory translated into action via techniques) must be evolved according to the unique client, problem, and situation. That is, the helping approach should be tailored to the individual and should be decided upon by the professional helper's careful appraisal of the needs and characteristics of the helpee. This frame of reference has been termed the *Psychobehavioral* approach (Woody, 1968a, 1968b, 1969, 1971).

Since the dimensions of the psychobehavioral approach have been elaborated upon and the relevant clinical and experimental research presented in the book *Psychobehavioral Counseling and Therapy: Integrating Behavioral and Insight Techniques* (Woody, 1971), this chapter will simply summarize that more comprehensive source and posit the ramifications for professional helping directed at sexual, marital, and familial relations.

BEHAVIORISM VERSUS INSIGHT

Regrettable as it now seems, certain theorists and practitioners attempted to support their preferred approach by *denouncing the opposition* rather than by *presenting scientific documentation* for their respective positions. This was the case decades ago when the adherents of classic psychoanalysis openly feuded with the so-called neo-analysts, and more recently this was replayed in combat between the espousers of behaviorism (i.e. behavior therapists) and the espousers of psychodynamically-oriented approaches (i.e. psychotherapists). The behavior therapists, of course, believing that human behavior is conditioned, support a theoretical model based on learning theory. Their therapeutic techniques are aligned with reinforcement procedures. The psychotherapists, conversely, believe that learning theory or conditioning is too simplistic (that at best learning theory might explain the "tip of the iceberg") and that human behavior is a complex system of psychodynamics, representing primary and secondary needs, with the problem behaviors being manifestations of unfilled needs and/or emotional conflicts. Their therapeutic techniques, as might be anticipated, are aligned with increasing understanding via introspection and insight procedures.

With a great furor, the proponents of the opposing camps lashed out at each other, particularly through the weapon of *therapeutic efficacy*. That is, they each claimed that their efficacy for helping clients or patients was superior and that the opposition's efficacy was low or non-existent. Of course, the fact that was frequently ignored was that each camp had its unique set of criteria for improvement, and since the two sets of criteria were quite different, a comparison of efficacy was ill-founded. The behaviorist maintained that if he eliminated or alleviated the problem behavior that brought the person to treatment, he was successful. The insightist maintained that the problem that brought the person to treatment was secondary to the undoubtedly present underlying emotional conflict; the criterion of success would be increasing the person's self-understanding (through insight) and it was irrelevant whether the person lost the actual problem that brought him to treatment (for example, it could be, according to the insightist, that the person would decide that the so-called "problem" was actually a needed representation of "self" and would decide to keep it, but would do so free from guilt or anxiety).

Eventually, as more and more research was accumulated for both behavioral and insight approaches, it became evident that there were many commonalities. Even though Dollard and Miller (1950) had earlier offered a thorough translation of psychodynamic principles into a learning theory system for psychotherapy, this was neglected until about a decade-and-a-half later, with many unnecessary, hostile accusations and professional cleavages occurring in the meantime. The behavioristic impact hit the insight therapies in the late fifties and early sixties (Eysenck, 1952, 1965; Wolpe, 1964). This was followed by scholarly analyses of the issue of alleged "superiority in efficacy" (Breger and McGaugh, 1965; Kiesler, 1966). Then finally the commonalities were recognized, and the possibility of a behavioral-insight integration was explored. Mowrer (1964, 1966) presented astute comparative analyses, and Marks and Gelder (1966) acknowledged the "common ground" between behavior therapy and psychotherapy and indicated that the two approaches: were not theoretically independent, reciprocally influenced each other, and were both potentially valuable for evolving a treatment plan for the helpee. This led to the development of the psychobehavioral framework (Woody, 1968a, 1968b, 1969, 1971). Subsequently, although some die-hards are still maintaining the fallacy of theoretical supremacy (note Wolpe, 1969a, 1969b), it has now become more widely accepted that some of the attributes of psychotherapy can contribute beneficially to behavior therapy and vice versa; note the change reflected in the writings of Lazarus from his early position (Wolpe and Lazarus, 1966) to his most recent position (Lazarus, 1970).

ELECTICISM

The idea of integrating seemingly diverse approaches to therapeutic interventions is certainly nothing new. Indeed, it is quite likely that in actual practice every professional helper actually integrates elements of various theories, but in his verbal description of his professional stance he may perceive his practice based on a well delineated single theory. There are, however, still great differences among professional helpers in the amount of electicism that they consciously attempt.

Any discussion of eclecticism should start with noting the contributions of Thorne, who has the distinction of holding doctorates in both medicine and psychology, and who has unrelentingly opposed rigid adherence to a single theory. This emphasis has been accompanied by his assertion that clinical judgment is highly vulnerable to bias and error and that it is necessary to recognize the limitations of clinical practice: Clinical helping should be offered as being simply the "best available at the moment"; consequently there should be a constant search of further empirical documentation. Thorne has synthesized his beliefs into the so-called *integrative psychology* approach (Thorne, 1967). He states:

> *Eclectic-therapies* hypothesize a wide spectrum of etiologic factors potentially causing disorder, and therefore postulate that it is necessary to have a wide therapeutic armamentarium of methods suited to specific indications and contraindications (Thorne, 1967, p. 322).

He also states:

> The basic strategy of eclectic therapy is to differentiate all the possible etiologic causes of disorder and then to select appropriate methods specifically indicated to modify specific etiologic factors. This is not an hodge-podge approach, experimenting with shot-gun methods on a hit-or-miss basis (which sometimes has spectacular results). It is a rational method based on knowledge of valid indications and contraindications with reference to any specific etiologic equation (Thorne, 1967, p. 322).

And in one of his numerous denunciations of persons who perceive themselves as being near-infallible, he states:

> Particularly suspect are professionals who identify with limited viewpoints such as the various schools and systems of psychology, religionist psychologists, and all the orientations whose labels imply special interests or commitments which can influence clinical judgment. Only the thorough-going eclectic has a chance of being uninfluenced by potentially distorting irrelevant value considerations (Thorne, 1969, p. 231).

Thorne's point about special allegiances, such as being a strong proponent of a singular theoretical approach to therapy, is extensively documented in Chapter 1 of *Clinical Assessment in Counseling and Psychotherapy* (Woody and Woody, 1972).

PSYCHOBEHAVIORISM

Psychobehaviorism should not be construed as a theory: to do so would be to cast it into company it attempts to avoid. Psychobehaviorism is simply a theoretical frame of reference, a conceptual set for viewing the integration of behavioral and insight theories and techniques.

Psychobehaviorism *per se* emphasizes the technical aspects, but since all techniques have explicit or implicit theoretical assumptions, there is naturally some relevance to theoretical integration. Lazarus (1972) objects to the fact that the psychobehavioral framework posits an eclectic theoretical stance; his preference is to emphasize the technical:

> Why must we turn to the intrinsically untestable and semimystical constructs of psychodynamic theory? Let us by all means employ those very few empirically validated procedures that have long been part of traditional psychotherapy, but in so doing, let us not become ensnared in their epistemological fallacies (p. 140).

Elsewhere, Lazarus (1969) endorses what he calls "broad-spectrum behavior therapy" and supports "technical eclecticism" (Lazarus, 1967). It seems obvious that technical eclecticism can be more easily achieved than theoretical eclecticism, but such technical eclecticism has, as was mentioned, inherent theoretical constructs. Not to state them or not to define their existence does not remove them. Beneath a systematic technical integration there are theoretical factors and these too must be integrated. So in approaching psychobehaviorism, it should be acknowledged that this is but a technical frame of reference, but the movement should be toward theoretical integration as well (much research and theoretical evolution will be required to accomplish this). Although several theorists, such as Dollard and Miller (1950) and Thorne (1967), have made significant strides toward theoretical integration at all levels of conceptualization, it would appear that the current state of affairs still necessitates that each practitioner make his own idiosyncratic formulations.

Psychobehavioral Assumptions

There are at least ten assumptions that seem to set the stage for the technical frame of reference of psychobehaviorism:

ASSUMPTION I. SINGLE THEORY INADEQUACY. No one theoretical approach can optimally serve all helpees.

ASSUMPTION II. MAINTENANCE OF A PREFERRED THEORY. A given theoretical position can be principally maintained and techniques from other positions can be used adjunctively.

ASSUMPTION III. BEHAVIORAL AND INSIGHT RECIPROCITY. Behavioral and insight-oriented approaches hold the potential to be mutually beneficial; there is theoretical reciprocity.

ASSUMPTION IV. ELIMINATION OF FAILURES IN BEHAVIORAL INTERVENTIONS. Despite its claim to a high degree of therapeutic efficacy, behavior therapy does fail. The four primary reasons for failure seem to be: opposition to treatment in general, resistance to behavior therapy in specific, misdiagnosis (i.e. faulty identification and formulation of reinforcement contingencies), and transference phenomena (even in behavior therapy!). Insight-related procedures can reduce and/or eliminate many (and probably most) of these behavioral intervention failures.

ASSUMPTION V. ELIMINATION OF FAILURES IN INSIGHT-ORIENTED INTERVENTIONS. Insight-oriented approaches sometimes fail to produce desired changes. The reasons are many, but often it is because the helpee is unable to attain the quality of introspection necessary to gain adequate insight into his psychodynamic composite and because the helpee is unable to muster the resources to pursue an alternative behavioral path to achieve desired change; e.g. he cannot make adequate commitment to maintain plans that could lead potentially to more rewarding, fulfilling psychological and behavioral characteristics. In these instances, behavioral procedures can be valuable adjuncts to the psychotherapeutic procedures.

ASSUMPTION VI. NEED FOR FACILITATING CONDITIONS. The facilitating conditions (as described in Chapter 3) optimize the chances of effective helping, regardless of which theoretical approach is espoused.

ASSUMPTION VII. NEED FOR CLINICAL ASSESSMENT. Clinical assessment of possible causations, current situations, and prognostic outcomes should be made, regardless of primary theoretical allegiance and regardless of the nosology (be it in reinforcement or psychodynamic terms).

ASSUMPTION VIII. MINIMIZING NEGATIVE TERMINATION EFFECTS. Regardless of theoretical position, steps should be taken to assure minimal adverse effects from the conclusion of therapeutic intervention; commonly this would include focusing on termination feelings, milieu factors, and follow-up plans.

ASSUMPTION IX. DEVELOPMENT OF THE PROFESSIONAL SELF CONCEPT. The professional helper's personal characteristics cannot and should not be eliminated; rather he should hold his personal needs in abeyance while working with the helpee. Particularly critical is the requirement that the professional helper evolve a compatible synthesis between his professional self concept and his personal self concept: a dissonant relationship between these two forms of self concept will probably lead to poor functioning in professional activities and in personal life. Thus an "examined life" is recommended.

ASSUMPTION X. RESPONSIBILITY OF THE HELPEE. The objectives of therapy should remain primarily the responsibility of the helpee, but the professional helper has a responsibility to both the helpee and society to attempt to provide a realistic awareness of behavioral consequences, to safeguard the personal integrity of all concerned (the helper, the helpee, and society), and to cultivate an ability within the helpee to fulfill the ultimate criterion: personal responsibility and a repertoire of actions that can be effectively implemented to alleviate and eliminate undesirable conditions in one's individually/socially determined life style.

These assumptions are but briefly outlined. They are intended to provide the structural components for the technical actions of the professional helper; additional relevant material may, of course, be found in the previously mentioned primary sources (Woody, 1971).

Psychobehavioral Guidelines

Given the preceding backdrop, there seem to be three basic guidelines for making use of an integrated technical frame of reference.

GUIDELINE I. FACILITATION AND ACCELERATION OF PROFESSIONAL HELPING. There are many clinical instances in which the ongoing treatment approach may be attaining benefits for the helpee, but it becomes evident that there is a sense of urgency to achieve a relatively great deal of change. For example, a helpee might be engaged in a sexual activity that is creating a strong risk of his being arrested (e.g. involved in homosexual activities in a public restroom); or a helpee might have preference for an activity like sadomasochism or transvestism that is causing a spouse to threaten a divorce, etc.); or a couple might be experiencing such a tremendous marital strain that is causing one partner to have severe depression or suicide ideation. In situations like these, it seems imperative that all technical possibilities should be considered. Although there is definitely the possibility of theoretical reciprocity, most often this guideline seems to come into effect when insight-oriented procedures need a boost in acceleration from a behavioral procedure (such as those described in Chapter Five).

GUIDELINE II. ELIMINATION OF UNCOMFORTABLE SYMPTOMS. Here again there is an element of acceleration, in that the approach to treatment currently being used is found to be inadequate for bringing prompt, immediate relief to a symptom that is creating a significant disturbance or defeating condition for the helpee. For example, in the case of a person who experiences extreme anxiety in a sexual situation and who can scarcely work effectively on improving a sexual relationship, a specialized anxiety-reducing technique could be integrated into an existing treatment format. Or if a client has an obsession with some condition, such as preoccupation with his spouse's past infidelity, he can scarcely enter into a meaningful exploration of his marital relationship; so a specialized technique focusing on the obsession would seem appropriate. In situations of this nature, the specialized technique is integrated into the intervention approach with the understanding that it is but a partial treatment, and that the elimination of the target symptom, although it may bring welcomed relief, should not be interpreted by the helpee as negating the need to deal with other aspects of the overall problem situation (such a decision should be based on the analysis of both the helper and the helpee).

GUIDELINE III. TREATMENT OF THERAPEUTICALLY UNRESPONSIVE HELPEE. Inevitably there will be some helpees who fail to benefit from the seemingly most preferred form of treatment. In some instances the failure might be due to resistance to change, but in other instances the failure may stem from the helpee's characteristics; e.g. he may possess a cultural set toward psychotherapy that negates effectiveness or he may be lacking in the ability to fulfill the expectations of psychotherapy (such as to enter into introspection and verbal exploration of abstract concepts). Certainly it would be preferable professionally if an optimally logical, academically-based treatment scheme could be maintained, but reality (with the logistical limitations imposed by actual practice) is not always accommodating. When the preferred treatment prescription and the equally feasible alternative have failed to obtain the helping objectives, the helper should seek to achieve desired changes by essentially any legal and ethical means (assuming that the objectives are deemed proper from professional, social, and individual vantage points). One of the most common examples is to make use of a behavioral technique which may seem too superficial or too narrow to accomplish the total helping goal, but which might bring relief, satisfaction, or comfort to the helpee. For example, a marital intervention may fail to reorder the majority of interactions between spouses (i.e. they have failed, even after extensive treatment, to attain significant compatibility), and a procedure could be used to bring another accomplishment, albeit a more limited one (e.g. reinforcing a reasonably non-hostile, non-destructive relationship and/or some immediate gratification from each other, such as through sexual activity).

These guidelines are obviously quite global, but it is intended that decisions about technical integration not be predetermined by fixed criteria: decisions about technical integration must rely upon the clinical expertise of the professional helper and the personal views of the helpee.

PROFESSIONAL POSTURE

Comments made previously have pointed out how the professional helper dealing with sexual, marital, and familial relations must go beyond the posture required of professional helpers in general. In addition to the multitude of knowledge, skills, and qualities that are requisite to be an effective professional helper, dealing with sexual, marital, and familial relations requires a whole new repertoire of academic knowledge, a coterie of specialized techniques, and an array of application considerations.

As though all of these additional required acquisitions were not enough, there is probably no other form of professional helping, including individual and group psychotherapy, that holds as much potential for the presence of potent transference and counter-transference phenomena. Part of this unmatched potential probably stems from the fact that the topics of sexuality, marriage, and family "hit close to home" for everyone, including the professional helper. Also relevant is the fact that the format for helping with these issues (as elaborated upon in Chapter Two) frequently encompasses all parties of a relationship, i.e. combinations of persons (such as both the husband and wife being present with the professional helper) that would not always be part of other forms of therapeutic interventions.

All of the foregoing factors combine to create a unique press for the professional helper who wants to be effective in serving helpees for sexual, marital, and familial relations. There is a pronounced need for a well developed, healthy professional posture.

This desired and mandatory professional posture can and should come through several avenues. Most basic, of course, is the academic knowledge: there must be an academic understanding of the physiological, psychological, and sociological aspects of sexual, marital, and familial relations. Another avenue is the related technical knowledge: there must be an awareness of and facility with the intervention techniques unique to sexual, marital, and familial problems, as well as an adaptation of the more generic techniques for these problems.

Beyond this academic-technical sphere is the professional self. As has been mentioned, the professional helper's self concept must be compatible with the professional self concept, and this required synthesis is not always easily attained. Of course academic-professional preparation is helpful, but many find that specialized experiences, such as supervision and experiential workshops or seminars, are necessary in order to move into a compatible position. An "examined life" may be attained by a variety of methods, and it would be inappropriate to elaborate extensively on these alternatives at this juncture. Suffice it to say, it is essential that the professional helper achieve a degree of self-understanding that facilitates his working effectively with helpees and that guarantees him (and his family) that his professional activities will not jeopardize his own happiness and fulfillment.

Another essential part of professional posture is the manifestation of professional responsibility. This is more than assuming a professional stance verbally; it necessitates a willingness and ability to *implement actions.* All too often professional helpers and helpees alike tend to expect someone else to assume the load of responsible action. Responsible action involves, to some extent, risk-taking behavior, and some professionals would rather tacitly sit back and point to the helpee to have full responsibility for change rather than share this challenge with the helpee. Change can best be attained by shared responsibility and by unflinching follow-through with action–action that is appropriately defined by the integrity and rights of the professional helper, the helpee, and the contemporary society.

REFERENCES

Breger, L. and McGaugh, J. L.: A critique and reformulation of "learning theory" approaches to psychotherapy and neuroses. *Psychological Bulletin, 63*:335-358, 1965.

Dollard, J. and Miller, N. E.: *Personality and psychotherapy: an analysis in terms of learning, thinking, and culture.* New York, McGraw-Hill, 1950.

Eysenck, H. J.: The effects of psychotherapy: an evaluation. *Journal of Consulting Psychology, 16*:319-324, 1952.

Eysenck, H. J.: The effects of psychotherapy. *International Journal of Psychiatry, 1*:99-142, 1965.

Kiesler, D. J.: Some myths of psychotherapy research and the search for a paradigm. *Psychological Bulletin, 65*:110-136, 1966.

Lazarus, A. A.: In support of technical eclecticism. *Psychological Reports, 21*:415-416, 1967.

Lazarus, A. A.: Broad-spectrum behavior therapy. *Newsletter of the Association for Advancement of Behavior Therapy, 4*:5-6, 1969.

Lazarus, A. A.: *Behavior therapy and beyond.* New York, McGraw-Hill, 1971.

Lazarus, A. A.: Book review of R. H. Woody's *Psychobehavioral counseling and therapy: integrating behavioral and insight techniques. Behavior Therapy, 3*:140-142, 1972.

Marks, I. M. and Gelder, M. G.: Common ground between behaviour therapy and psychodynamic methods. *British Journal of Medical Psychology, 39*:11-23, 1966.

Mowrer, O. J.: Freudianism, behavior therapy and self-disclosure. *Behaviour Research and Therapy, 1*:321-337, 1964.

Mowrer, O. H.: The behavior therapies with special reference to modeling and imitation. *American Journal of Psychotherapy, 20*:439-461, 1966.

Thorne, F. C.: *Integrative psychology: a systematic clinical viewpoint.* Brandon, Vt., Clinical Psychology, 1967.

Thorne, F. C.: Editorial opinion: value factors in clinical judgment. *Journal of Clinical Psychology, 25*:231, 1969.

Wolpe, J.: The comparative clinical status of conditioning therapies and psychoanalysis. In J. Wolpe, A. Salter, and L. J. Reyna (Eds.), *The conditioning therapies.* New York, Holt, Rinehart and Winston, 5-20, 1964.

Wolpe, J.: *The practice of behavior therapy.* New York, Pergamon, (a), 1969.

Wolpe, J.: Therapist and technique variable in behavior therapy of neurosis. *Comprehensive Psychiatry, 10*:44-49 (b), 1969.

Wolpe, J. and Lazarus, A. A.: *Behavior therapy techniques.* New York, Pergamon, 1966.

Woody, R. H.: Integrating behaviour therapy and psychotherapy. *British Journal of Medical Psychology, 41*:261-266 (a), 1968.

Woody, R. H.: Toward a rationale for psychobehavioral therapy. *Archives of General Psychiatry, 19*:197-204 (b), 1968.

Woody, R. H.: *Behavioral problem children in the schools: recognition, diagnosis, and behavioral modification.* New York, Appleton-Century-Crofts, 1969.

Woody, R. H.: *Psychobehavioral counseling and therapy: integrating behavioral and insight techniques.* New York, Appleton-Century-Crofts, 1971.

Woody, R. H. and Woody, Jane D.: (Eds.). *Clinical assessment in counseling and psychotherapy.* New York, Appleton-Century-Crofts, 1972.

AUTHOR INDEX

271

SUBJECT INDEX

A

Abortion-reform groups, 8
Adolescence, 15
Adult development tasks, discussion of, 30
Affect, heightened
  acceptance, inability of, 212
    effects of, 212
  development of
    methods of, 214-220
    tape recording affecting, video, 217-218
  levels, discussion of, 212
Affect stimulation, 227
  description of, 218-219
  evolution of, 218
  helper, role of professional, 219
  rationale of, 219
  social modeling and, relationship between, 220
Aggression, excessive, 167
Agorphobia, definition of, 202
Alcoholism
  treatment of, aversion therapy, 210-211, 231
  treatment of, covert sensitization, 208
Algorithms, 189
American Group Psychotherapy Association, 46, 47, 64
  ethics of, code of, 52, 54
American Society
  see Society, American
Anger
  causes, recognition of, 146
  consequences, recognition of, 146
  coping, methods of, 146
Anxiety
  desensitization of, systematic
    approach, hierarchy of, 201-202
    approach, progressive, 201
    helper, role of, 201

    relaxation affecting, 201
    stimuli during, 202
  forms of, 199
  recognition of, helpee, 200
  transformation of, 199
  universality, discussion of, 199
Anxiety, sexual
  desensitization, application of systematic, 202, 227
    approaches to, 204-205
    effects of, 203, 205
    problems of, 204
  hierarchy of, 203-204
  implosive therapy treatment, 229
  negative practice treatment, 228
  relaxation affecting, muscular, 227
  satiation therapy treatment, verbal, 228-229
  satiation treatment, 227-228
Anxiety, social
  aversion therapy treatment, 211
  definition of, 202
  description of, 202-203
  desensitization, application of systematic, 202
  effects of, 205
  phobia and, relationship between, 202
Approach, integrative psychology, 262
Approach, psychobehavioral, definition of, 259
Approach, therapeutic
  definition of, 259
  selection, factors affecting, 259
Approach integration, psychobehaviorism and, relationship between, 262-263
Assertive practice, 226
  application of, 217
  approach to, 217
  description of, 216-217

success, factors affecting, 161, 163-
164
use of, sensitive, 160-161
approaches to, familial, conditions
affecting, 160
approaches to, successive sieves, description of, 161
function of, 159
methods of, factors affecting, 159-
160
types, description of, 161-163
use of, 173
factors affecting, 159-160
timing, discussion of, 159
Principle of interdependence
see Interdependence, principle of
Problems, emotional
causes, behavior theory of, 181
causes, insight-oriented theory of,
181
treatment, behavior theory of, 181
Problems, familial
behavior modification procedures,
application of, effectiveness of,
183
causes, discussion of, 191-192
desensitization, application of systematic, approach to, 200-201
prevention of, programs, guidelines
for, 34
reinforcement of, 183-184, 191
sexuality and, 221
solutions to, destructive, 135
treatment, Gestalt therapy
description of, 250
helper during, role of, 250
treatment, training group, 245
Problems, marital
behavior modification procedures,
application of, effectiveness of,
183
causes, discussion of, 191-192
desensitization, application of systematic, approach to, 200-201
reinforcement of, 184, 191
sexuality and, 221
solutions to, destructive, 135
treatment, training group, 245

objectives of, change, 245-246
Problems, relationship
approaches to, 12
discussion of, 3-4
socio-cultural change affecting, 3-7
classification of, 4
Problems, sexual
desensitization, application of systematic, approach to, 200-201
treatment, training group, 245
Psychiatry, responsibility of, public, viii
"Psychic high," 255
Psychobehavioral approach
see Approach, psychobehavioral
Psychobehavioral counseling and therapy, 57
Psychobehavioral frame of reference, ix,
186, 189, 251
definition of, 57
development, basis for, 260-261
Psychobehaviorism
application, guidelines for, 265-267
assumptions, basic, 263-265
description of, 262-263
Psychodrama, 195, 240, 252
uses of, 196
Psychodynamic composite, 264
Psychology, responsibility of, public,
viii
Psychopathology, 170
Psychosis, 255
Psycho-social framework
see Family, frameworks of
Psychotherapy
see also Therapy
description of, 252
therapy affecting, behavior, 56
Psychotherapy, group, description of,
44-45
Puberty, 15

R

Racism, 4
"Rap groups"
see also Therapy, group
description of, 47
Rapport, 249
see also Control